Rape Fantasies

Rape Fantasies

Rape Culture and the Persistence of Sexual Violence

ALISA KESSEL

OXFORD
UNIVERSITY PRESS

Oxford University Press is a department of the University of Oxford. It furthers the University's objective of excellence in research, scholarship, and education by publishing worldwide. Oxford is a registered trade mark of Oxford University Press in the UK and in certain other countries.

Published in the United States of America by Oxford University Press
198 Madison Avenue, New York, NY 10016, United States of America.

Library of Congress Cataloging-in-Publication Data
Names: Kessel, Alisa Susan, 1975– author
Title: Rape fantasies : rape culture and the persistence of
sexual violence / Alisa Kessel.
Description: New York, NY : Oxford University Press, [2025] |
Includes bibliographical references and index.
Identifiers: LCCN 2025016200 (print) | LCCN 2025016201 (ebook) |
ISBN 9780197797822 paperback | ISBN 9780197797815 hardback |
ISBN 9780197797846 epub | ISBN 9780197797839 pdf |
ISBN 9780197797853 online
Subjects: LCSH: Rape—Political aspects | Rape culture |
Sex crimes—Prevention
Classification: LCC HV6558 .K396 2025 (print) | LCC HV6558 (ebook) |
DDC 362.88392–dc23/eng/20250606
LC record available at https://lccn.loc.gov/2025016200
LC ebook record available at https://lccn.loc.gov/2025016201

DOI: 10.1093/oso/9780197797815.001.0001

Paperback printed by Integrated Books International, United States of America
Hardback printed by Bridgeport National Bindery, Inc., United States of America

The manufacturer's authorised representative in the EU for product safety is Oxford University Press España S.A., Parque Empresarial San Fernando de Henares, Avenida de Castilla, 2 – 28830 Madrid (www.oup.es/en or product.safety@oup.com). OUP España S.A. also acts as importer into Spain of products made by the manufacturer.

For my parents, Ellarita and James Kessel

with love and gratitude, always

Contents

Acknowledgments

I am fortunate to have a rich community of family, friends, and colleagues who support and love me. I have also been gifted with wonderful teachers who instilled in me a sense of my own worth and intellect. This is a strong foundation, and I do not take it lightly. As I contemplate writing the "acknowledgments" for a book, I realize that I will never be able to acknowledge every individual whose kindness, encouragement, or critical insight has made this book possible; but I am grateful for every intervention that has helped me finish it.

This book is inspired by my students at the University of Puget Sound, both on the main Tacoma campus and at the Washington Corrections Center for Women (WCCW). I still remember the day a student came to my office to share that they had struggled with Carole Pateman's "Women and Consent" because it surfaced memories of being raped by an intimate partner. That conversation was a catalyst for my work on sexual violence. As I completed the manuscript many years later, I supervised the senior capstones of the first graduating class of the FEPPS Bacholor of Arts (Freedom Education Project Puget Sound) program at WCCW. Like the student who came to my office many years before, these students shared themselves and their experiences of violence openly and with critical insight, and they reminded me what is at stake in this work. Between these two bookends are scores of other students with whom I have been fortunate to think and learn.

I have also benefited from generous scholars and friends. The partnership between the University of Puget Sound and Universität Passau (Germany) has been especially fruitful. Karsten Fitz and Michael Oswald have invited me to teach and present my work. Karsten, Alexandra Hauke, and Bettina Huber have read and commented on chapters of this book. Grit Grigoleit-Richter is a generous interlocutor and collaborator. Through these engagements, and over many meals and cups of coffee, I have found a second scholarly home among my American studies and political science colleagues at Uni Passau.

Closer to home, I am lucky to be part of a community of political theory scholars who are relentlessly generous. Joel Schlosser read an early draft of my work on consent and helped me find my way to a framework for the book. Shirin Deylami and Vicki Hsueh gave me an intellectual community in Washington State and invited me to give my first talk on this topic at Western Washington University. Later, Michaele Ferguson and Zoe Moss invited me to the University of Colorado Boulder to give a talk as well. Libby Anker, Courtney Berger, and Jeanne Morefield generously read and commented on the book proposal. Jeanne has also become a mentor (whether she intended to or not), who is always available to help me think about how to approach my work. Incredible reviewers and editors at the *American Political Science Review* and *Contemporary Political Theory* helped me see where I need to push and rethink my ideas. Thanks to many colleagues who have taught my work or shared a positive post about it on social media. Those encouragements have helped me feel like this project is useful.

The communities of scholars at the Association for Political Theory and the Western Political Science Association have been especially welcoming and important for me, not just in terms of this book but in terms of pedagogy, community, and professional development. I leave every conference inspired by my colleagues and sporting a long list of new things to read. I also draw inspiration and insight from my colleagues on Facebook, who share resources and insights about political theory scholarship and pedagogy.

The idea for a book about rape culture was born at the Whiteley Center in Friday Harbor, Washington. It is a beautiful and inspiring place to work, and I am grateful that the board continues to welcome me back. The University of Puget Sound has also supported my work: much of the book manuscript was composed during a yearlong sabbatical in 2021–22, the University Enrichment Committee has supported conference travel and editing support for the manuscript, and the Department of Politics and Government has filled in funding gaps whenever possible. Finally, the Daedalus Committee kindly invited me to give a lecture in 2021, which was both an honor and a joy. Last year, I participated in a writing retreat sponsored by the Faculty Development Center at Puget Sound, which proved serendipitous: that retreat was the beginning of the "Spillers Salon," a small group of wayward scholars who meet weekly to read and discuss scholarship. Wind Woods and Regina Duthely, thank you for co-creating this intellectual space with me.

One advantage of teaching at a small college like the University of Puget Sound is that there are many opportunities for interdisciplinary engagement and friendship. I have talked about or shared this work with several brilliant people who have given me feedback, ideas, reading recommendations, or gentle nudges about how to approach this topic thoughtfully. Thank you, dear colleagues: LaToya Brackett, Katherine Crocker, Monica DeHart, Rachel DeMotts, Regina Duthely, Dexter Gordon, Suzanne Holland, Robin Jacobson, Grace Livingston, Tiffany MacBain, Renee Simms, Alison Tracy Hale, and Seth Weinberger. Thanks also to our research librarians, Andrea Klyn and Charlene Floyd, who respond to my queries helpfully, happily, and quickly (so quickly that I have finally learned to ask first rather than descend down the rabbit hole!). Thank you to Irene Lim and Theresa Williams-Chow for ongoing support in all things. Finally, I will forever be grateful to my late friend and colleague Marta Palmquist Cady for her example and advocacy.

Although I am fortunate to have broad support, I can also say, unequivocally, that this book would not have come into being if not for my "writing group"—Giunia Gatta, Jonathan Havercroft, Michael Illuzzi, and Amit Ron. My dear friends, I cannot thank you enough for the support, criticism, and encouragement over these past five years. Thank you for fostering analytical clarity (Amit), keeping me from overthinking (Jonathan), reminding me of the human stakes of this project (Giunia), and never letting me forget what my argument really is (Mike). I'm grateful to you all.

Thank you to my colleagues at Oxford University Press for helping make this book a reality. The two anonymous reviewers were generously critical. Thank you both for recommendations that improved the manuscript considerably and for seeing value in the project. Thank you to Angela Chnapko and Alexcee Bechthold at Oxford University Press for shepherding this project with enthusiasm and care, Abishayareddy Vijaybabu for thoughtful collaboration on the production of the book, Kelley Friel at KRF Research for careful editing of the entire manuscript, and Birgitte Necessary for constructing the index.

Writing a book about sexual violence is taxing, and I am lucky to live in a place of natural beauty that humbles and inspires me. I am also surrounded by loving friends and family. I thank my friends, especially Victoria Defrancesco Soto, Claire Kramer, Jorge Bravo, Efrén Pérez, Tammy Pérez del Cano, Natalie Masuoka, Ali Aslam, Stefan Dolgert, Carol Atkinson, and Giacomo Chiozza for true friendships that have persisted far beyond graduate school. To the "Seattle group" of Arizona transplants, thank you for adventures on land and sea; thanks to the Tacoma "dinner group" for culinary inspiration; and to my hiking and backpacking friends, thank you for adventuring with me into the woods. Colette Lescantz, you are my sister, and your lifelong commitment to caring for women and their bodies inspires me and keeps me grounded. Thank you for sharing yourself, your experiences, and your knowledge so generously.

I have an extended family that I get to travel, laugh, sit around, walk around, talk about the dogs and cats, and eat and drink with. For over twenty years, I have felt welcomed and loved by the entire Alvey–Cook–Mauk clan and have created many happy memories with Carol, Monty, Jeri, Erica, Cassie, and the several Steves. Tyler Mauk is my soulmate-nephew and has brought me joy and love since we first met when he was five. To my brother, Kevin, and his spouse Fran, thank you for support and love in good and hard times over the years. I am grateful to have you all in my life.

I wrote this book under the watchful eyes of our dogs, Dewey and Gracie, and amidst the antics of two orange tabbies, Mango and Enzo. Final revisions of this book were undertaken under the supervision of Dahlia Louise Pettibone, whose daily displays of joyful abandon have been essential for reminding me of the good things.

My dearest love is Ben Mauk, who has supported me and my work with love, generosity, and laughter. I cannot imagine a better life partner, and I will be forever grateful that he decided to drive the Penske truck across the country from Arizona to North Carolina . . . and then stayed to build a life with me. Ben, I tell you this all the time because it's true: you are my absolute favorite.

Finally, I dedicate this book to my parents—my late father, James, and my mother, Ellarita—for their relentless love and support, for teaching me to care about politics, and for supporting me and my "blazing pen" ever since I wrote my first protest letter in kindergarten.

Chapter One
Rape Culture and the Politics of Sexual Violence

The Meaning of Rape

The popular video game series *Grand Theft Auto* (*GTA*) depicts a world of misogynist, heteropatriarchal, white supremacist violence. Until the sixth edition, which will be released in 2025, the only protagonists in the game have been male.[1],[2] Players try to evade authorities and murder, steal, pimp, and assault their way from "street-level hustlers" to "kingpins."[3] Although players can kill or injure their adversaries, *GTA* does not permit players to rape one another. Yet, shortly after *GTA V* came out in 2013, some players modified the game's code to allow their avatars to rape other avatars,[4] even though this did not earn them any material advantage in the game. Note that these players didn't modify the game to allow other players' avatars to *be raped*; they changed it to allow their own avatars to *commit rape*. For them, the ability to rape represented a more tantalizing exercise of power than theft, assault, or murder. The homophobic and misogynistic inferences associated with rape made it uniquely appealing: through rape, players could "own" their opponents in a way they could not when using the other forms of violence sanctioned in the game.

In 2021, Nina Jane Patel was an executive at an immersive technology company who had been asked to beta-test a virtual reality (VR) game called *Horizon Worlds* (developed by Meta). She reported that within a minute of entering the virtual game space, three or four male avatars verbally and sexually harassed and then gang-raped her avatar. VR is designed to feel like an embodied experience, and Patel reported being traumatized by the virtual assault and even described it using terms that are common to many victims of sexual assault: she said she "froze" as her avatar was raped. The assailants expressed a "you know you want it" sensibility about this virtual rape: they took screenshots and said, "don't pretend you didn't love it," justifying their virtual violence on the grounds that all women enjoy sexualized violence and violent domination.[5] Their actions reveal the power of using non-consensual sex to dominate a space. When Patel wrote about the incident on her blog, some commenters said it was her fault for selecting a female avatar, while others chided her for her naivete and even discounted her experience with comments such as "you've obviously never played fortnite" and "avatars don't have lower bodies to assault."[6] Some noted that female avatars are responsible for putting a "safety barrier" in place to protect themselves from the threat of sexualized violence, which is used—even in a digital space—to remind them that they do not belong there, while male avatars are free to exercise unlimited agency. The virtual assailants were conveying the message that in VR, as in the real world, females exist to be dominated by males.

My starting point for this book is that rape is enacted to assert a political claim to control and domination. The meaning of rape is determined by the ideological context in which it is imagined, threatened, and enacted. *Rape culture* is this context; it does not tell us what rape *is*, exactly, but rather what it *means*. US rape culture employs myths, discourse, and practices related to sexual violence to preserve hierarchies of race, gender, sexuality, and class. Thus, sexual violence is always a political act: it is an exercise of power rather than a behavioral or biological phenomenon.[7] In other words, in US rape culture, rape *means* that individuals who inflict sexual violence do so because they understand themselves—and are understood by others—to be entitled to dominate.[8]

I think about domination as feminist philosopher Iris Young does, as an inhibition on self-determination that is structurally supported but also individually or collectively enacted.[9] Dominability is a feature of the raped or rapeable body: being raped or rapeable is evidence that one was (or is) dominable, often because one is already marginalized in US society in some other way. The myths, discourses, and practices of rape culture identify *who is dominable* and *who is entitled to dominate.* Thus, even when a culture condemns and criminalizes rape, rape culture identifies and preserves relations of domination.

The imperative to dominate through rape or the threat of rape is unique among crimes. While other violent crimes (such as theft or murder) can be committed out of a material need or desire for security, and may even have political motivations, theft and murder are not exclusively motivated by a desire to dominate others. Rape is different because it is always an expression of domination and control: a potential rapist must first identify a suitable victim—someone who could *be raped* but could not *commit rape* against *them*. This is why the *GTA* hackers and the *Horizon World* players sought to "rape": being able to rape demonstrates their capacity to dominate others. In a rape culture, existing structures of domination determine a person's "rapeability," which may be one reason why so many heterosexual men find it so hard to believe that men can be raped. In a sense, a rape victim is not made dominable by *being raped*; the perpetrator must have already identified the victim as dominable in order commit rape.

To understand how both rape and the threat of rape perpetuate political domination in the United States and elsewhere, we must acknowledge that sexual violence is pervasive and requires systematic analysis. Yet such analysis often disregards individuals' specific experiences of sexual violence and the threat of sexual violence, which require care, compassion, and attention. I explore the political meaning of rape in order to better understand how sexual violence persists but *not* to dictate how individual survivors should understand their experiences. After they are targeted as objects of domination, rape victims suffer from the specific violence they endure and then suffer again because of the broader meanings that US rape culture assigns to them as victims. The trauma of sexual violence shapes victims' lives, sometimes across generations; in many communities, rape is a historical trauma as well as a personal one. Preventing sexual violence requires acknowledging that rape is not triggered by natural sexual appetites, simple miscommunication, or ethical breaches. Sexual violence is a political act, a form of violence that is also, as feminist scholar Jacqueline Rose puts it, "a form of entitlement" that is more difficult to grasp than privilege because it "relies for its persistence on a refusal to acknowledge that it is even there."[10] Sexual violence is born out of a political claim—an entitlement—to dominate, a willingness to use another person for one's own gratification, and oftentimes a fervent denial that this exercise of privilege has been undertaken at all.

I conclude that rape is undertaken with the aim to dominate for two reasons. First, the selection of another person to dominate for one's own gratification is never accidental. An individual chooses a target for rape out of a sense of power and control rooted in either an overt belief in their own superiority and dominance or a more subverted sense that they have a claim to gratification. Second, and more to the point, rape victimization is too systematic to be accidental. The groups of people who are most likely to be raped already face ongoing oppression in US culture, such as those who are subordinated by white supremacy, cisgender heteropatriarchy, and settler capitalism. This means that, because rape can be perpetuated in any situation in which one person believes they are empowered to dominate another, it is possible (though uncommon) for a woman to rape a man. The meaning of rape is the same in this uncommon scenario: the rapist is a person who has targeted another to dominate through sexual violence. What changes is the basis on which the domination is justified (socioeconomic class, age, or race, for example, rather than gender). Those who are already in a position of control give themselves permission to enact domination through rape. Often, the act of rape or sexual violence affirms to them that they are able to subordinate others. In this sense, rape signifies a profound ability to dominate.

Some might challenge my argument by suggesting that the issue at hand is not the politicization of the meaning of rape but rather a corrupted form of sexual desire that is distorted by rape culture.[11] Feminist philosopher Amia Srinivasan has recently revisited the politics of sexual desire, which some feminist debates about sex positivity and desire under patriarchy have not satisfactorily addressed. Srinivasan is interested in the tension at the heart of these debates, which she describes as an acceptance that "no one is obliged to desire anyone else, that no one has a right to be desired, but also that who is desired and who isn't is a political question, a question often answered by more general patterns of domination and exclusion."[12] There are important connections between the politicized meaning of rape, as articulated by rape culture, and Srinivasan's explanation of the politics of sexual desire. Both are structured by those "general patterns of domination and exclusion." I agree with Srinivasan that "facts about 'fuckability'—not whose bodies are seen as sexually available (in the sense black women, trans women, and disabled women are all *too* fuckable), but whose bodies confer status on those who have sex with them—are political facts."[13] However, I want to consider what makes those particular bodies "all *too* fuckable." Why are some violent assaults called rape, while others don't seem to count as rape? Why are some victims extended care and attention, while others are blamed or are not recognized as having been raped at all? Answering these questions requires a political and—as I explain later in the chapter—an intersectional analytical frame for analyzing rape culture.

Entitlement to Sex and Entitlement to Dominate

Elliot Rodger was a college student who murdered six people and injured fourteen more before taking his own life in Isla Vista, California, in 2014. His planned "Day of Retribution" to avenge his status as a virgin exemplifies a patriarchal "entitlement to sex." Rodger has become a hero among incels, who lionize him and who now believe that "[they are] owed sex, and . . . [are subsequently] enraged by the women who deprive [them] of it."[14] Rodger responded violently to his ostensible sexual deprivation, which he blamed on multiple factors including the women who rejected or failed to notice him, the alpha males who got laid without even trying, and his own attributes: his biraciality, bad haircut, unfashionable clothes, and shyness. Rodger said he eventually "realized that I would be a virgin forever, condemned to suffer rejection and humiliation at the hands of women because they don't fancy me, because their sexual attractions are flawed. They are attracted to the wrong type of male."[15]

I agree with Srinivasan and Kate Manne (2020), who characterize Rodger as expressing an "entitlement to sex." I note, however, that his sense of entitlement did not lead Rodger to commit rape to get what he thought he was owed. Although Rodger believed he was entitled to sex, he had foreclosed the possibility that, as a beta loser, he was *entitled to dominate* via rape. He did not doubt or deny that alphas were empowered to dominate via rape, but in his mind, he was no alpha. Resigned to his status as a permanent virgin, Rodger determined that he "would rather die than suffer such an existence, and [he] knew that if it came to that, [he] would exact [his] revenge upon the world in the most catastrophic way possible."[16] Murderous, nonsexual violence would allow him to achieve the retribution he sought and would vindicate him as a man. His weapons empowered him to kill because, according to his logic, this is the only way he could become an alpha: "After I picked up the handgun, I brought it back to my room and felt a new sense of power. I was now armed. *Who's the alpha male now, bitches.*"[17]

Although Rodger did not believe he could dominate via rape, his incel fans understand things differently today. They discuss strategies to make it "legal for incels to rape women."[18] Some of his "beta" fans now claim a right to rape, insisting on a legal entitlement to dominate by virtue of their perceived (yet unsatisfied) entitlement to sex.[19] This example (and shifting attitudes among incels about what Rodger was entitled to) illustrates that in US popular culture, rape *signifies who is entitled to dominate.* A rapist has demonstrated that they are entitled to sex and are entitled to dominate via rape to get it; they have demonstrated that they are the dominator, not the dominated. That is what it means to commit rape in US rape culture.

Rape culture is the interpretive framework that identifies who is *dominable* via rape and who is *entitled to dominate.* By identifying a set of paradigmatic myths with victims and perpetrators who share particular traits, a rape culture conceals persistent forms of rape victimization and perpetration, renders some victims unworthy of recognition or care, and indemnifies some perpetrators against rape allegations. This culture fosters discourses and practices beyond rape (such as street harassment, romanticization of manipulation and violence, and norms of appropriate styles of dress) that reinforce the ubiquitous threat of rape and regulate the behavior of potential victims. This *political* work occurs across multiple axes of oppression, including white supremacist, heteropatriarchal, cisgender, settler colonial, and capitalist axes. Rape culture draws on these axes to form an interpretative framework through which US society collectively distinguishes between rape and sex, victims and liars, and rapists and "good guys." Rape culture is both cause and effect: it shapes and is shaped by an interpretive framework that facilitates sexual violence. Acts of sexual violence, representations of rape in popular culture, and shifts in popular attitudes all contour the evolving rape culture.

This book's thesis is that the interpretive framework of US rape culture sustains white male control over all the subordinates of white heteropatriarchy by evolving and expanding to apply to any group that threatens this control. My argument that rape culture evolves and expands echoes scholar of gender and sexuality studies and cultural studies Rana M. Jaleel's sentiment that "rape as a concept offers a fiction of coherence."[20] I suggest that the meaning of rape is a moving target that seems to be "coherent" (e.g., that non-consensual sex is rape) but is in fact incoherent over time (e.g., either that non-consensual marital sex is not rape because it is necessarily consensual or that sexual consent is always implied unless expressly rescinded). This incoherence is managed by the contortions of a rape culture that specifies who can be raped and who can rape. I am not saying that "only white males commit rape" or that "only white males benefit from sexual violence." My argument is that the *meaning* that US rape culture ascribes to rape always preserves white male economic supremacy over US society. Analysis of rape culture must therefore extend beyond men's dominance of women to include other forms of political domination (such as white supremacy, heteronormativity, cisnormativity, capitalist exploitation, and settler colonialism) and how these forms interact. This type of intersectional analysis is often missing from recent explorations of rape culture, which tend to undertake what Beth Ritchie calls an "everywoman analysis," seeking to provide critical insights into struggles that all women experience (such as domestic violence and sexual violence) but implicitly reflecting and relating to the particular experiences of white, middle-class women.[21] The explicit focus on male domination and the implicit formulation of the white, middle-class woman as the target of sexual violence obscure the fact that rape culture sustains many structures of domination, including white supremacy and heteronormativity—an insight that slave abolitionists, Black feminists, and intersectional theorists have long described, even if they did not always label it as a "rape culture."[22] In the next section, I trace the emergence of an explicit concept of rape culture in order to develop a more capacious account of the concept that will help us unpack the myriad ways in which rape signifies and reinforces structures of domination.

The Emergence of the Concept of Rape Culture

The phrase "rape culture" is relatively new to feminist analysis, and it seemed to arise in feminist scholarly and activist literatures in the mid-1970s. In the mid-1990s, use of the term expanded, and it eventually migrated to the mainstream: in the 2010s, Google searches for "rape culture" in the United States increased exponentially.[23] In this mainstream US discourse, "rape culture" is typically defined as a culture that normalizes aggressive heterosexual male violence toward women.[24]

Although mainstream sources acknowledge that women are not the only victims of rape, most accounts of rape culture refer to the normalization of sexual violence *by men against women*. This framing of rape culture does political work in its own right: it obscures the scale and scope of sexual violence throughout the culture and conceals many of the targets of sexualized violence. Journalist Amanda Taub defines the concept as "a culture in which sexual violence is treated as the norm and victims are blamed for their own assaults. It's not just about sexual violence itself, but about cultural norms and institutions that protect rapists, promote impunity, shame victims, and demand that women make unreasonable sacrifices to avoid sexual assault."[25] This definition usefully notes that sexual violence is normalized through culture and institutions but centers women as its targets. This centering, common to most accounts of rape culture, is a feature of rape culture itself: a singular focus on patriarchy conceals the victimization of those who do not fit within its normalized account of rape, particularly those who are (or are *also*) subordinated by systemic white supremacy, settler colonialism, capitalist exploitation, and heteronormativity.

Some of the earliest invocations of the concept (if not the term) "rape culture" are undeniably intersectional in orientation. In these analyses, rape, the threat of rape, and accusations of rape are understood to be exertions and reflections of political power. These analyses seeded the ground for the eventual emergence of a concept of rape culture that articulates how myths, discourses, and practices shape and reinforce popular ideas about what rape is, who a rape victim is, and who a rape perpetrator is. To demonstrate what this intersectional work reveals, I first explore the myth of the Black male rapist who threatens white femininity, which emerged during the post–Civil War Reconstruction period in the United States (1865–77) to justify lynching. Second, I explore the myth of the "bad man" rapist that regained prominence in some conservative feminist circles in the mid-1970s as they sought anti-rape reforms. Third, I discuss the places where the term "rape culture" began to appear explicitly in the mid-1970s within anti-rape analysis and activism. These brief explorations are not meant to reveal a straight line of analysis or to provide a complete genealogy. Rather, they reflect what critical legal scholar Kimberlé Crenshaw describes as tracing the *travels* of an idea.[26]

These travels reveal how the concept of rape culture emerged and why an intersectional analysis of rape culture is essential if we want to eliminate sexual violence. US rape culture relies on structures of domination beyond patriarchy, including white supremacy, heteronormativity, cisnormativity, and capitalist, settler colonial exploitation. Due to the entanglement of varied structures of domination—and the reinforcement of their entanglement through the myths, discourses, and practices of rape culture—sexual violence, particularly against marginalized persons, continues largely unacknowledged, unreported, and unabated, despite widespread public condemnation of rape. An intersectional approach exposes these entanglements and provides us with resources to oppose them.

I begin to trace the travels of the idea of a rape culture by turning to Ida B. Wells's and Frederick Douglass's potent political analyses of rape and the rape allegation. In the late nineteenth century, they observed the consequences of an emerging myth that Black men posed a violent, sexual threat to white women. This myth had not existed prior to the abolition of slavery but arose after the emancipation of enslaved people during the Reconstruction–Redemption period to justify the latest strategy of white terror: lynching.[27] During the antebellum and Civil War periods, there is no evidence of widespread concerns about enslaved Black men raping white women.[28] Yet, Wells notes, once Black persons could no longer be owned and controlled via the system of chattel slavery, "a new system of intimidation came into vogue; the Negro was not only whipped and scourged; he was killed."[29] This system required moral justification: white men and women promoted the myth of the Black male rapist as the salacious and sensationalistic ground to justify the torture and murder of newly emancipated Black men and boys.

According to Angela Y. Davis, white men began disciplining Black citizens through lynching not only to maintain political supremacy; they also used the myth of the Black male rapist to their economic advantage. Davis argues that after the Civil War, the North needed a strategy to continue to exploit Black labor while pitting white and Black working-class individuals against each other to sustain control of the southern economy.[30] Lynching "Black male rapists" did both: it disciplined Black persons whose economic successes threatened white economic dominance *and* gave the white working class a spurious rationale to avoid solidarity with the Black working class.

The Tulsa Massacre of 1921 that destroyed the thriving "Black Wall Street" illustrates how this myth was used to consolidate white working-class economic dominance over Black persons. An alleged sexual assault involving a young Black man (Dick Rowland) and a white woman (Sarah Page) provided the spark for the massacre. Reports compiled by the Oklahoma Commission (2001) and the Department of Justice (2025) find no evidence that Page ever made such an allegation when she was interviewed by police. The evidence of sexual assault was so thin, in fact, that police did not even arrest Rowland until the next day.[31] Yet locals, enraged by unsubstantiated rumors, took matters into their own hands,[32] destroying the Greenwood area of Tulsa and killing or injuring a still unknown number of Black residents.[33] Here, as elsewhere, the myth of the Black male rapist justified the destruction of the Black economic success that threatened local white economic and political supremacy.

In *The Red Record*, Wells explains that rape is used to justify lynching of Black men who rape white women but not white men who rape

Black women. The rape of a Black Baltimore woman by a group of white men was a meager "color line justice": although the rape should have been "a deed dastardly enough to arouse Southern blood, which gives its horror of rape as excuse for lawlessness . . . *she was a colored woman*," and so the men were acquitted.[34] Wells also explains that the moral outrage of white mobs is not actually directed at the crime of rape itself. This collective action is directed only at rape (or even consensual sex) when it threatens *whiteness* by challenging the white man's claim to control "his" women as property. The white woman's body was the vessel of whiteness, and white male supremacist power was enlisted to protect whiteness—not individual women. The practices of "protecting" white reproductive power (as white femininity) and disciplining Black masculinity were two sides of the same coin.

Eventually, white women also sounded the call to protect white femininity; despite the past solidarity between the slave abolitionist and women's movements, the myth of the Black male rapist took root in the white supremacy of the women's movement. According to philosopher Tommy J. Curry, "the dawn of the twentieth century birthed a feminist activist that used the myth of the Black male rapist as a bridge between white women's moral capacities and more visible political presence and engagement with societal problems."[35] Many white women activists—including Rebecca Latimer Felton, Charlotte Gilman, and Jane Addams—accepted the myth of the Black male rapist and, in some cases, even defended lynching.[36] Curry demonstrates that white men and white women both used the myth of the Black male rapist who poses a dangerous threat to white women, albeit in different ways, to exert political power and contribute to a collective discourse of Black men and boys as irreducibly immoral and criminal. The myth has persisted far beyond Reconstruction, from a fictional rape in *Birth of a Nation* (1915) to the false rape allegations against Black men and boys by white women—including the Scottsboro Boys (1931), Emmett Till (1955), and the Central Park Five (1989)—and, more recently, to the accusation that Amy Cooper leveled at birdwatcher Christian Cooper (no relation) in Central Park in May 2020.[37]

A second mythic figure—the sinister white male rapist who targets defenseless white female victims—gained special attention from anti-rape activists in the 1960s and 1970s who sought broad public support for their cause.[38] Historian Christine Stansell suggests that, due to their concern over radical feminist arguments for women's bodily autonomy during the abortion rights debates in the 1960s and 1970s, more conservative feminists adopted a different approach when advocating anti-rape initiatives related to date rape, marital rape, and rape shield laws. Popular support of anti-rape initiatives was predicated on the assertion that most rape involved a violent, predatory male rapist (often a stranger) who attacks a defenseless female.[39] Stansell suggests that this myth gained traction in feminist "body politics" circles by reaffirming radical feminist arguments about the ubiquity of violent masculinity, but it then moved to a more conservative mainstream by bypassing the argument for sexual autonomy in order to reaffirm female victimhood and weakness: "it was easier to invoke feminism when it meant protecting women than when it meant ensuring they could protect themselves from the adverse consequences of sex."[40] In this debate, political expediency eclipsed radical feminist principles, at great cost to anti-rape efforts. Contrary to the crucial radical feminist insight that the normalization of sexual violence was essential to the maintenance of white supremacist and heteropatriarchal power, this myth suggested that only "bad apples" committed rape.

This myth of the "bad apple/bad man rapist" obscures the everydayness of rape; perpetrators who are outwardly judged to be "good guys" are largely presumed to be incapable of rape. The myth that only deviant white men rape and the rest are just misunderstood "good guys" endures. Brock Turner was a white, wealthy 19-year-old Stanford athlete in 2015 when he raped Chanel Miller, a recent college graduate and a non-white, mixed-race woman. His father made a public appeal to Brock's goodness and remorse to suggest that a sentence involving incarceration was a "steep price to pay" for "twenty minutes of action" and that the guilty verdict had already "broken and shattered [Brock] and our family." Brock's father did not mention the victim, only the harm done to his son;[41] at sentencing, the judge justified the light sentence on the grounds that prison would have a "severe" impact on Turner.[42] When the perpetrator is a "good guy," the consequences on *his* life, not the victim's, are the real tragedy.

Black women are differently trapped in the narrow space between the myth of the "bad apple" rapist and the Black male rapist. First, as Deborah K. King writes, Black women's "institutionalized exploitation as the concubines, mistresses, and sexual slaves of white males distinguished our experience from that of white females' sexual oppression because it could only have existed in relation to racist and classist forms of domination."[43] Black women often work in close proximity to white men within white households. Because white men within a domestic space are presumed to be "good guys," rather than "bad apples," they do not pose a threat to anyone. Thus, Black women are rarely assumed to require protection from the white men with whom they are most often in contact. At the same time, Black women, like Black men, are construed as both hypersexual and inhumanly strong;[44] and this is a second reason they are not afforded protection from sexual predators. Instead, it is presumed that if she had not been engaging in welcome sex, a Black woman would have overwhelmed her attackers by herself. Political scientist Melissa Harris-Perry notes that many Black women refigure themselves as asexual (e.g., as a Mammy figure) in order to create modest protection from white male sexual violence.[45] Taken together, these two mythic rapist figures have facilitated the centuries-long sexual victimization of Black women at the hands of white men by structuring Black women as if they were impossible to victimize.

The two mythic assailants (the Black male and the bad apple)—both of whom are presumed to attack undeserving, defenseless, white, middle- and upper-class women—justify ongoing white male dominance in the popular US imagination in two ways: (1) by empowering white men to use violence to protect "their" women from external threats and (2) by deflecting attention away from the ubiquity of white male rape. But they also nourish other, related myths, such as the hypersexualized and unrapeable Black woman, which in turn supports the myth of the unvictimizable tease (who is often poor and white). In effect, these myths perpetuate a culture in which individuals are only recognized as rape victims if they are deemed good enough, innocent enough, or helpless enough, while others are only recognized as perpetrators if they are deviant enough, criminal enough, or inhuman enough. The construction (and reconstruction) of these myths imposes specific political meaning on the threat or act of rape. This was the foundation of the concept of "rape culture," though anti-rape activists had not yet found the words to name it.

In April 1971, the New York Radical Feminists hosted a "speak-out" on rape, which prompted a compilation of "facts and figures on the extent to which society ignores, tolerates, and even encourages repeated acts of rape and sexual exploitation."[46] The group argued that societal forces subjected all women to patriarchal oppression, which meant rape was an essential matter "to be dealt with in feminist terms for female liberation."[47] Although the analysis published after the speak-out focused on rape as a tool of male domination, it offered two other insights that signal the importance of intersectional analysis. First, it acknowledged in general terms that there were differences across women's experiences, which were revealed through consciousness raising;[48] in contrast, more "mainstream" analysis tended to universalize white women's experiences as all women's experiences. Second, by identifying a range of experiences with sexual violence (not only rape), the New York Radical Feminists argued that "rape, as an issue, was a means of analyzing the psychological and political structures of oppression in our society."[49] These two insights paved the way toward examining how previous analyses of rape centered the experiences of white women and treated rape as an individual-level phenomenon and toward thinking instead about differences across experiences of rape and evaluating the broader structures at work. But at their speak-out in 1971, they had not yet deeply engaged these questions.

That same year, Susan Griffin published her essay "Rape: An All-American Crime," which does not use the phrase "rape culture" but explains that cultural discourses about male aggression and female passivity translate into an assertion that overwhelming male sexual desire is natural and uncontrollable and that women are simultaneously modest and secretly harbor rape fantasies.[50] Griffin argues that, while laws do not formally uphold these contradictory discourses, "the fact that rape is against the law should not be considered proof that rape is not in fact encouraged as part of our culture."[51] In other words, rape can be unlawful and still be normalized in a popular culture. Although her essay starts from the position that all women are vulnerable to being raped, Griffin's analysis incorporates race when it notes that rape myths and discourses benefit white men in particular. For example, Griffin explores the myth of the Black male rapist, citing Douglass's argument about its emergence during Reconstruction, and notes the precarity of Black women and the heteropatriarchal terms of the protection of white women: "The white male's open rape of black women, coupled with his overweening concern for the chastity and protection of his wife and daughters, represents an extreme of sexist and racist hypocrisy."[52] Griffin's exploration of the dynamic relationship between race and gender approaches intersectional analysis at a time when other white feminists treated race and gender as discrete structures of domination, rather than as interlocking ones.

The 1975 documentary *Rape Culture* (which may be the first place the term is used formally) also approaches an intersectional account of the concept. Although the film—which was revised and re-released in 1983—never defines rape culture, the contributors note that the sexual allure of rape—typically, to men—is "programmed by the . . . mass media" (4:57) and constitutes a "total process of socialization" (7:12) that reinforces broadly accepted ideas about rape. Although the dominant assumption of the film is that only men can rape, it offers a more capacious account of victimhood than other analyses at the time. The contributors affirm that rape victims can be men or women and from any class and that Black, Asian, and Indigenous women are all considered rapeable but are sexualized in distinct ways.[53]

Two years later, the Combahee River Collective affirmed the notion that rape combines oppressive relations to sustain white male supremacy: "racial–sexual oppression . . . is neither solely racial nor solely sexual, e.g., the history of rape of Black women by white men as a weapon of political repression."[54] The members of the collective identified the politicization of rape, explicitly accounting for its racial and gendered dimensions and implicitly referencing its heterosexist and capitalist-exploitative ones.[55] They understood rape as a political strategy, and their analysis suggests an intersectional understanding of how this weapon was wielded. Yet, this analysis did not seem to inspire a comprehensive, intersectional account of rape *culture* from other feminists. Instead, the biologized account of rape from some radical feminists seeded a gender-dominant analysis of rape culture that eventually made its way to the mainstream.

The Mainstream Account of Rape Culture and Its Shortcomings

If Black feminist and some radical feminist analyses were considering rape culture in intersectional terms, why did the mainstream fail to push its understanding of rape and rape culture in the same direction? Why has rape culture been defined and analyzed in the mainstream as what intersectional theorists call a "single-axis" issue, understood almost entirely in terms of the male subordination of women? Susan Brownmiller's *Against Our Will* declared that only men rape (since male genitalia has been weaponized against women since "prehistoric times") and only women are rape victims. Her book, which has not been out of print since its publication in 1975, advances an explicitly patriarchal analysis of rape, which she defines as "a conscious process of intimidation by which *all men* keep *all women* in a state of fear."[56] Brownmiller does not use the term "rape culture" but describes rape as both an exercise of power in itself and a process of control that extends beyond the act of rape. Her analysis crucially explores rape as an exertion of power codified in laws, fortified by institutions, carried out on battlefields and in bedrooms, and permeated as a threat in the daily lives of all women. It brought anti-rape analysis activism into mainstream conversations in ways that few earlier interventions had and emphasized the gendered dimension of rape.

Yet Brownmiller's account may have been a little *too* influential in focusing on gendered analysis, and this influence has endured. A 2015 *Time* article about her book noted: "What today's feminists describe as 'rape culture' has its roots in Brownmiller's theory of rape as a means of social control, her emphasis on gender role socialization and her critique of the glorification of sexual violence in the media."[57] The allegations against Harvey Weinstein at that time, and the resulting growth of the #MeToo movement, prompted *The Guardian* to observe that "Brownmiller's work is suddenly crisp again, its prescience and enduring relevance noted anew by anyone old enough, or well read enough, to be familiar with it."[58] David Remnick wrote in a 2017 *New Yorker* article that "'Against Our Will' remains an important prod to our understanding of the social order."[59] In short, her book remains profoundly important to mainstream feminism's critical analysis of rape. But its problems have migrated into mainstream feminist analysis of rape *culture*.

Though her work is focused on patriarchal relations, Brownmiller takes questions of race, settler colonialism, and class seriously. However, her analysis of the Scottsboro Boys and Emmett Till replicates white supremacist anxieties about the Black male rapist.[60] For example, she claims that "the recurrent nightmare in the eighteenth-century slaveholding South had been the white male dream of black men rising up to rape 'their' women,"[61] a claim that, as I have noted, is not supported by the historical record. Brownmiller is appalled by the murder of Till and the acquittal of Bryant and Milam but writes: "rarely has one single case exposed so clearly as Till's the underlying group-male antagonisms over access to women, for what began in Bryant's store should not be misconstrued as an innocent flirtation."[62] She maintains that Till was trying to show his friends that he could "get a white woman. Till's action was more than a kid's brash prank and his murder was more than a husband's revenge."[63] Brownmiller attributed male sexual desire to Till, who was only 12 years old. His Blackness allowed her to categorize Till as a criminally adult male rather than as the child he was—much less a child from Chicago who did not know there were things he simply could not do and survive a family visit to rural Mississippi. She thus implicitly upholds the myth of the Black male rapist, which she uses to defend Carolyn

Bryant's accusation—an accusation which Bryant later recanted. According to Brownmiller, Bryant is worthy of defense and her motives are above reproach, while Till behaves like a typical man—or, worse, like a Black man.

Yet Carolyn Bryant's motives were complicated and suggest that she traded on the power she enjoyed by virtue of her race to protect her from the domination exerted upon her by virtue of her sex. She was likely protecting herself from a physically abusive husband,[64] which does not justify her accusation against Till but clarifies why a white woman might appeal to the myth of the Black male rapist to protect herself and illustrates how patriarchy draws on white supremacy to preserve both. Griffin similarly explains that if "a black man was found to be having sexual relations with a white woman, the white woman could exercise skin-privilege, and claim that she had been raped, in which case the black man was lynched. But if she did not claim rape, she herself was subject to lynching."[65] In this context, patriarchy and white supremacy work together to maintain white male control; white women invoke the myth for their own self-preservation—at tremendous cost to the Black men they accuse. White women are subject to the fear of rape and the myths and discourses that normalize sexual violence, but the interlocking structures of race and gender make them both victims and beneficiaries of a rape culture that protected them above all others. Yet Griffin does not offer in-depth exploration of the critical role that white women play in perpetuating rape culture. Like many white feminists, she was likely wary of casting doubt on the veracity of women's claims to being raped, given how easily women's accusations are dismissed. Yet this choice conceals the ways in which white women use rape culture to carve out a degree of power or control for themselves in a patriarchal, misogynistic context and, in doing so, re-seed the ground from which sexual violence and their own victimization can grow.

The "single-axis" approach to thinking about rape culture is to regard sexual violence purely as a function of patriarchy. Two problems emerge from this kind of thinking about rape and rape culture, which does not recognize structures of domination as multiple, simultaneous, and interlocking. The first is political: single-axis thinking isolates marginalized groups from one another. In the *Rape Culture* documentary, rape education consultant Karla M. Jackson emphasizes that rape is an exercise of violence with a specific political intent: "when we talk about rape, we talk about violence and the threat of violence that is used to keep people in their place, just like racism is used to keep people in their place. . . . That place may be in the lower socioeconomic strata, in a particular neighborhood, in their houses, *afraid*" (24:10). Jackson's analysis explicitly connects rape, race, and socioeconomic status and implicitly references the geographic control of marginalized groups in ghettos, which Michelle Alexander and Loïc Wacquant identify as central to the ongoing disciplining and control of African Americans.[66] The documentary argues that the reason rape controls subordinate groups so effectively is that the myths, discourses, and practices of rape culture isolate groups by virtue of race, ethnicity, class, gender, and sexuality and teach each group to fear or hate the others. White heteropatriarchal and cisgender men benefit from this isolation and are comparatively unscathed by rape culture.

The second problem associated with oversimplifying sexual violence as only related to the patriarchy is analytical: single-axis analyses simply cannot expose how rape culture isolates marginalized groups *and* pits them against each other. Brownmiller's text is a case in point. Angela Y. Davis writes: "In pretending to defend the cause of all women, [Brownmiller] sometimes boxes herself into the position of defending the particular cause of *white* women."[67] It is not surprising that Brownmiller yields to this temptation, having been raised in a rape culture that taught her to believe it, nor is her faulty analysis grounds to reject her work out of hand (Davis, a pointed critic of Brownmiller, is also unwilling to draw that conclusion). But why is Brownmiller, despite her commitment to unearthing the structural, political bases of rape, drawn into white supremacist analysis? Davis suggests that what's missing from Brownmiller's (and subsequent white feminist) analyses of rape culture is the insight that the myths and discourses that comprise a rape culture—those that "make meaning" of sexual violence—do so by pitting marginalized groups against one another. The social conditions for rape are not limited to heteropatriarchy but are simultaneously structured by white supremacy and settler capitalism.[68] Addressing this analytical problem requires a framework that can reveal the "pitting": it must uncover what the myths, discourses, and practices of rape culture are, how they are reinforced, and whom they empower.

Rape culture sustains white male control over all the subordinates of white capitalist heteropatriarchy by evolving and expanding to apply to any group that threatens this control. Davis calls the myth of the Black male rapist "an aggression against Black people as a whole" because "the mythical rapist [also] implies the mythical whore" and therefore implicates Black women.[69] She also argues that "racism nourishes sexism, causing white women to be indirectly victimized by the special oppression aimed at their sisters of color."[70] Taken together, Davis's two points contain the intersectional insight that structures of domination interact to reassert control that is both white and heteropatriarchal. The myths of the Black male rapist and Black hypersexualized woman are used to discipline Black people as well as other oppressed groups, including white women. Because "racism nourishes sexism" through the myths of rape culture, it is only a small jump from the mythic hypersexualized Black woman to the mythic "white trash" tease who is "asking for it."

Despite the critical, intersectional insights of anti-rape activists and analysts, the mainstream account of rape culture (including Brownmiller's influential but incomplete analysis) continues to conceptualize it as primarily a phenomenon of male domination of women. This misconception of rape culture reproduces misunderstandings of sexual violence, as intersectional feminist Patricia Hill Collins explains, "because theories *explain* the social world, they *affect* the social world."[71] When mainstream feminists declare that rape culture is about gender, they are not just theorizing; they are also doing political work. Their misconception of rape culture amplifies a cultural understanding of rape that fails to recognize it as a multifaceted strategy of control.[72] Put differently, the gendered framing of rape culture that dominates mainstream discourse confines the "meaning" of rape to a "single axis"[73] and obscures its white supremacist, capitalist, cisnormative, heteronormative, and settler colonial dimensions. The mainstream account of rape culture thus impedes the recognition that rape and the threat of rape are exertions of power (specifically, of discipline and control) over *anyone* in a structurally subordinate position within US society.

Restoring an Intersectional Concept of Rape Culture

Defining US rape culture in single-axis terms—as primarily or exclusively pertaining to gender—obscures the complex interactions that reinforce relationships of subordination and normalize sexual violence across many marginalized groups of people. By contrast, an intersectional analysis of rape culture reveals how rape is politicized in order to reinforce relations of subordination across multiple axes of oppression. I define rape culture as *the set of myths, discourses, and practices that normalizes rape and other forms of sexual violence (such as sexual abuse or harassment) as techniques of political domination that can be used against anyone who threatens existing structures of political domination. In a rape culture, rape and other forms of sexual violence are employed to reinforce these structures and preserve relations of subordination.* In the United States, these structures of domination include (but are not limited to) white supremacist, heteropatriarchal, cisnormative, settler colonial, and capitalist forms of domination. Using this more expansive and intersectional definition allows us to investigate how a rape culture is cultivated and what its effects are.

A rape culture collectively defines what "counts" as rape. While rape culture may influence how victims and perpetrators understand their individual experiences, it primarily reveals an entire culture's understanding of subordination and sexual violence. The myths, discourses, and practices of a rape culture shape how it interprets rape victimhood and perpetration, distinguishes rape from consensual sex, and assigns innocence and blame. When confronted with an incident of sexual violence, those living within a rape culture will decide whether they believe an individual was a "real" victim rather than someone who was "asking for it" or whether a perpetrator is a "real" rapist rather than a good person on the wrong side of a misunderstanding. Individuals render these judgments largely based on shared myths and discourses. While I do not draw a bright line between myths and discourses, I note that rape culture relies on both the *specific figuration* of certain people (or kinds of people) and the reproduction of *more general* attitudes and beliefs that justify sexual violence.

Myths are the specific and archetypal stories about rape. Mythic figures—like the Black male rapist, the "bad apple," the stranger in the bushes, the innocent virgin, or the teasing whore—are paradigms of rape perpetrators and victims that draw on and reinforce existing structures of domination. Because myths are used to classify perpetrators and victims, they also reveal who does not fit the archetype of perpetrator or victim. Those who do not are most likely to go unnoticed by the broader culture.

Discourses, by contrast, are prevalent attitudes that implicitly normalize sexual violence—for example, that male sexual aggression and violence are inevitable, that women wield control over men through sex, or that consent is always implied until expressly rescinded. None of these discourses reflects a specific account of rape, but each contributes to the justification and logic of being entitled to dominate another through sex.[74] Some discourses of a rape culture may seem distantly related to sexual violence, but their prevalence throughout a culture can help justify sexual violence. Taken together, myths and discourses form the substantive core of a rape culture.

Practices are individual activities that reinforce subordination and normalize sexual violence. Anthropologist Sherry Ortner's practice theory emphasizes that culture is "the production of the world through human practice"[75] and that *actions*, not just norms or ideals, (re)produce a culture. Rape culture is supported by individual actions (and, sometimes, inactions) that, when replicated throughout a culture, reinforce the interpretive framework about what counts as, and who is responsible for, sexual violence. Rape itself is a practice of rape culture, and it would be absurd to suggest otherwise; but it would also be a mistake to assume that rape is the only practice of rape culture. A rape culture relies on individual, non-violent practices that facilitate, obscure, or normalize sexual violence, including the self-regulating behaviors of persons in at-risk groups, the objectification of certain bodies through personal interactions and media representation, the stigmatization of certain kinds of people,[76] and the (understandably self-protective) decision of many victims not to report being raped. I call these "practices" because although they are individual actions that reflect the myths and discourses of a rape culture, they are commonly enacted and therefore contribute to the widespread reproduction of rape culture. The concept of a rape culture allows us to evaluate discourses and practices that do not seem, superficially, to be about sexual violence so that we can identify how they nevertheless support the conditions that normalize sexual violence.

Ortner's practice theory is similar to Pierre Bourdieu's but invites a "dialectical synthesis"[77] of the agent–structure problem, which is essential in thinking about rape culture. Some critics of the concept of rape culture have argued that it denies the individual responsibility of perpetrators;[78] others say it implies that rape is an inescapable fact of life.[79] A practice theory of rape culture addresses these criticisms by emphasizing its structural *and* individual aspects and explains how social actors can support a context for sexual violence even when they do not commit sexual violence. Practice theory "constructs people as particular kinds of social actors . . . [who] through their living, on-the-ground, variable practices, reproduce or transform—and usually some of each—the culture that made them."[80] Ortner identifies both agents and structures as essential to a theory of culture, which reflects the intersectional emphasis on both the structural nature of oppression and the particularities of lived assertions and experiences of it. To argue that we live in a rape culture, especially if we grapple with the complexities and contradictions of that culture, does not deny the individual culpability of rapists or the perpetuators of rape culture. On the contrary, it invites acknowledgment and resistance of the structures that have been collectively sustained through individual and shared practices.

The practices of rape culture extend beyond popular reflections on sexual violence. Rape culture also finds its way into institutions—even those that are imagined to be immune to such intrusion. For example, a legal statute about rape will attempt to distinguish precisely between sex and rape. Yet when a prosecutor decides *not* to prosecute a rape case, they may do so based on a judgment about whose story a jury will find convincing. This decision is not rendered explicitly on the basis of what the law requires, or even what the evidence proves, but on the ways in which myths and discourses of rape culture shape how social actors (re)act to rape allegations. When enacted in light of rape myths and discourses, prosecutorial discretion thus reproduces a culture that facilitates sexual violence.[81] While rape culture is not always determinative, we cannot understand and oppose sexual violence unless we understand how sexual violence is culturally articulated and normalized, both inside and outside institutions.

Some may wonder why I use the term "practice" rather than "norm." A cultural norm is a "societal rule, value, or standard that delineates an accepted and appropriate behavior within a culture,"[82] while a practice is the "actual application or use of an idea, belief, or method, as opposed to the theory or principles of it,"[83] whether normative or not. Practices account for both the normative and non-normative, which is important in two respects. First, the idea that a rape culture reflects "appropriate behavior" begs the question of intersectional analysis. Norms are determined by one's positionality; the behaviors that are normatively "appropriate" for white women and Black women in US society are not the same. The language of norms may obscure the differential analysis necessary to understand the myriad practices of a rape culture that sustain white male control over subordinates of white heteropatriarchy, which apply to each group in a different way. Second, I have noted that in a rape culture, rape is culturally supported even though it is legally denounced. This contradiction is possible because many of the practices of a rape culture that are *not* considered socially acceptable are nonetheless commonplace. For example, Marcus identifies "microstrategies of oppression"[84] that take advantage of cultural norms to protect perpetrators, like the advice on men's rights activist websites *Thumotic* or *Return of Kings* to encourage men to get "proof" of consent after the fact (e.g., by sending texts saying "last night was fun"). This practice manipulates a norm of female politeness to protect men against accusation.[85] The concept of "norms" captures only the first aspect of this dynamic; the second aspect is not normative but is nevertheless a feature of rape culture.

The myths, discourses, and practices of rape culture (re)define who is a victim and who cannot be one, as well as who is a perpetrator—and who cannot be one. These kinds of judgments reinforce specific structures of domination within a culture.[86] Because these structures often overlap and can reinforce each other, one cannot critically analyze rape culture in a non-intersectional way. I am not suggesting that the interpretations borne by a rape culture are monolithic or that cultures do not shift over time. I argue that it is both possible and necessary in a rape culture to identify the persistent myths, discourses, and practices that make it possible for rape and other forms of sexual violence to serve as techniques of political domination.

Outline of the Book

This book explores select manifestations of US rape culture to identify myths, discourses, and practices that perpetuate it and to demonstrate how rape culture reinforces existing structures of domination—namely heteropatriarchal, cisnormative, white supremacist, settler colonial, and neoliberal capitalist ones. A rape culture is necessarily context-specific, but the myths, discourses, and practices of one rape culture can migrate and shape another, particularly when distributed through media, popular culture, the law, and other colonial and imperial structures.[87] Each context requires its own interrogation by those who live in and understand it, but the intersectional framework I lay out in this book is designed to support critical analysis of all rape cultures. I have chosen five specific examples of how rape culture operates in the United States, but I could have chosen others, such as the discourses and practices of racialized securitization and economic exploitation at the southern US border or the myths and discourses of male sexuality and homophobia in US jails and prisons or the myths and practices of heteropatriarchal exotification of Asian and Pacific Islander women through US military action and tourism in the Pacific. I encourage other scholars to adapt this analytical framework to continue uncovering the intersectional operations of US rape culture and exposing the ways in which it perpetuates structures of domination and relations of subordination.

The book's title is admittedly provocative, and it is meant to challenge the harmful contention that women and other feminized people actually desire to be raped. US popular culture often treats the rape fantasy as if it were inevitable or natural rather than questioning whether such a desire is sincere—and if it is, what it would tell us about a political context that suggests to many people that desirable sex must be forced and violent. The rape fantasy has been used to justify sexual violence on the grounds that "no" doesn't really mean "no," that being treated with violence is a mark of passion and desire, and that violence is part of a "normal" or "natural" sexual encounter. Against this discourse, I seek to reclaim the language of the "fantastical" to point out how a rape culture is comprised of convenient axioms and imagined truths that both conceal and enable sexual violence.

The *Oxford English Dictionary* defines "fantastical" as "fabulous, imaginary, unreal."[88] This definition gets at the heart of the work a rape culture does when it constructs and reinforces unreal and imagined stories about rape. These stories are fantastical, and they teach an entire culture what rape means. Each chapter of the book analyzes a different manifestation of US rape culture to highlight some of the fantastical mythic figures, discourses, and practices that must persist for rape to be used as a tool of political domination. These fantasies are collective mischaracterizations, like the misconception that "good guys" cannot rape or that personal behavior is a viable strategy of rape prevention. Fantastical stories about rape and the mythic figures who play a leading role in them allow an entire culture to stipulate who can be dominated and who is entitled to dominate using sexual violence. Each chapter addresses a specific story—an invented fantasy—about rape in the United States.

Chapter Two focuses on the anti-trans bathroom debates to articulate a crucial discourse of US rape culture: the discourse of white male protection, practiced through violent and non-violent means. At the intersections of gender, sexuality, race, and religion in the United States, white men have exerted legal and extra-legal violence to protect "their" women and children from perceived sexual threats. These threats are often perceived through the myths and discourses of US rape culture, such as the sexually deviant "bad apple" I mentioned above. In the context of this myth, protective violence can be legitimized through a discourse that identifies certain strong men as protector-citizens who inflict righteous violence on "aggressors" whose foreignness, non-whiteness, or non-normativity poses a threat. I conclude that, counterintuitive as it may seem, anti-trans bathroom bills, championed on the (false) promise that they will protect women and children from sexual violence, actually *facilitate* sexual violence: such legislation increases the risk of violence against trans persons; relegates the authority to exert violence to righteous "protectors" who are, invariably, white, cisgender, heterosexual men; and blurs the distinction between protectors and aggressors. In effect, the discourses and practices of "protection" justify the heteropatriarchal, violent masculinity that causes sexual violence in the first place.

Chapter Three applies the logic of violent masculinity to the "frontier." In US rape culture, popular sympathy and care are typically reserved for victims of sexual violence who fit the paradigm of white, virginal, cisgender female vulnerability. Non-paradigmatic victims—those who are not white, are perceived to be promiscuous, or do not adopt heteropatriarchal sexual mores—are disbelieved and disregarded. By concealing these victims of sexual violence, a rape culture reinforces systems of dominance that subject some people to persistent violence and premature death. This chapter explores the confluence of settler colonialism, capitalist exploitation, and sexual violence on the Bakken oil formation near Fort Berthold, North Dakota. The construction of Indigenous persons as sexualized and wastable mirrors the "wastelanding" of land through fracking and other extractive processes. Through the myth of the sq*aw,[89] the discourses and practices of extraction, and the practices of frontier masculinity, Indigenous persons and lands are "wastelanded" while oil workers—fashioned as present-day frontiersmen—seem to have impunity to act violently, at least some of the time. US rape culture conceals the Indigenous women, queer, trans, Two Spirit, and others who are assaulted or destroyed as "collateral damage" in service to ongoing heteropatriarchal settler control and capitalist exploitation of land, resources, and people.

Chapter Four investigates sexual consent, which is often perceived as a strategy to mitigate sexual violence. Although social contracts and standard contracts have long been a "technology" of consent, contract language has only recently been invoked as a way to guarantee sexual consent. Recent technological interventions—apps, text messages, photographs, and video recordings—seek to *document* and *contractualize* sexual consent. This may seem promising to some, but I contend that this new approach to consent emerges to protect the falsely accused—a mythic figure who stokes fear in everyone from concerned parents to misogynistic "red pillers" (men's rights activists), all of whom are eager to find ways to protect men from false rape accusations. Far from mitigating sexual violence, the sexual consent contract intensifies the myth of the false (female) rape accuser who must be corralled into a contractual obligation because she cannot be trusted otherwise. This new practice of consent—and its attendant technologies—reveals a desire to prevent rape *allegations*, rather than to prevent rape. Such technology, if adopted widely, could foster even greater mistrust of sexual assault survivors and make it easier for certain perpetrators to avoid criminal prosecution under the protective power of an ostensible contract to have sex.

Chapter Five asks how direct-to-subscriber services like OnlyFans, when mediated through neoliberal capitalism, contribute to US rape culture. I do not argue that porn is bad or that it cannot be empowering, but I do believe that within the exploitative context of neoliberal capitalism, any move toward ethical porn is likely to be co-opted in ways that create new avenues of exploitation. I focus on direct-to-subscriber services which, while liberating for content creators in many respects, create an imperative to "scale up" to remain profitable. First, I discuss the promise of ethical porn and the distinctive consequences of trying to "scale up" within a neoliberal free market. Second, I establish how the myths and discourses of rape culture are reinforced when competing content creators try to build a following and keep their followers engaged with promises of 24/7 availability. Third, I show that when direct-to-subscriber services like OnlyFans mediate intimacy, authenticity, and accessibility, these desires reinforce male entitlement to care and sexual attention. I conclude this chapter by reflecting on the implications of the emergence of artificial intelligence chatbots that might further intensify the male entitlement to sex that is intrinsic to US rape culture.

Chapter Six explores how to dismantle rape culture. I argue that the only way to change an entire culture is to adopt relational practices that challenge the myths, discourses, and practices of rape culture and resist the interlocking structures of oppression that sustain it. We must change our interpersonal practices and sociopolitical structures and build communal practices and storytelling opportunities that support a multiplicity of voices, experiences, and practices to challenge the hegemonic stories of US rape culture. In the last chapter, I turn to Black feminist and Indigenous scholars and activists, whose countercultural vantage points afford them critical insights into what it takes to disrupt and dismantle US rape culture. Their survivor-led, culturally specific practices invite and inspire the radical reconfiguration of US rape culture into one that refuses to use sexual violence as a tool of political domination.

Conclusion

Rape and sexual violence persist because they are sustained by broadly accepted myths and discourses and widely enacted practices about race, gender, settler capitalist exploitation, and sexuality. A critical stance on rape culture is possible and can reveal a path toward a world without persistent, commonplace sexual violence. I argue that rape is political and that rape culture constructs the meaning of rape in order to preserve structures of domination over marginalized groups. Rape culture provides an interpretive framework through which judgments about victimhood and perpetration are made, both individually and collectively. It extends beyond gender to substantiate white heteropatriarchy and settler capitalist exploitation. Maintaining these systems allows sexual violence to persist in US culture, and resisting and rejecting those structures require analyzing rape culture to determine how systems of domination intermingle to ensnare and discipline some bodies but not others.

US rape culture asserts that—on average—only deviants are rapists, all men will always to want to "get some," women and children are weak and inherently victimizable, and most victims are at least partially responsible for being raped. These assertions contradict the facts about who the victims and perpetrators of sexual violence in the United States really are, yet they are reliably reproduced as if they reflect truth(s) about rape. An intersectional reconceptualization of rape culture is needed, which can reveal how rape culture evolves and expands to discipline any group that threatens white heteropatriarchal control. Otherwise, cultural myths, discourses, and practices will continue to structure collective interpretations of who can be raped (or not), who can rape (or not), and what "counts" as rape (or not). Rape culture conceals the reality that rape is endured by individuals of every race, class, gender, age, sexuality, or other identity (whenever they occupy positions of relative powerlessness); and it obscures the fact that sexual violence is an essential political strategy to preserve and, often, to embolden white, settler capitalist heteropatriarchy.

Chapter Two
The Politics of Protection

Introduction

In 2015, after several US cities passed anti-discrimination ordinances that included provisions to require public institutions to provide gender-neutral bathrooms, some state legislatures doubled down on public restroom segregation on the basis of biological sex.[1] At the time, sixteen states were considering "bathroom bills," which would require individuals to use the public restrooms, changing rooms, and locker rooms that corresponded to their sex as assigned at birth. While North Carolina was the only state to pass a bathroom bill in 2016,[2] new forms of anti-transgender (trans) legislation surfaced in state legislatures across the United States in 2021, which included further regulation of public bathroom use by trans people. Between 2015 and 2020, an average of twenty-one bathroom bills were introduced in state legislatures each year. That number grew to an average of eighty bills each year between 2021 and 2023 and continues to rise.[3]

A common justification for these bathroom bills is that regulation is necessary to protect women and children from the threat of sexual predators who disguise themselves as trans to enter public restrooms and changing rooms in order to gain access to victims.[4] At first glance, it might seem promising that several state legislatures are taking steps to protect people from sexual violence. One might imagine that these interventions are evidence of increasing political attention to rape. Yet sexual violence is often invoked as a policy issue when doing so supports white heteropatriarchal authority, and the bathroom bills are no different.[5] Counterintuitive as it may seem, bathroom bills actually help *normalize* sexual violence. They cast sexual predation in terms that mis-associate[6] trans persons with sexual predators to deflect attention from the frequency with which sexual violence is committed *against* trans people and *by* white, cisgender men.

In the United States, a cynical discourse of protection frequently appeals to fears about sexual violence to justify legal and extra-legal violence to protect "our" women and children from perceived threats, especially sexual ones. In this discourse, "protectors" are figured as honorable citizens who use violence judiciously and righteously against "aggressors" who are outsiders, usually due to their foreignness, non-whiteness, or non-normativity. The issue of rape is often invoked in this discourse to preserve the distinction between protector and aggressor, which also corresponds to the distinction between insiders and outsiders. As a feature of US rape culture, this discourse of protection reinforces collective interpretations about who can be a victim or perpetrator and who is empowered to enact symbolic or physical violence to protect those who are (supposedly) inherently victimizable. The bathroom debates strategically wield the threat of sexual violence to justify what sociologists of religion Philip Gorski and Samuel Perry would call a reactionary conservative "Christian nationalist" political agenda[7] that directly endangers trans people and indirectly endangers other vulnerable people. According to Gorski and Perry, Christian nationalists believe libertarian freedom is reserved for Christians and that they are entitled to maintain the hierarchical (white, Christian, and heteropatriarchal) order by domination, which only white Christian men are free to enact.[8]

The discourse of protection has been employed to justify actions to prevent or seek retribution for sexual violence in many contexts. It invokes righteous opposition to sexual violence (1) when it can be attributed to an (often racialized or non-normative) Other and (2) so that it can be used to justify violence against that Other. For example, political theorist Jeanne Morefield is investigating a deep archive of twentieth-century materials to explore how liberal imperialists and contemporary liberals use the threat of sex trafficking to construct a universal, global subject (women and children who are vulnerable to trafficking) *and* a global Other (non-white and Jewish men who traffic). Morefield observes that this discourse of protection against sex trafficking is *generative* in the sense that it constructs a universal vulnerable subject and universal Other, over whom the "protectors" are justified in wielding violence to maintain control.[9] In a recent social media post, political theorist Hagar Kotef noted that the violent attacks of October 7, 2023, which included sexual violence against Israeli women, should neither be used to justify retribution in Gaza nor erased or denied as part of support of liberatory resistance. Like Morefield and Kotef, I obviously do not deny the existence or significance of sexual violence. Instead, we are all identifying the politics at work when the prevention of (or retribution for) sexual violence is invoked cynically, typically by men in power, to justify violent actions they have already decided to take against people they have already decided to dominate with violence. Ironically, the discourse of protection justifies violence but is unlikely to prevent it. On the contrary, the focus on a non-normative Other who perpetrates sexual violence does deflective work: those who fashion themselves as the "protectors" are often perpetrators of gendered and sexual violence themselves, but they are rarely held accountable.

In Chapter One, I defined rape culture as an interpretive framework that relies on myths, discourses, and practices to assign characteristics to victims and perpetrators and to distinguish the innocent from the guilty and the dominators from the dominated. In this chapter, I explore the discourse of protection in the context of the "bathroom debates" of 2015 and 2021, which aligns with a paradigmatic and mythic story of rape. This story features a triad of key figures: the deviant and dangerous rapist, the heroic and chivalrous protector, and the weak and endangered victim. In this account, protectors are valorized for being righteously violent and virile, while rapists are vilified for being dangerously violent and appetitive.

But in what ways are "good" violence and healthy sexual appetite distinguished from bad? In this chapter, I establish that the discourse of protection, particularly when it aligns with the triadic rape story, distinguishes the rapist from the sexually appetitive protector by identifying him as a racialized or non-normative *Other*. This othering justifies legal or extralegal violence against the Other and conceals the dangers posed by the protectors, who are heralded for their judicious use of violence and who are owed sexual satisfaction from their wives. In other words, the discourse of protection empowers "protectors" to adopt practices of regulation, surveillance, and violence to discipline non-normative bodies and protect white heteropatriarchy, all while enabling the conditions for ongoing sexual violence.

The Bathroom Bills

In 2014, a Christian legal defense fund called the Alliance Defending Freedom (ADF)[10] reached out to public school districts across the United States to encourage them to enact policies requiring trans students to use private bathrooms or multi-occupant bathrooms that corresponded to their sex as assigned at birth. The next year, the ADF developed model legislation that would mandate this policy and shared it with state legislators across the country.[11] In the months that followed, legislators in several states introduced "bathroom bills" that closely resembled the ADF template.[12]

Motivated by the ADF model, the 2015 round of bathroom bills adopted a common legislative approach: to codify a biological sex binary, regulate the use of certain public spaces (public restrooms and changing rooms or public school restrooms and locker rooms), and challenge local anti-discrimination measures, all as part of a broader legal effort that would permit discrimination against people (including queer and trans people) as a matter of religious liberty.[13] The bills were often justified via a discourse of protection which alleged that trans persons (or individuals who disguised themselves as trans) were sexual predators. Barnett et al. identified three rhetorical justifications for this round of bills: (1) being trans is a symptom of mental illness, therefore trans people are inherently dangerous; (2) trans persons are more likely than cisgender persons to commit sexual violence; and (3) cisgender men with "sexual disorders" will pose as trans to gain access to women and children.[14] The conflation of trans persons with sexual predators is neither inconsequential nor unintentional. When conservative Christian organizations like the Family Research Council (FRC) assert that the bills target cisgender men posing as trans,[15] their argument treats trans people as sexually deviant. In a rape culture, this presumptive deviance is often coded as violent and unsafe.

North Carolina was the only state to pass a bathroom bill in 2016. On March 23, House Bill 2 (HB2, the Public Facilities Privacy and Security Act) was introduced to the General Assembly, debated after a 30-minute public comment period, and signed into law by then-governor Pat McCrory—all on the same day.[16] The bill was ostensibly about mandating "single-sex" multiple occupancy public restrooms throughout the state as a matter of personal security but in fact had a much broader purpose. Section 3.1 of HB2 prevented cities in North Carolina from expanding statewide workplace discrimination laws, which did not include protection on the basis of sexual orientation or gender identity.[17] The bill was an immediate response to a Charlotte municipal ordinance passed on February 22 that was set to go into effect on April 1, 2016, which would have expanded anti-discrimination protections for queer and trans persons.[18] The bathroom bill revised state law to stipulate that only the state's General Assembly could prohibit workplace discrimination on the basis of sexuality or gender, thus nullifying municipal codes designed to prohibit discrimination.[19] Although it did not mention religious liberty, HB2 revised North Carolina's anti-discrimination laws in ways that enabled a now common legal strategy to allow private organizations to lawfully discriminate against trans and queer people on the basis of religious liberty.[20]

Because the 2015–16 round of bathroom bills was largely unsuccessful, a new round of anti-trans legislation, including several revised bathroom bills, has emerged since 2021. Like their earlier counterparts, these proposals aim to codify a biological, binary definition of sex, undermine anti-discrimination measures on the basis of gender and sexuality as part of a broader project to seek "generational wins,"[21] and focus on public schools as a site of regulation.[22] Yet they adopt a more defensive approach to discrimination questions: now, it is Christian conservatives who need protection from the "homosexual agenda." Since 2021, anti-trans legislation has focused on public school regulations, gender-affirming care, and competitive sports—a strategic shift that seems designed to rally conservative voters and drive a wedge between progressives who might defend trans-exclusive policies in the name of equal access for women (that is, women who are assigned female at birth) and those who advocate trans-inclusive policies in the name of gender parity.[23] This new approach again invokes the discourse of protection to justify discrimination and nurture a sense of embattlement among Christian traditionalists: now it is not just "our" women and children who are under threat but "our" Christian values as well.[24]

Adopting this new approach, the Tennessee General Assembly passed five pieces of anti-trans legislation in 2021, including a prohibition on trans athletes competing in girls' sports and a bathroom bill that makes public schools independently liable if they enact gender-congruent (i.e., corresponding to one's gender identity) bathroom policies.[25] In May of that year, the state passed HB1182, another statewide "bathroom bill," in defense of those who claim a principled right to segregate *themselves* on the basis of sex or gender. Rather than require individuals to use the public restroom that corresponds to their sex as assigned at birth, HB1182 requires any private business that permits gender-congruent public restroom use to post a sign that states "This facility maintains a policy of allowing the use of this facility by either biological sex, regardless of the designation of the restroom."

Early in the legislative deliberations, HB1182's sponsor, Representative Tim Rudd, asserted that the bill was designed to protect "'women and children against sexual predators that could be taking advantage of policies, executive orders or legislation that may allow the opposite sex to enter a restroom, shower or locker room that allows more than one person in the facility at a time.'"[26] Unlike the FRC's position, which I mentioned above and will discuss in more detail below, Rudd's statement does not distinguish between trans persons and sexual predators; Rudd suggests that "women and children" must be protected from the shadowy figure of the sexual predator who is either trans or disguised as trans. In other words, gender "confusion" is considered the cause of predation. Rudd's binary language (evident here in the dualistic phrase "opposite sex") suggests that those who enter the "wrong" bathroom are gender-confused and therefore dangerous.[27]

Rudd partly defends HB1182's targeting and discriminating against trans people by suggesting it is *good* for trans folks. He argues that the bill prevents violence, but what he means is that it prevents the violence we should expect from someone who happens upon a trans person in the "wrong" bathroom and who justifiably responds violently. He maintains that the signs protect "both sexes":

> It's very shocking and [can] endanger people when they walk into a restroom that's marked "men" or "women" and the opposite sex is standing there. It could scare 'em, it could provoke violence. This way at least it lets people know that are using the facility, for both sides . . . that it, uh, that it protects them not to just be surprised by it. At least it makes a *minimal* effort to let people know.[28]

Rudd's legislation, like so many other trans-exclusive bills, reveals the underlying logic of protective discourses: he makes clear that he knows that some people, namely white cisgender heterosexual men, feel justifiably entitled to exert violence anytime they see someone who threatens the traditional, heteropatriarchal order (particularly as this order is understood in the Christian nationalist frame described by Gorski and Perry and by historian Kristin Kobes Du Mez).

Further, Rudd's language reveals how the legislation reinforces a sex binary in which people are either in the "right" or "wrong" restroom, that this distinction is legible and evident because one is or is not "opposite" to the sex specified on the door, and that—as the word "provocation" suggests—those who enter the "wrong" door are asking for what is coming to them. Implicit in this framing is Rudd's assumption about whose assessment of the threat matters: he is certainly not suggesting that a trans person encountering a cisgender person would be justified in exerting self-defensive violence on grounds that the cisgender person is somehow of "the opposite sex." Only righteous protectors can transgress the "wrong" bathroom to protect those in danger.

In the context of the "traditional" Christian family that the ADF seeks to defend from secular humanist persecution, the righteous protector is the patriarch who is called by God to protect "his" women and children because they are too weak to protect themselves. To safeguard women and children from sexual violence in women's public restrooms, patriarchal protectors might have to invade these restrooms, even if they do not conform to the sex placard on the door. Yet based on this logic, *their* invasion of the "wrong" bathroom and violence is understandable. The problem, then, is not really trespass into public restrooms by "the opposite sex": it is trespass by those the "protectors" deem threatening to their values—those they have mis-associated with criminality, danger, and immorality.

Rudd invoked the threat of sexual violence to promote his bathroom bill, but he is (as others in this debate are) primarily concerned about sexual violence against those they deem worthy of protection: "their" women and children. When upheld, bathroom bills like HB1182 are likely to facilitate violence and sexual assault against trans persons by forcing them into unsafe conditions (e.g., a trans woman required to use a "male" public restroom). When proponents of the bathroom bills selectively and cynically invoke the discourse of protection, they deflect attention away from ubiquitous forms of sexual assault by relying on the triad of mythological "characters" of sexual assault: the perpetrator (deviant and non-normative), the protector (heroic even when he is violent), and the victim (always innocent but only if it is the right kind of victim). This discourse reinforces the "protector's" right to engage in violence by virtue of his authority as a white, heterosexual, and cisgender man—the same authority that enables him to exert sexual violence to satisfy his sexual needs. This discourse therefore blurs the line between protective violence and sexual violence: those who are empowered to exert protective violence are structurally the very same people who are entitled to commit sexual violence.

Deviants, Heroes, and Victims: The Rape "Triad" and the Discourse of Protection

Although incidents of sexual violence do not require the presence of all three figures in the triad described above, this story is widespread—especially in fictional representations of rape or near-rape. Its replication reinforces common expectations and imaginings of sexual violence, victimization, and predation. The triadic story of rape, and the discourse of protection that accompanies it, is often used to justify white heteropatriarchal aggression and violence in the name of protection.

Throughout the book, I use the composite term "white heteropatriarchy" to refer to a set of mutually reinforcing relations of domination sculpted out of the categories of race, sexuality, and gender and their interplay. Some will argue that such a term is too expansive to be useful, arguing instead, as Wendy Brown does, that we can best understand the operations of power (such as state power) by disentangling the ways in which the state racializes, affirms bourgeois logics, or is gendered.[29] I don't find fault with Brown's advice, but I think we need to pay attention to the power that is exerted *in* and *by* the tangling as well. I adopt an intersectional approach which aims to illustrate how these operations can rely on white supremacy, heteronormativity, and patriarchal rule simultaneously; can generate a series of permutations that reinforce each element; and will, in combination, multiply and sustain the effects of one another. These power relations are in some ways independent but, like different gears in an interlocking mechanism, also interdependent. The gears work together to keep the whole mechanism moving; if one gear falters, the others will ensure continued movement. My goal is to describe how systems like white supremacy, patriarchy, or heteronormativity interact in ways that compound their effects.

This intersectional approach usefully complicates our understanding of the operations of power. Paisley Currah warns against theoretical approaches that "naturalize the state, and attach certain properties to 'it'—a totalizing logic, an ordered hierarchy, a comprehensive rationality, a unity of purpose and execution" and instead encourages scholars to uncover various modes and mechanisms of governmentality.[30] For example, Currah notes that states identify, document, and regulate biological sex through a tangle of contradictions and variation across agencies and levels of government that each do political work in their own right, rendering the question of identity both immutable (in the sense that it is presumed to be fixed, permanent, and knowable) and contestable (i.e., every governing agency brings its own approach to fix or challenge it). Likewise, the entanglements of white supremacy, heteronormativity, and patriarchy in institutional arrangements, political practices, and cultural norms—at various levels of enactment—allow them, collectively, to endure.

For example, the enduring ideal of the "traditional" family in the United States is a white, heteropatriarchal, middle-class ideal, with two heterosexual parents: a breadwinning father and a caregiving, stay-at-home mother.[31] This set of relations is *heteronormative* in the sense that it is "dependent upon an absolute split between male and female gender identities, their circulation, repetition, and recitation in the social milieu"[32] and reinforces a social order predicated on the centrality of sexual reproduction. It is *patriarchal* because it features a "traditional" family headed by a male protector whose women and children are his subordinates and protectorates.[33] It is functionally (though not exclusively) *white* because, in the US context, those who are able to claim safety for themselves (and those they wish to protect) and to wield legal or extra-legal violence with impunity are typically white.[34] It is also "white" and bourgeois in the sense that Hortense Spillers describes, as "the *vertical* transfer of bloodline, of a patronymic, of titles and entitlements, of real estate and the prerogatives of 'cold cash,' from *fathers* to *sons*,"[35] a relationship reserved for those who were eligible to hold a title or own property. Crucially, white heteropatriarchy is not enacted solely by white, heterosexual, cisgender men; it is a broad phenomenon sanctioned and sustained by many people. Non-white persons can be heteronormative or patriarchal; non-men, non-cis, and non-hetero persons can be, too. Yet, irrespective of who replicates them, the intermingling myths, discourses, and practices of US rape culture sustain white heteropatriarchy.

At the center of white heteropatriarchy in the United States, Du Mez notes, is the strongman protector who is emboldened by a Christian nationalism which asserts that Christians are singularly embattled because of their religious identity.[36] To redress this persecution, Christians must defend the United States as "God's chosen nation."[37] Their nationalism rests on an ideal of patriarchal authority and militant masculinity that connects a father's dominion over his home to the leadership of a nation state that must repel all threats to the Christian ideal.[38] Du Mez explains that it also rests on racial hierarchy: "the heroic Christian man was a white man, and not infrequently a white man who defended against the threat of nonwhite men and foreigners."[39]

Du Mez identifies two related qualities of the strongman protector in the white evangelical "traditional" family that are essential to the discourse of protection in US rape culture (and to Christian nationalism). First, she describes a strong association between the aggressive leadership of strong men and an aggressive male sex drive,[40] which necessitates wives' ongoing efforts to satisfy their husbands' sexual needs. One evangelical Christian sex manual cautions that when a wife fails to satisfy her husband's sexual desires, she should expect him to be "'carnal, nasty, and insulting.'"[41] While a husband's sexual needs must be gratified, women's needs—sexual and otherwise—are subordinate.

The second, related feature of the white evangelical "traditional" family is that the husband is the protector and the wife and children are the objects of protection.[42] This expressly authoritarian relationship[43] is also emphatically non-democratic, as suggested by *The Homosexual Agenda*, co-authored by ADF co-founder/former president Alan Sears and Craig Osten, who discredit any portrayal of marriage as egalitarian; they argue instead that marriage should be structured around the father's "claim to dominion or control . . . instead [of] equality and respect."[44] Christian evangelical activists from Phyllis Schlafly to Tim and Beverly LaHaye have defended women's rights as the rights "to have babies and to be protected";[45] they argue that protection should be provided to women by the men in their families, who should be empowered to use violence (even over other family members) when necessary. Taken together, these two qualities—between an aggressive sex drive and an obligation to enact aggressive protection—confound the boundary between acceptable and unacceptable uses of violence and suggest that the aggressive male has exclusive authority to police the boundary. As Du Mez notes, "evangelical 'family values' entailed the reassertion of patriarchal authority; at its most basic level, family values politics was about sex and power,"[46] and the white Christian male was entitled to dominate to obtain both.

Organizations like the ADF have committed to defending a traditional, patriarchal family, which is a strategy that (re)secures white male control over biological and social reproduction. *The Homosexual Agenda* paints an anxious picture of the decline of the traditional, two-parent, heterosexual household, which the authors attribute to the homosexual political agenda; no-fault divorce; and radical feminism.[47] They argue that alternative parenting or family relations, which lack the structure of patriarchal authority, harm children and pave the road to "pederasty, adultery, bestiality, and incest" by fostering confusion and "sexual dysfunction" when these children become adults.[48] The 2021 documentary *Pray Away* reveals that proponents of conversion therapy (to "cure" homosexuality) blame the "choice" to "[live] a homosexual lifestyle" on abuse, poor parenting, and confused parental sex roles (e.g., when a child's same-sex parent does not display adequate masculine or feminine characteristics).[49] Evangelical opposition to homosexuality reflects anxiety about gender confusion, weakness, vulnerability (the latter two of which are presumably acceptable in women but not in men), and non-reproductive sex. Like homophobia, "gender ideology" is now considered a threat to the traditional (Christian) family.[50] Anti-trans bathroom bills and other anti-trans legislation have gained traction in several US states in response to this perception of threat, and proposed regulations have focused on aggressive protection of this conception of a family.

False Targets: Trans Persons in the Bathroom Debate

Former Arkansas governor Mike Huckabee's off-putting joke about a proposed bathroom bill in 2015 unwittingly exposed the hypocrisy of framing the bathroom debate as a matter of patriarchal protection: "I wish that someone had told me when I was in high school that I could have felt like a woman when it came time to take showers in PE. I'm pretty sure I would've found my feminine side and said, 'Coach, I think I'd rather shower with the girls today.'"[51] Huckabee meant to make a joke of trans identity by suggesting that being trans is a matter of confusion at best or deception at worst. But the joke only works because it depends on an implicit admission that, as a young, white, evangelical Christian man, Huckabee would have engaged in deceit just to see a naked girl or woman. In other words, it's a joke only if we accept that a young, white, Christian male like Huckabee would engage in sexual predation if given half a chance.[52] Uncontrolled sexual desire is understood as a natural element of strongman masculinity, so policies must be put in place that address that risk. For instance, school dress codes require women and girls to dress in ways that do not "distract" boys. Boys' uncontrolled sex urges are accepted as given; the appropriate policy response is to regulate the behavior of non-boys rather than to address the behavior of boys, which is why the bathroom bills target trans persons, rather than the cisgender men who are apparently sexually aggressive by nature.

As I note above, debates about the bathroom bills treat trans persons as predatory threats to women and children, an association that is not substantiated by empirical evidence.[53] The conservative rhetoric of the 2015–16 bathroom debates, as reflected in *The Homosexual Agenda* and *Pray Away*, represent trans persons as mentally ill, as sexual predators in their own right, or as cisgender men with sexual disorders who disguise themselves as trans.[54] With respect to the first two of these justifications, Barnett et al. conclude that "there is no current evidence that granting trans individuals access to gender-corresponding restrooms results in an increase of sexual offenses."[55] With respect to the third, they searched news stories from the United States, Canada, Japan, and the United Kingdom from 2003 to 2016 and found only one incident of trans individuals using gender-incongruent restrooms to gain access to women and children; they identified nineteen cases involving cisgender men dressed as women.[56]

But as Mike Huckabee's joke makes clear, even many defenders of the bathroom bills don't really believe trans people pose a threat to women and children. To support the anti-trans legislative efforts, the FRC published an "incident brief" in 2017 on anti-discrimination laws and argued that public safety was threatened when individuals were permitted to use gender-congruent restrooms. The report began with a statement worth reproducing at length:

> "Gender identity" non-discrimination laws—particularly those that apply to schools and "public accommodations"—authorize people to use sex-separated facilities (such as restrooms, locker rooms, and showers) that correspond to their subjective, psychological "gender identity," rather than their objective, biological sex.
>
> This has led to concerns that such policies—particularly insofar as they permit biological males to use facilities designated for women or girls—could threaten the privacy and safety of the general public, and even lead to an increase in voyeurism and sexual assault. **It is important to note that the concern is not that transgendered individuals are more likely to be sexual predators, but rather that sexual predators could exploit such laws by posing as transgendered in order to gain access to women and girls.** Beyond this, when companies such as Target implement any-sex bathroom/dressing room policies, it encourages criminals to take advantage of these policies to commit crimes.[57]

The statement begins with an indictment of gender non-discrimination laws, which it suggests are the motivating force behind the more specific restroom policies that the FRC critiques. The scare quotes around the phrase "gender identity"—repeated in the statement and juxtaposed with the "objective" concept of biological sex—aim to cast doubt on the concept of gender identity. Indeed, as many scholars note, biological sex is not "objective" in the sense that the FRC suggests here (i.e., as a permanent, binary category).[58] By suggesting that criminals often disguise themselves as trans, the FRC statement feeds the mis-association between trans identity and predatory criminality. The FRC report emphasizes (in its own boldfaced type) that the real risk of sexual violence comes from "biological males" pretending to be trans. Still, this proclamation does not constitute FRC support for trans persons, who—the brief admits—are not likely to be sexual predators. Instead, the FRC statement suggests that gender-congruent bathroom policies facilitate criminal behavior and only a trans-exclusive, biologically determinist public restroom policy can deter voyeurism and sexual assault. The bills target trans people (whom they often admit are not predators) and, in so doing, deflect attention from those most likely to perpetrate sexual violence—cisgender men.

The FRC brief replicates a discursive move made by many conservatives in the bathroom debate and other anti-trans discourses: associating trans personhood with deception.[59] The FRC brief characterizes trans (and other gender-non-conforming) persons as indistinguishable from voyeurs, assailants, predators, and criminals. This mis-associates being trans with being a cisgender male sexual predator. The FRC report lists twenty-five news stories of "men violating the privacy of women" in public restrooms and changing rooms (a problem the FRC report says trans activists do not take seriously, another mark of the danger of trans persons and the permissive "homosexual agenda"). The unsystematic list provides no meaningful distinctions between examples, and the news stories themselves often only report what witnesses claim to have seen. For example, the witnesses see "a man dressed as a woman" but do not (certainly, *cannot*) know whether this person is simply wearing what they want, a gender-non-conforming or trans person, a cis person in disguise, or someone else. The uncertainty is, of course, precisely the point. The adjacency of the imagined "trans person" with the imagined "predator" throughout the statement creates an association in the reader's mind that trans people are not to be trusted since they are always indistinguishable from predatory criminals. In the FRC brief, trans people are constructed as appropriate targets of protectors' vigilance; their proximity to danger and violence justifies danger and violence being visited upon them. Transphobic violence is motivated by trans personhood as a site of *deception* such that, even when the FRC is ostensibly disavowing transphobia, it does so by putting trans persons in the position of having to defend themselves against presumptions of deception, violence, and predatory threats.[60]

In US rape culture, collective imaginings of victimhood or perpetration often conceal actual, persistent victimization and perpetration by suggesting that only the very worst people commit sexual violence. In the bathroom debates, the trans person has become conflated with the "bad man rapist," a myth of rape culture that suggests sexual violence is perpetrated only rarely, and only by obviously deviant men. This myth is at least as ancient as the story of the rape of Lucretia. In current US rape culture, this "bad man" is a "stranger in the bushes" who lays in wait for a victim or the obsessed stalker of crime novels and movies who watches from the shadows until he finds the right moment to pounce. Obviously, I am not arguing that strangers and stalkers are incapable of sexual violence, but these instances of sexual violence are comparatively rare. Most sexual violence is committed by someone the victim knows—often an intimate partner. Only 7% of rapes reported in the US Department of Justice's National Crime Victimization Survey between 2010 and 2016 were committed by strangers of the victim.[61] When trans people are mis-associated with violent predation in the bathroom debates, trans people are endangered by the mis-association, while the most common form of sexual violence—committed by someone the victim knows, often intimately—goes unaddressed.

The "bad man"/deviant rapist myth deflects attention from the everydayness of sexual violence. The rhetoric supporting the bathroom bills often portrays trans persons as dangerous predators rather than exposing the ways rape and other forms of sexual violence are commonplace. Even when trans persons are not considered deceptive, they are thought to be "gender-confused" and are not to be believed, to their peril: "Indeed, it is precisely the fact that trans people often do not have their self-identifications taken seriously that is so deeply bound up with the transphobic hostility and violence."[62] In the face of trans deception or confusion, as "bathroom bills" like Tennessee's HB1182 suggest, a violent response is understandable and expected but only from righteous protectors.

Largely as a result of the deep distrust of trans persons fostered by the persistent mis-association of trans identity with violent criminality and sexual deviance, trans individuals are frequent victims of sexual and other forms of violence in the United States. Nearly half (46%) of respondents to the 2015 US Transgender Survey (USTS) reported being verbally harassed in the past year as a result of being trans; one in nine reported being physically assaulted.[63] In the same study, 47% of respondents reported they had been sexually assaulted; 10% had been sexually assaulted within the past year.[64] Public bathrooms are a common site of victimization. Barnett et al. point out that 59% of USTS respondents had avoided public restrooms in the past year due to fears of violent confrontation or other dangerous experiences.[65] Law enforcement officials—who may be summoned if a person suspects a bathroom law has been violated—also pose a risk to trans persons. Over half (58%) of USTS respondents said law enforcement officers had mistreated them in the past year (including misgendering, verbal harassment, and physical and sexual assault), and 57% were somewhat or very uncomfortable asking the police for help.[66]

Indeed, the bathroom bills did not emerge out of widespread public outcry against these high rates of sexual violence perpetrated against trans persons—in public restrooms or anywhere else—or in response to a wave of sexual assaults in public restrooms.[67] Even in legislative deliberations about HB1182, Tim Rudd admitted that the bill emerged out of concerns about the rise of "executive orders and policies"—*not* in response to evidence that public restrooms are a common site of sexual violence or to widespread public pressure for the bill.[68]

Instead, the bathroom bills are part of an intentional, "traditional" Christian political agenda justified by claims of ongoing Christian persecution in the United States. The ADF does not dedicate substantive energy to ending sexual violence in its most common manifestations (within the family) but is more interested in legal "generational wins" that change the culture in favor of a more traditional, patriarchal, Christian orientation.[69] These wins—couched in terms of protecting religious liberty—are unambiguously anti-queer and anti-trans. The Southern Poverty Law Center has designated the ADF a "hate group."[70] It notes that *The Homosexual Agenda*, which praises the ADF's involvement in legal victories protecting "traditional marriage," links homosexuality to pedophilia and claims that homosexual behavior is predatory and should be prohibited by law.[71] In addition to its efforts to challenge anti-discrimination regulations in the

United States (such as its central involvement in significant US court cases including *Masterpiece Cakeshop*, *Arlene's Flowers*, and *Hobby Lobby*), the ADF has supported efforts to ban homosexual sex in Belize, prohibit same-sex marriage in Romania, and defend anti-sodomy laws in Jamaica.[72] In fact, ADF staffers and affiliated attorneys have long decried the "homosexual agenda" as degrading human culture by undermining the family. Because gender and sexuality are so deeply entangled in the Christian evangelical imagination, "gender confusion" is understood to be the cause of homosexuality. Thus, it is reasonable to conclude that long-standing anxiety about a "homosexual agenda" is motivating this new wave of anxiety about "gender ideology."[73]

The bathroom bills, like other policies and initiatives advanced by the ADF and other Christian nationalist groups, are designed to *create* fear of trans identity and *encourage* symbolic and physical violence against trans persons in four ways. First, by fostering a mis-association between trans persons and perpetrators of sexual violence, the discourse of protection creates conditions for ongoing violence against trans persons who are perceived to be predatory threats to the "innocent" victims of sexual assault: "women and children." Legal scholar and activist Dean Spade notes that "administrative systems that classify people [in this case, as safe or dangerous] actually invent and produce meaning for the categories they administer, and . . . those categories manage both the population and the distribution of security and vulnerability.[74] The administrative system at work here—which codifies a biological sex binary and renders trans persons "guilty by association" with sexual predators—encourages targeting trans persons rather than sexual violence, a strategy that puts trans persons at sustained risk of violence and death. Under the guise of preventing extra-legal physical violence (of the kind Rudd expects unless HB1182 is passed), bathroom bills exert a legal form of symbolic violence on trans persons. Because of the mis-association between trans persons and sexual predators, the bills may encourage even more extra-legal physical violence against trans persons. At the very least, by requiring persons to use gender-incongruent bathrooms and—by virtue of the discourse of protection—thus implying that trans and gender-non-conforming persons are sexual predators, HB1182 exacerbates the vulnerability of trans persons, who face ongoing distrust, threats, and physical danger.

Second, the mis-association of trans persons as deceivers perpetuates willful ignorance in US rape culture about who is a paradigmatic sexual predator. As I note above, for many conservative Christians, the primary explanation for "homosexual behavior" is "gender confusion." Based on this logic, trans persons are indistinguishable from cisgender sexual predators *disguised* as trans: to find predators, one must look for trans persons. This mis-association helps normalize sexual assault by implying that "normal" (i.e., cisgender, heterosexual) people are not confused or deviant, and therefore are unlikely to perpetrate sexual violence. In a rape culture where some people are deemed more or less "believable" and some people are coded as "normal" while others are "deviant," the mis-association proves dangerous: sexual predators who do not "look" deviant can repeatedly victimize others, while victims who do not "look" innocent are subjected to sexual violence again and again.

Third, the bathroom bills and other anti-trans legislation supported by the ADF, FRC, and other right-wing evangelical Christian groups reinforce a biologically deterministic sex binary that serves patriarchal interests by strictly regulating the boundaries of what counts as "male" and "female." This kind of regulation requires ad hoc surveillance by those who the law implicitly empowers to police the sex boundary—gender-conforming (normative) people who are eligible to perform surveillance and boundary-setting work.[75] As historian A. Finn Enke explains, "social spaces that depend on identity categories—as most do—are constituted through surveillance and policing of those within. The presence of 'difference' from the operative identity category is simultaneously invoked and erased: social spaces suggest that all people within them *pass* as *really being* members of the social category that the space thereby helps produce."[76] The state is called upon to enforce regulations only after a complaint has been filed. At that point, theorist Toby Beauchamp notes, agents who enforce the laws require a way to make a more formal determination of non-compliance, usually through formal documentation or biometric identification—tools of state surveillance that more deeply entrench a biological sex binary that sustains the heteropatriarchal order and stunts the political possibility of more capacious imaginings of gender identity and fluidity.[77]

Finally, bathroom bills regulate and surveil trans persons *not* because they are threats to women and children but because they are threats to the heteropatriarchal order and to those who benefit from it. Despite their promise to prevent sexual violence, bathroom bills increase danger—of sexual violence and other forms of symbolic and physical violence—for trans persons. Yet this violence is of little concern to the bills' proponents. Rather than mark a systematic commitment to ending sexual violence, this discourse of protection is cynically deployed to secure white heteropatriarchal normativity. The actual threat to victims of sexual violence that Huckabee's joke reveals is not "[feeling] like a woman" or challenging heteronormativity; it is the entitlement (or at least the ostensibly uncontrollable desire) of "biological males" to manipulate circumstances for their own sexual gratification or predatory purposes.

The Heroes: Men as Protectors

In 2018, when speaking at a University of Miami "It's On Us" rally to end sexual violence, Joe Biden said that if, as a young man, he had heard Donald Trump bragging about how he treats women, Biden would have "take[n Trump] behind the gym and beat[en] the hell out of him." Trump, always one to take the bait, responded that if Biden had tried anything, he would have "go[ne] down . . . crying."[78] Biden asserted that Trump was a sexual predator[79] who needed to be put in his place and that a younger, less restrained Biden would have been justified in using violence to protect women from him. Yet Biden's assertion that he could discipline a bully by being a bully only makes sense if he believes that any violence he exerts to protect someone else from violence is somehow righteous.

In effect, Biden and Trump exhibited the same logic of white masculinity that empowers white men to use physical domination to address threats. When Biden identified himself as a worthy executor of a righteous kind of violence that would combat an unrighteous kind, he reinforced an idea central to the preservation of white heteropatriarchy[80]: that white, heterosexual, cisgender men are entitled to use violence in situations in which others are not, that being a violent bully is okay if you are a *righteous* bully, and that a righteous bully can use his power to decide when to offer protection to others. Biden's threat of violence and Trump's rejoinder both conjure the image of the righteous, strong, white protector—an image that pervades US rape culture.

I use the term "protector" to encompass the myriad ways the discourse of protection is invoked and sustained, sometimes by the very people who are imperiled by the discourse. Some may invoke the discourse of protection to get protection (in Schlafly's sense, in which "women's rights" means a right to be protected), while others invoke it to justify their use of violence. Self-designated protectors are not only white men: sometimes they are non-white, non-hetero, non-men. What these protectors have in common is that they feel empowered—in some contexts, at least—to use violence to protect what is theirs. In US rape culture, these are often, but not always, white, heterosexual, cisgender men. These protectors enact physical and symbolic violence legally, through laws and regulations (including "stand your ground" laws), and extra-legally, by taking the law into their own hands.

Iris Young's 2003 essay "The Logic of Masculinist Protection" provides useful insight into the model of the strongman protector. Though Young's argument is about the justification of the security state, her analysis of the archetypal righteous protector emerges from the logic of chivalry, according to which the male is empowered to defend weak and otherwise defenseless people from outside aggression. Two competing masculine figures emerge from this logic: the "man as aggressor" and "man as protector."[81] The chivalrous protector marshals the righteous power and violence of his position to challenge the aggressor, who threatens the vulnerable. Both are aggressive, so the distinction between them is not about whether aggression is exerted but whether it is exerted *rightly*. Right-wing Christian, evangelical nationalists have made similar associations between a strong man patriarchal protector at home and a strong security state abroad.[82]

What Young calls the logic of masculinist protection requires weak, feminized figures who need protecting, such as women and children, who are in "a subordinate position of dependence and obedience."[83] Subordinates accept protection from the protectors, but in return for this security, subordinates must be obedient and subservient. Although Young acknowledges that most feminist critiques are right to challenge the construction of masculinity as a claim to domination (especially sexual domination), she draws on the logic of chivalry to make a further point: that masculinist protection relies on the assumption of a benign, honorable protector who must be trusted and *obeyed* by those he protects.[84]

The logic of chivalry—at both the national and household levels—is elemental to Christian nationalist ideals, which require warrior defenders. These ideals are predicated on militant masculinity and feminized weakness that explicitly links the protector state and the protector. Du Mez argues that the political split between left and right Christian evangelicals began to emerge *not* from theological disagreement but because "Christian nationalism, militarism, and gender 'traditionalism' came to define conservative evangelical identity and dictate ideological allies."[85] On this reading, militarism is associated with righteous governing. The beneficent patriarch, like the hegemon, is necessarily violent at times but only when called to defend the weak from a dangerous threat. His own violence, including sexual violence, can be justified as elemental to his strongman status.

According to Young's account, the protector's "virtuous masculinity depends on its constitutive relation to the presumption of evil others."[86] The protector will assume that the violence he exerts is good because he has already determined that he is good and that the aggressor is dangerous. When the discourse of protection pertains to sexual violence, collective judgments of US rape culture help determine whose violence is acceptable and whose is unacceptable. These judgments help the protector identify who is a fellow protector, who is a worthy protectee, and who is a dangerous threat. In other words: good guys enact good violence to prevent bad guys from enacting bad violence, but only the good guys get to decide who the bad guys are. Structurally, the protectors and aggressors are therefore often indistinguishable: both are cisgender, heterosexual, white men with voracious sexual appetites who feel empowered to use violence for their personal gratification.

When they do not employ extra-legal physical violence, strongman protectors often use the law to enact symbolic violence against those they have deemed dangerous. The problem is that the powerful are the ones deciding who poses a danger—*not* those who are most vulnerable to systemic violence. Criminology and legal studies scholar Beth Richie explains that when "protectors" decide that they are the "good guy" protectors and that other kinds of people are the "bad guy" aggressors, the "good guys" may enact legislation to address some kinds of patriarchal abuse instead of other (often more endemic) types. Using the law for these ends is not a new strategy. Richie notes, for example, that "the target of . . . legal and legislative reforms [of the 1980s and 1990s] was the direct physical assault or sexual abuse and stalking, *not* the forms of violence that are more closely linked to other fundamental aspects of patriarchal power abuse, such as forced sterilization or police brutality."[87] In these reforms, the law was understood by many to be neutral and benign[88] but in fact does intentional political work. In the guise of colorblindness, these reforms disproportionately target people of color and aim to distinguish "unacceptable" kinds of patriarchal abuse from "acceptable" kinds. Acceptable violence can be enacted in the name of protecting and disciplining the white, middle-class, Christian "women and children" who are subservient to their white, strongmen protectors.

The ADF has pursued legal reform to protect the "traditional" family. It fashions itself as an agent of "good guys" and seeks to ban gender-congruent bathroom use by mis-associating trans identity with criminality, thus transforming trans people into "bad guys." The ADF is not alone. In recent years, some Christian traditionalist groups, including the ADF, have collaborated with the Women's Liberation Front (WoLF), a radical feminist group. Although the ADF and WoLF are miles apart on their positions regarding reproductive rights, they have worked together on several anti-trans legislative efforts. The ADF reportedly gave WoLF a $15,000 grant to support an anti-trans legal effort,[89] and WoLF members have been involved in bills designed to ban transitional care for trans youth.[90] WoLF's objection to gender-congruent bathroom use appears to be at least partly rooted in members' belief that trans women are not really women since women are biologically female, assigned female at birth, and raised within the strictures of patriarchy. They contend that the "biological differences between the sexes leave females more physically vulnerable than males to specific forms of violence, including sexual violence."[91] Thus, members of WoLF and other trans-exclusive radical feminists seem to believe that an *essential* feature of being female is that women and girls are always in danger of sexual violence. Trans women, if they were raised as male, are not recognized as "real" women because they have not and do not live under threat of sexual violence (an incorrect view, as the USTS data shows) and may in fact be "real" men because they want to use gender-congruent bathroom policies to gain access to women and girls to further perpetrate sexual violence. Like the ADF and FRC, trans-exclusive radical feminists seem to accept that heterosexual, cisgender men are the likely perpetrators of sexual violence and agree with these organizations that the solution is to target trans persons and mis-associate them with criminality.

I disagree with WoLF's position for three reasons. First, the argument biologizes a sociocultural phenomenon: it says that there are two biological sexes and that an individual is either (1) always a potential *victim* of sexual violence (and therefore biologically female) or (2) always a potential *perpetrator* of it (and therefore biologically male). If I accepted this view, this book would be pointless because it would mean there is nothing to do about sexual violence but accept its inevitability. Instead, I argue that the conditions that normalize sexual violence are neither inevitable nor natural.[92] Second,

WoLF's view necessarily ignores the fact that trans people disproportionately experience sexual and other forms of violence in the United States. Defending policies that target trans people for further violence by forcing them to use the bathrooms that correspond to their sex as assigned at birth, particularly when they are enduring so many forms of violence including sexual violence, is indefensible. Third, WoLF makes the same mistake the ADF and FRC do, albeit for different reasons: WoLF and other radical feminists are concerned that cisgender men will take advantage of gender-congruent bathroom policies to "act trans" and perpetuate violence against women and girls.[93] But by advocating policies that mis-associate trans people with sexual predators and by aligning with the ADF, they contribute to a heteropatriarchal, Christian nationalist, and homophobic discourse of heteropatriarchal protection (that is also, of course, transphobic). As I note, those who fashion themselves as the "protectors" are structurally the same as perpetrators of gendered and sexual violence and are rarely held accountable. By misidentifying the perpetrators of sexual violence, WoLF inadvertently protects the source of violence it seeks to dismantle.

Ultimately, bathroom bills are used to target "trans behavior" rather than sexual violence. They endanger trans persons and ignore the factors that normalize sexual violence. The cynical discourse of protection awards would-be protectors an exclusive claim to exert righteous violence to address the issues it deems worthy (and in defense of those it considers worthy) and to punish those it wishes to cast out. This process reinforces the strength of the so-called protectors, leaving them free to enact violence through legal or extra-legal means to defend what is theirs.

Justifying extra-legal violence via a discourse of protection also has a long (white supremacist) history. Political theorist Cristina Beltrán argues that "performances of whiteness and white supremacy have often involved practices of violence, domination, control, and deference related to the control of women's bodies that are deeply patriarchal in nature."[94] The romanticization of strong white men enacting "frontier justice" to protect their women and children has long been part of some evangelical traditions (frontier masculinity is discussed further in Chapter Three).[95] Indeed, Donald Trump launched his 2016 presidential campaign by proclaiming his candidacy a reaction to dangerous foreigners who threatened the American way of life by threatening American women: "They're bringing drugs. They're bringing crime. They're rapists. And some, I assume, are good people. . . . It's coming from more than Mexico. It's coming from all over South and Latin America, and it's coming probably—probably—from the Middle East."[96] The next day, Dylann Roof opened fire in a Charleston, South Carolina, church and killed nine Black Americans while reportedly declaring, "I have to do it. You rape our women and you're taking over our country. And you have to go."[97] While there is a distinction between racist rhetoric and racially motivated murder, they rest on the same protective logic: Trump and Roof both saw themselves as protectors who were entitled to use violence against non-white aggressors who threaten "their" (white) women. The real threat, however, was to their own status as white, heterosexual men. They considered themselves righteous protectors who are entitled both to judge and to execute judgment; their words and actions reinforced the ideal of the white, male heroic protector, which is culturally constructed (and re-constructed) in the discourses of heroism, innocence, and guilt that reproduce white male supremacy.

In fact, the bathroom bills are not about preventing sexual violence. They are designed to codify a sex binary that supports a heteropatriarchal conception of the family while simultaneously mis-associating trans persons with deceptive, sexually violent aggressors. These bills endanger trans persons for merely being gender-non-conforming and place them at risk of violence if they use the bathroom that corresponds to their gender identity. The bathroom bills are justified on a discourse of protection which says that men-as-protectors can enact righteous violence against anyone who threatens the white heteropatriarchal order. Everyone—from Mike Huckabee to the FRC and WoLF—openly declares that the sources of sexual violence are straight, white, cisgender men. Yet the discourse of protection that they invoke empowers those same men to use righteous violence to protect what is theirs and enforce obedience to their way of life.

Innocent Victims: "Women and Children"

In this section, I discuss the third category in the triad of rape: the "women and children" who are often portrayed as the innocent victims of sexual violence. I combine them into a single category to highlight how they are always connected in the heteropatriarchal order as irredeemably weak and vulnerable people who require protection. That said, each figure does different work to support the heteropatriarchal order. For example, women are presumed to be the primary caregivers of children even though they are sometimes treated as children themselves, as incapable of self-determination or self-protection. Both figures help preserve a heteropatriarchal order in which sexual violence is condemned when it threatens white heteropatriarchal rule and is normalized when it doesn't.

When video footage surfaced in October 2016 capturing Donald Trump boasting that he could "do anything" to women and get away with it, from kissing them without permission to "grab[bing] 'em by the pussy,"[98] Trump's critics—and even some supporters—responded with predictably righteous indignation. "I am sickened by what I heard today. Women are to be championed and revered, not objectified," said then-House speaker Paul Ryan (R-WI). Senator Ted Cruz (R-TX) similarly declared, "Every wife, mother, daughter—every person—deserves to be treated with dignity and respect." Senator Thom Tillis (R-NC) responded, "As a proud husband and father of a daughter, I find Donald Trump's comments indefensible." Senator John Cornyn (R-TX) was "disgusted by Mr. Trump's words about women: our daughters, sisters and mothers." And former Governor Mitt Romney added, "Hitting on married women? Condoning assault? Such vile degradations demean our wives and daughters and corrupt America's face to the world."[99]

While these remarks held women in special status (worthy of reverence and respect), the men who spoke them reserved that status—and the indignation it inspired—for their own mothers, daughters, sisters, and wives. Trump's critics did *not* express outrage on behalf of US congresswomen, witnesses who testify before that body, friends and acquaintances, or female congressional staffers. Their outrage—and the protection from sexual violence that such outrage might offer—was rooted in their own status as righteous protectors of the women who matter to *them*: mothers, daughters, sisters, and wives. The remarks reveal that those who are deemed worthy of protection, respectful discourse, reverence, and non-violent treatment are those whose identities are affirmed by—and whose identities undergird—a white supremacist, patriarchal, and heteronormative family.

Sex segregation of public restrooms has also been—since its inception—rooted in this same desire to segregate and protect women (the weaker sex) from men (the stronger). As legal scholar Terry Kogan notes, this logic of protection sought to preserve a "separate spheres" ideology by identifying (and, in effect, privatizing) spaces in which upper-class white women could safely rest when they ventured out of the ostensible safety of their homes and into the ever-present dangers of the public sphere.[100] The motivation for laws requiring sex-segregated restrooms, Kogan explains, was not to protect women from dangerous and predatory men but "to further early nineteenth century moral ideology that dictated the appropriate role and place for women in society,"[101] which reaffirmed who the public realm was safe for: normatively white, heterosexual men. If a public space was safe for white men, it was both figuratively unsafe for middle- and upper-class women and their children (in the sense that it was figured as an unsafe space) and literally unsafe, particularly for non-white and working-class persons who had to venture out to work. For example, when public restrooms in the Jim Crow period offered only three options—"ladies," "gentlemen," or "colored"—the labels reflect a politics of both race and class that was partially reinforced through the sex segregation of public restrooms. Non-white women were not afforded the same privacy, safety, and protection as white women; there was no separate restroom for "colored" *women*, who were presumed not to need special treatment and could use the sexless, "colored" restroom. Kimberlé Crenshaw and Angela Davis have argued that narratives about white feminine innocence reinforce a pernicious narrative of sexual promiscuity among Black women.[102] Crenshaw argues that "Black women are essentially prepackaged as bad women within cultural narratives about good women who can be raped and bad women who cannot."[103] Conversely, some white women are prepackaged as good women but only if they also comply with heteropatriarchal expectations—namely, that they are mothers, daughters, or wives and that they are taking care of the children. Through a discourse of protection, then, white men simultaneously confirmed their security as righteous defenders of the weak and innocent *who matter to them* and whose weakness is a predicate of heteropatriarchy, reinforced the insecurity of those who were not powerful enough to enact protection (by themselves or others), and reaffirmed who in the political order did not require protection. This multifaceted discourse of protection has extended beyond the security of the public restroom to infuse US rape culture and popular responses to sexual violence.

When the United States reformed its legal codes in the 1980s and 1990s to address sexual violence, the enactment of protection depended on the construction of "innocent victims of male violence who *deserve* protection by the state and its agencies."[104] As Richie notes, those constructions of innocence are rooted in class, gender, and racial myths and discourses that allow the protectors to marshal state power to protect only some victims of sexual violence, some of the time, and to punish only some perpetrators of sexual violence. These myths and discourses depended on an assumption of innocence on the part of victims: common victims of rape, such as incarcerated men, are not afforded such care and concern. Wendy Brown makes a similar point about class: "Protection codes are . . . key technologies in regulating privileged women as well as in intensifying the vulnerability and degradation of those on the unprotected side of the constructed divide between light and dark, wives and prostitutes, good girls and bad ones."[105] A rape culture thus creates an interpretive framework that justifies a distinction between the women who are worthy of protection and those who are not.

The child is the other vulnerable protectee. At least since Anita Bryant's anti-queer "Save Our Children" campaign, the impulse to protect children's innocence against an increasingly liberal, sexually permissive culture has stoked conservative ire. It was in the name of protecting the innocence of children that Representative Fred Deutsch (R) introduced a bill in the South Dakota state legislature in 2016 to require public school students to use the multi-use restrooms corresponding to their biological sex as assigned at birth.[106] Deutsch, a religious conservative, shares many of the values of the ADF, FRC, and other Christian conservative groups. In a section of his website called "Defending Traditional Values," he asserts that the religious liberty of American Christians is under threat, as are the values of life (from "conception to natural death"), family values, and traditional marriage between a man and a woman.[107]

In his defense of HB1008, Deutsch did not declare the need to protect children from sexual assault as some other proponents of bathroom bills have done. (For example, the NC Values Coalition's executive director, Tami Fitzgerald, raised these concerns in her statement about an NCAA boycott threat in advance of the repeal of HB2 in 2016–17; the ADF has also made statements along these lines[108]). Deutsch instead worried about "the *innocence* of children. . . . How do we protect their minds and hearts and eyes while they're showering and changing?"[109] "I don't want our children to be exposed to the anatomy of other genders," he clarified in another 2016 statement, most likely in reference to a biological sex binary, as determined by the presence of either a penis or a vagina. The South Dakota bill focused on public school bathrooms; presumably some kinds of exposure to "other anatomies" is okay. When, for example, a mother takes her young son into a family restroom, or her young son and daughter together, each child is being exposed to another anatomy. This exposure—within the controlled environment of a heteropatriarchal, "traditional" family—is not cause for the same kind of concern.

Deutsch's statements reflect the same logic as groups (like the ADF) determined to prevent children's exposure to non-normative bodies or gender expression, which are perceived as gateways to sinfulness. These groups believe public bathrooms are essential sites of regulation to maintain the existing social order, which is why they work so hard to preserve them as sex-segregated spaces. In *Queering Bathrooms*, sociologist Sheila Cavanagh argues that the physical space of the public restroom and its configuration as a site of segregation mirror the normative social order. In this context, exposure to a previously unseen or unknown Other reveals a rift between the normative and non-normative, thereby opening up the possibility of non-normativity: "when the perceiving subject is uncertain about the body of the intercepted by sight, the viewer may come to be uncertain about his or her own gendered body and postural schema."[110] The transphobia that motivates bathroom bills and other anti-trans legislation, Cavanagh's analysis and Deutsch's words suggest, is inspired by an anxiety that mere exposure to non-normativity will lead the viewer to call sex, gender, and the regulatory scheme of the public restroom into question. The only acceptable mirror—the one that hangs on walls in sex-segregated public restrooms—is the one that reaffirms the norms and hierarchies of white heteropatriarchy.

If the deep-seated fear of trans or gender-non-conforming people is that "exposure" facilitates a loss of innocence and then sinfulness, then the discourse of protection that claims to want to prevent sexual violence is disingenuous. Preventing exposure to the "opposite sex" does not address child sexual abuse, which is commonplace in the United States: according to the Centers for Disease Control (CDC), 1 in 4 girls and 1 in 13 boys is a victim of child sexual abuse.[111] This risk is unevenly distributed, and low-income and at-risk children are more likely to be victims.[112] The CDC reported in 2021 that 91% of US child sexual abuse is committed by someone the child's family knows,[113] rather than strangers (such as those in public restrooms). According to Seto et al., a third of all child sexual abuse is perpetrated by a family member—most often fathers and stepfathers.[114] Far from being the great protectors of child victims, then, fathers and father figures (the patriarchs) are very often the perpetrators.

But rather than focus on the causes and effects of this systematic and relentlessly consistent form of sexual violence, those who employ the discourse of protection do so to induce a moral panic directed at transgender people—who, the evidence suggests, do not pose a significant or persistent threat of sexual violence toward children. The issue of child sexual assault is frequently used strategically to either affirm the myth of the deviant male rapist (i.e., that child sexual abuse, like other forms of sexual violence, is rare and perpetrated by sexual deviants) or reinforce other discourses of sexual deviancy in order to justify homophobia and transphobia. Prominent child sexual abusers like Jerry Sandusky and Larry Nassar were often described as if they were monstrous outliers, when in fact their grooming techniques were quite mundane. Roman Catholic Church sexual abuse is almost always discussed in homophobic terms regarding male clergy and boys and usually downplays the perpetration by nuns and the victimization of girls.

The traditional imperative to protect children from sexual violence is more likely an imperative to protect "The Child," an abstraction that literary critic Lee Edelman argues represents the social order and its future endurance.[115] The Child allows a social order to sacrifice people, including specific children, to preserve itself and its future. Violence is justifiable when it protects The Child and can be used against anyone who threatens the social order. Edelman argues that we should expect the endangerment of actual children, or of trans and queer persons, or of *anyone* who challenges the social order, to be of less concern to the heteropatriarchal order than the endangerment of The Child—which is to say, endangerment of the future of the order.[116] The reproductive imperative at the heart of heteronormativity and its defense of The Child (what Edelman calls "reproductive futurity") is evinced not only in Deutsch's anxiety about The Child's exposure to the non-normative and non-innocent but also in the ADF's stated agenda to promote "generational wins" with legislative and judicial actions that will profoundly alter the US culture toward its (heteropatriarchal) "family-centered" view. According to this view, US society can protect The Child by preserving the structure of the traditional family, even though most sexual assault of children occurs in such families and households and is perpetrated by fathers and father figures.

Because aggressive violence against *all* perpetrators of child sexual abuse—in defense of children rather than The Child—would rupture the white heteropatriarchal social order, only non-normative figures (like trans people) can be depicted as the real threat. With the bathroom bills, the guardians of heteropatriarchy target trans people precisely because the violence must be directed *somewhere*, and if the heteropatriarchy is to blame, it can hardly be expected to exert violence upon itself. The order is predicated on a strongman patriarch who is entitled to use righteous violence to defend his home and homeland. As Du Mez argues, this Christian nationalist worldview revels in some kinds of brutality and empowers men to use their own judgment to determine whether the use of violence is justified.

While not all evangelical Christians adopt this view or commit violence against their loved ones, it is clear that—despite what church teachings might advise—intrafamilial violence and sexual violence are commonplace within a white supremacist, heteropatriarchal, cisgender order. Churchgoers will blame gender confusion, but the empirical evidence overwhelmingly suggests that children are at far higher risk of sexual violence committed by a family member than by a transgender person in a gender-congruent public restroom. Preserving this order, to empower those at its head to continue to enact violence in defense of what they deem valuable or worth protecting, is an essential aspect of the discourse of protection that normalizes sexual violence through concealment and deflection. Those who deploy this discourse with a promise to protect children from sexual violence do not address the conditions of widespread sexual violence—which might require addressing white supremacy, poverty, patriarchy, homophobia, and transphobia.

Conclusion

The discourse of protection is evident in many aspects of US political life, from law enforcement and public safety (it has been used to justify "stand your ground" or "stop and frisk" laws) to immigration policy (to justify a southern US border wall). Yet, I am not suggesting that every strategy of protection in politics preserves heteropatriarchal violence. Indeed, there are powerful forms of protective politics, particularly related to land, water, and wildlife protection, such as when water protectors resisted the Dakota Access Pipeline in Standing Rock, South Dakota, or the Coastal GasLink Pipeline in Wet'suwet'en (British Columbia). In moments of real danger during Black Lives Matter protests, Black activists have called upon white activists to form human shields to protect them from law enforcement officers. We must distinguish such coalitional strategies of protective politics from the cynical discourse of protection through which so-called protectors invoke their power to protect *in order to perpetuate their domination of others.* The core distinction I am drawing is between instances when protection is deployed to *maintain* dominance and when it is offered, via coalitional commitments, to *resist* it.[117] This distinction allows us to theorize a strategy of protection that does not replicate the myths, discourse, and practices of rape culture that enable sexual violence.

I condemn legislators' cynical discourse of protection that involves introducing bills that harm trans people under the guise of protecting women and children from sexual predation. The unvarnished truth at the heart of the bathroom bill legislation—which the FRC and Mike Huckabee openly admitted—is that cisgender men are the ones who seek to enter women's bathrooms and changing rooms to engage in sexual predation. These legislative efforts focus on trans persons, even though they rest on the assumption that opportunistic, cisgender men are predatory. Yet the bills punish trans persons by forcing them into dangerous situations that increase their own risk of sexual assault. The irony is that the bathroom bills emphasize and bolster the ostensible non-normativity of transgender people, which in effect reinforces the profound normativity of sexual violence in the white, heteropatriarchal US rape culture.

In US rape culture, the discourse of protection reflects a white, cisgender, heteropatriarchal idealization of the family. As Du Mez has argued, this understanding might also, in some right-wing Christian evangelical circles, locate an insatiable male sexual appetite alongside righteous exertions of male violence. In addition to other forms of protective violence, this association can justify a version of "frontier justice."[118] On the "frontier" (i.e., the uncivilized spaces that exist at various levels of remove from the domestic sphere), those who have historically been forced to gratify white male sexual desire—such as enslaved women, commercial sex workers, or Indigenous persons—are not worthy of protection. Moreover, the status of the white woman as worthy of protection in the white heteropatriarchy depends on her disassociation with those who can be used to satisfy male sexual desire, who are in turn regarded as invulnerable or unworthy of care. In order to determine which bodies to protect, white heteropatriarchal men need to identify which bodies they can violate—in the name of either protecting their women and children or satisfying their sexual desires. The ostensible right to use violence in either case is justified by the righteous judgments of the heteropatriarchy. It needs bodies on whom to enact the protective impulses through violence and bodies to protect. In the next chapter I turn to the "frontier" of the Bakken oil formation in the United States to explore how, precisely because US rape culture does not deem them worthy of protection, Indigenous people are disproportionately subjected to all forms of violence, including sexual violence.

Chapter Three

"A process of history"

Sexual Violence and the Settler Colonial Project

"No one knows"

Wind River is a 2017 film about the rape and murder of a young Arapaho woman at an oil drilling site adjacent to the Wind River Indian Reservation in Wyoming. It highlights the ongoing crisis of violence against Indigenous[1] women and girls and the jurisdictional challenges of pursuing criminal investigations on or near reservations.[2] While the film goes to great lengths to humanize Indigenous experiences of violence, and succeeds in many ways, its closing title returns to the familiar trope that the scope of settler violence is unknown: "While missing person statistics are compiled for every other demographic, none exist for Native American women. No one knows how many are missing."

While this ending is meant to inspire a sense of injustice, the claim that "no one knows" is not quite accurate for two reasons. First, missing persons statistics have been compiled and disaggregated by race (including a category for Native Americans) since 1999, according to Muscogee (Creek) legal scholar and MacArthur Fellow Sarah Deer.[3] The problem is that data collected by US government agencies, including local law enforcement and the FBI, drastically undercounts the number of missing and murdered Indigenous persons. In response to these failures, Indigenous-led organizations like the Sovereign Bodies Institute and Urban Indian Health Institute (UIHI) have sought to decolonize data by using their own methods of collection and presentation. Their work highlights the inadequacies of the US government approach to data collection from Indigenous populations, which is often based on self-reports to local law enforcement.[4]

Second, the proclamation that "no one knows" makes sense only if one centers the settler gaze. For example, the "discoveries" of mass burial sites at Indian schools in the United States and Canada were not revelations to the families and communities who lost their children to the boarding school system, who knew with intimate certainty that their children were missing or dead because they had never returned home. Nor were their disappearances unknown to the administrators of the settler state, who knew where the bodies were buried because they had, in fact, buried the bodies. Declaring this information unknown or unknowable is tantamount to saying that since the scope of the problem cannot be determined by the white settler state, there is little to be done about it. This willful ignorance implies that violence against Indigenous persons has somehow escaped the notice of the settlers who enact that violence daily and that, while white heterosexual women and children are objects of protection violence in the white settler state, Indigenous people are afforded little protection or care.

The denial of settler violence in the forms of murder, disappearance, and gendered violence mirrors another kind of denial—climate change denial—which is invoked to justify selective inaction by way of ignorance. Both types of denial enable unbridled economic growth and are bound together: violation of and violence toward people, cultures, and the natural environment can be tolerated if they satisfy a collective appetite for natural resources. As it turns out, reservation lands are more valuable than the US federal government once thought: they contain "approximately half of the nation's uranium, one-third of its low-sulfur strippable coal, and a decent percentage of its oil shale and natural gas."[5] What was once considered undesirable land, fit only for Indigenous inhabitants, is now eagerly reclaimed by the US settler state to support its own economic growth.

Wind River is set on and near the reservation lands of the Shoshone and Arapaho Nations, and the significant action takes place at a hydraulic fracturing (fracking) site. Like the nearby Bakken oil formation—located in North Dakota, Montana, Saskatchewan, and Manitoba, and including Fort Peck, Montana, home to the Assiniboine and Sioux Nations, and Fort Berthold, North Dakota, home to the Three Affiliated Tribes of the Mandan, Hidatsa, and Arikara (Sahnish) Nations (the MHA Nation)—the Wind River Basin sits atop a multilayered formation of shale and sandstone that contains large deposits of oil and gas. Fracking pipes, up to 2 miles long and encased in concrete, penetrate these shale layers buried deep beneath the earth's surface. Explosives are detonated in this "wellbore" to fracture the shale, and a mixture of water, sand, and toxic chemicals floods the wellbore to expand the "fractures" through seismic ruptures that release oil and gas, which is then extracted from deep underground and transported to Illinois via the Dakota Access Pipeline.

Like the violence against Indigenous peoples, the violence of extraction by fracking is hidden: it occurs far below the earth's surface. It generates significant environmental risks including groundwater pollution, toxification of the land through chemical dumping, and increased seismic activity.[6] Social risks also emerge as oil and gas workers migrate to places like the Bakken to work temporarily: they overcrowd social services, drive up housing costs, commit crimes, and make long-term residents feel unsafe.[7] The arrival of this workforce has overwhelmed the region with drug- and alcohol-related problems and increased rates of rape and other forms of sexual violence, including human trafficking.[8] The local residents, many of whom are Indigenous, bear these costs.

According to anthropologist Patrick Wolfe, settler colonial invasion is a "structure" rather than an "event";[9] settler invasion is ongoing in the sense that settlers come to stay. During the booms of resource extraction (characterized by housing encampments and short-term stays) and the eventual busts, invasion has taken at least two forms: both land and bodies are invaded. First, resource extraction at an industrial scale exerts slow violence on the natural environment. According to environmental historian Traci Brynne Voyles, this violence occurs in places that have been "wastelanded"—constructed as both wasted and wastable through raced, gendered, and classed narratives that justify extraction and the toxification of spaces that are not otherwise "useful" to industrialized, settler, white society.[10] Second, professor of Native studies Kim Tallbear (citizen of Sisseton-Wahpeton Oyate) observes that the "wastelanding" of space corresponds to the wastelanding of bodies.[11]

More precisely, settler invasion is enacted through what Michi Saagiig Nishnaabeg scholar Leanne Betasomsake Simpson calls a "gendered structure and a *series of complex and overlapping processes*"[12] that buttress the settler colonial project, which are often enacted by people who may not recognize their role in the project (particularly since many of them are subordinated by the very project they are sustaining).[13] Recent sexual assault statistics point to a series of individual events, carried out in the "man camps" and towns that dot the Bakken, which comprise a structure of invasion.[14] We must account for the relationship between the structure of settler invasion writ large and the particular experiences of those who enact or endure particular settler "invasions" of body and land. I presume that many of the oil workers who temporarily migrate to the Bakken and commit violence against the people and land that sustain the settler colonial project do not recognize how their actions enable the whole structure of settler invasion. This is not to excuse their actions, or even to suggest that they would act differently if they were aware of their role in the settler project. It is simply a way to focus on what political anthropologist Audra Simpson (Kahnawà:ke Mohawk) observes: "*States* do not always have to kill" (or, we can add, commit rape or other forms of violence) because "its *citizens* can do that for it."[15]

In this chapter, I argue that individual actors draw on the collective myths, discourses, and practices of US rape culture to justify and conceal the structure of sexual and other forms of violence, particularly against Indigenous persons. US rape culture contributes to the settler colonial ideology that "wastelands" Indigenous people and land and gives white men the benefit of the doubt when they are accused of sexual violence. In order to designate the protectable bodies, the settler state requires unprotectable bodies as well. Intersectional analysis reveals that interconnected axes of domination provide multiple avenues to discount the allegations and deny the fundamental care needs of Indigenous women: their status as *Indigenous* means they are uncivilized and hypersexual, as *women* means they are not to be believed, as presumptively *impoverished* means they are dirty and unworthy of care. Against this single complex figure stands the frontier man who can be excused for committing violence in the process of domesticating the Wild West. His domination of Indigenous places and people is understandable, and in fact necessary, to carry out the settler project. In this chapter, I explore the myth of the "sq*aw,"[16] the discourses and practices of resource extraction, and the practices of frontier masculinity to demonstrate how US rape culture helps perpetuate sexual violence against Indigenous persons by protecting assailants and vilifying victims. Through this distorting "protective" politics, US popular culture conceals its participation in the ongoing structure of settler colonial violence against both Indigenous persons and the natural world.

"Those whose lives are negated or made illegible cannot have violence done to them."

I start with a note about language: the English word "women" denotes a settler category that is often essentialist and does not neatly or accurately map onto gender categories in other cultures and languages, including some Indigenous ones. I use it to refer to those whom the settler state considers "women" partly because, as a settler and English speaker myself, I don't have alternative language to draw upon and partly because it is accurate in a specific way: the term "women" invokes the heteropatriarchal framework that is pivotal to the settler colonial project. In other languages and cultural formations, "women" do not exist as such. For example, L. B. Simpson explains that in Anishinabee the term *kwe* "is different than the word *woman* because it recognizes a spectrum of gender expressions and it exists embedded in grounded normativity"; they suggest that the term may also have "the capacity to be inclusive of both cis and trans experiences."[17] Yet the ongoing settler desires to pretend that alternative formulations of gender and identity did not exist or that heteropatriarchy is natural are both part of what political theorist Kevin Bruyneel calls "the work of settler memory," which he describes as "a process of remembering and disavowing Indigenous political agency, colonialist dispossessions, and violence toward Indigenous peoples."[18] The disavowal of Indigenous agency, and in particular the agency of Indigenous women, is a legacy of settler colonialism that has enabled settler violence, including sexual violence; it renders Indigenous people and relations illegible to the settler state so the settler state can claim its own innocence. As Hunt notes, "those whose lives are negated or made illegible cannot have violence done to them."[19]

Before being confronted by settler heteropatriarchy and the ideal of Victorian (white, middle- or upper-class) womanhood, the women who lived on the land that is now called North America participated in active, meaningful ways in the political, economic, and social lives of their communities. Women were often valued, honored, equal participants in their communities who—because they were political orders unto themselves,[20] because they participated actively in the sustenance of their communities, and because they embodied sexual independence—posed an existential challenge to the white heteropatriarchy that grounded eighteenth- and nineteenth-century settler culture.[21] Settler violence was used to discipline Indigenous women, to prevent them from setting a paradigm-shifting example to the white women of the settler state, and to force them to comply with political, economic, and sexual subordination.[22] Of course, among European settlers, one consistent form of gendered violence is sexual violence. This is why activist and author Jacqueline Agtuca noted at the Alaska Native Women's Conference in 2005 that "Sexual assault rates and violence against Native American women did not just drop from the sky. They are a process of history,"[23] one that is ongoing.

Settlers used physical and legal violence to suppress the political agency of Indigenous women. They controlled reproduction through violence, murder, rape, forced sterilization, and the toxification of Indigenous lands.[24] They forced Indigenous communities into patrilinear organizational structures, which Audra Simpson calls "legal femicide."[25] Feminist scholar Andrea Smith links the "colonization of Native women" to "the project of strengthening white male ownership of white women."[26] In these ways, settler heteropatriarchy disrupted what Sarah Deer calls a "precolonial gender balance."[27] I use the past tense here to denote a past moment (or series of moments) but not to signify a "before" that is characterized by Indigenous female agency and an "after" that indicates an absence of such agency. L. B. Simpson, A. Simpson, and others explain that while the role of Indigenous women in the lives of their communities may have changed, it has never been suppressed, despite the best efforts of the settler colonial project.

The violent suppression of these alternate forms of agency is ongoing. According to a 2016 Department of Justice (DOJ) report, 84.3% of female and 81.6% of male American Indian and Alaska Native respondents have experienced some form of violence (including stalking and physical, intimate partner, and sexual violence); 56.1% and 27.5%, respectively, have experienced sexual violence.[28] Of these victims, "96% of women and 89% of men have experienced sexual violence by an interracial perpetrator,"[29] which is to say that sexual violence is most often perpetrated against Indigenous people by non-Indigenous people. Many victims of sexual violence are victimized more than once in their lifetimes, often by different people.[30] Additionally, violence against Indigenous persons is not confined to tribal land. Both rural and urban Indigenous women are disproportionately subjected to sexual violence, and, for reasons related to the unique jurisdictional constraints between local, tribal, and federal authorities, those who live in reservation border towns face unique challenges as well.[31] The UIHI, located in Seattle, Washington, reported that 94% of Native women living in the city had "been raped or coerced in sex at some point in their lives."[32] The UIHI identified 5,712 cases of missing and murdered Indigenous women and girls (MMIWG) reported in 2016, only 116 of which were logged in the DOJ database.[33] The UIHI also independently documented 506 cases of MMIWG in seventy-one cities across the United States; 153 of these were not found in any law enforcement database.[34]

We can connect these disproportionately high levels of sexual violence to settler violence because, regardless of where they live, an overwhelming majority of Indigenous women report having had at least one non-Indigenous assailant. Indigenous women also report disproportionately more violent assaults than non-Indigenous persons do.[35] Indigenous persons thus appear to be targeted by non-Indigenous persons as objects of violent sexual assault. Though incomplete, these statistics indicate that "violence against Indigenous women is structural, not coincidental."[36]

Sexual and other forms of violence are so common that feminist Indigenous scholars and activists often describe it as *normalized*.[37] In Chapter One, I noted that mainstream US feminists frequently describe rape culture as contributing to the "normalization" of sexual violence. In that context, I understand the term "normalization" to signal the normative ideal that desirous sex is violent sex and that it is "normal" for sex to be violent and non-consensual. But Sarah Hunt, Kwakwaka'wakw scholar of Indigenous political ecology, describes a more immediate and troubling "normalization" of sexual violence: that rape (not only the threat of it) among Indigenous persons is so "normal" that women, queer, non-binary, and two-spirit persons live in the knowledge that they will have to protect themselves and one another from gendered violence.[38] (Other marginalized [non-Indigenous] persons in the Bakken *also* live in fear of violence, particularly sexual violence; their sense of unsafety has its own self-regulating and mental/physical health effects on the region's long-term residents, as I discuss below.[39]) The effects of sexual violence affect many aspects of Indigenous life: survey respondents report inadequate access to (and a lack of culturally safe) medical and social services. They also report enduring poverty cycles and ongoing environmental violence.[40] Even for those who have not been subjected to sexual assault, the normalization of rape constitutes a historical trauma—"an enduring violence that spans generations"[41] that is both always-past and ever-present, an embodied history that is not always tended in culturally safe ways.[42] The *normalization* of sexual violence as inevitable for Indigenous women, queer, non-binary, and two-spirit people and the *internalization* of an expectation that sexual violence is a rule rather than an exception are possible because the settler state's project of elimination continuously normalizes violence to control Indigenous persons and their homelands. As Hunt notes, in settler rape culture, rape is "just life" for Indigenous persons—especially for women, queer, trans, and two-spirit Indigenous persons.[43]

To justify the political and material dispossession of Indigenous women, settlers depict(ed) them as dangerous to settler men and to the settler order,[44] in part through the long-standing myth of the "sq∗aw." The word "sq∗aw" still graces place names across the United States. Richard King notes that many of these place names are sniggeringly sexualized, combining "sq∗aw" with words like "butte," "tit," or "teat," and are often associated with the "frontier" or American West.[45]

Indigenous women understandably consider the term "sq∗aw" insulting, violent, and threatening. Although there are many stories about its meaning (and its meaning as a settler term), the most comprehensive account I have found suggests it is derived from words in the Algonquian language family which encompassed "all the ordinary words for woman," not pejorative ones; like some other Indigenous words, the simple term for woman was appropriated by the settler state and contorted to denote a sexually promiscuous, morally degraded, and savage woman.[46] King explains the implications of the "racialized and sexualized images" implicit in the most common understandings of the term as "a woman or wife," "an effeminate or weak person," or "a sexually promiscuous woman."[47] He notes that the latter definition "has not only sexualized Native American women as prostitutes, but also derogated female sexuality more generally, as in the Second World War when American soldiers used sq∗aw to refer to an ugly prostitute."[48] Audra Simpson maintains that the "sq∗aw" became a necessary figure to reinforce the existence of the "savage and prior other"[49] whose extermination, assimilation, and replacement continue to rationalize settlers' extraction of whatever they desire from the people and land they regard as wasted and wastable.

Among settlers, the nineteenth-century feminine ideal was structured by white heteropatriarchy and upward class aspirations. Sociologist Gail Hawkes explains that the "ideal of purity and sexual innocence [was] well fitted to the separation of spheres [and] underpinned the patriarchal power of the new ruling class."[50] The "separate spheres" ideology referenced in Chapter Two (which suggests that men belong in public and women in private) preserved a Victorian idea of where white women ought to be, where they could be safe, and who could keep them safe. Of course, the "protection" of separate spheres is only available to women of the middle or upper class, typically white, who do not need to work outside the home.

Settler culture justified the male exertion of legal and extra-legal violence to protect a pure and innocent white "bloodline" and "civilization."[51] Settler men wielded violence (including sexual violence) to protect whiteness and tame the frontier and to gratify themselves and dominate the "savages."

Feminist scholar Andrea Smith maintains that there is little evidence that Indigenous men used sexual violence in this way as a tool of political control. For instance, they do not appear to have assaulted their female settler prisoners:

> As William Apess (Pequot) once stated in the 1800s: "Where, in the records of Indian barbarity, can we point to a violated female?" (O'Connell 1992, 64). Brigadier General James Clinton of the Continental Army said to his soldiers as they were sent off to destroy the Iroquois nation in 1779: "Bad as the savages are, they never violate the chastity of any women, their prisoners" (cited in Wrone and Nelson 1982, 17). As Shoat and Stam argue, the real purpose behind this colonial terror "was not to force the indigenes to become Europeans, but to keep Europeans from becoming indigenes."[52]

Even in captivity narratives that sensationalize Indigenous persons as savages, including Mary Rowlandson's 1682 *Narrative of Captivity and Restoration of Mrs. Mary Rowlandson*, captured settler woman often insist that their captors did not sexually assault them. For example, in the recounting of her captivity, Rowlandson maintains that "not one of them ever offered me the least abuse of unchastity to me, in word or action."[53] My point is not to claim that Indigenous men did not ever inflict sexual violence on settler women but only to suggest that settlers *themselves* noticed a difference in practices between settlers and Indigenous persons at the time. This difference is significant: it suggests that rape is a political tool when deployed in certain cultural contexts but is not an inevitable outgrowth of a supposed natural, insatiable male sexual desire. For cultures in which sex does not signify control or power, sexual violence is not a technique of domination. Yet white settlers have consistently wielded it as a weapon to dominate the frontier and Indigenous people and to reproduce whiteness itself.

Before the arrival of white settler women to the frontier, Indigenous women were "used to satisfy what were perceived to be natural needs"[54] of settler men. Once white women joined their husbands in the settlements, Indigenous women had to be reconfigured as both *useable* to satisfy men's sexual needs and *condemnable* because they were incapable of the chaste womanhood of white settler women. Historian Jean Barman notes that "local [non-settler] women were used for sexual gratification [and] . . . so long as colonial women were absent."[55] Once settler women joined their husbands on the frontier, Native women would need to be cast out. By portraying Indigenous women as "sq*aws" with untamed, insatiable sexual appetites,[56] settlers juxtaposed them against white femininity, rendering Indigenous women antithetical to the preservation and reproduction of white heteropatriarchy and therefore subordinate to white women. Andrea Smith describes this "demonization of Native women" as "a strategy of white men to maintain control over white women" by reifying the binary sex hierarchy of heteropatriarchy and the racial hierarchy of white supremacy.[57]

Historian Rayna Green suggests that what distinguishes the sq*aw from other dehumanizing, misogynistic, and racialized mythic female figures in US rape culture is the existence of the desirable, rare, and unattainable "Indian princess" as a counterpoint—a noble savage who sacrifices herself for the white settler order.[58] In contrast to the mythical princess, the sq*aw is drunk, dirty, lazy, crude, and stupid and cannot be rescued, so she "does what white men want for money or lust."[59] While the Indian princess is valorized for becoming white, Christian, and "civilized," the mythic sq*aw can only ever be "a depersonalized object of scornful convenience,"[60] a wastelanded person who gratifies white settler sexual appetites before being discarded.

Finally, the sq*aw is constructed as a drudge who lacks agency, toils endlessly for others (typically for men), is dirty, and lacks the capacity for speech or autonomy.[61] The image of a "dirty Indian" justifies and normalizes the extreme poverty experienced by many Indigenous persons as a result of practices of dispossession, cultural assimilation, forced relocation, disease, and toxification of land.[62] The dirty Indigenous body also serves as point of contrast with the pure, chaste, white body of the Victorian ideal woman. Smith explains that "because Indian bodies are 'dirty,' they are considered sexually violable and 'rapable.' That is, in patriarchal thinking, only a body that is 'pure' can be violated. The rape of bodies that are considered inherently impure and dirty simply does not count."[63] To undermine alternative, non-binary, and potentially non-hierarchical political orders, the mythic figure of the sq*aw emerged to discipline white women and eliminate Indigenous women. White women had to comply with the settler heteropatriarchy (which insisted on white female chastity) in order to be protected. To satisfy its appetite for land expropriation, settler society extended neither care nor protection to the sq*aw. The mythic figure of the sq∗aw is thus sexually objectified and radically depoliticized. She is a stark contrast to the "relatively egalitarian nature of Native societies [that] belies patriarchy's claims to normality,"[64] such as the female members of the Cherokee who "had their own arena of power," the female Lenni Lenape who owned their own property,[65] and the Iroquois women who were and are "the political form of the Iroquois Confederacy."[66]

The construction of a male sq*aw was also part of a settler project to depict "Native peoples as hypersexual and nonheteronormative."[67] The male sq*aw or "dirty Indian" male is feminized and at times (homophobically) queered. Scholars Nancy Parezo and Angelina Jones explain that the term sq*aw "became a taunt associated with male weakness or was used disparagingly to ridicule an effeminate man who did women's work. (This included homosexuals in European American society as well as two-spirited individuals in Indian cultures)" and was synonymous with "coward."[68] The effeminization of Indigenous men accomplished two objectives. First, it justified the wastelanding and sexual victimization of their bodies. Indigenous men experience higher rates of sexual assault than men from other racial groups,[69] including increased incidents of male rape in the Bakken (which I discuss more below). Second, American studies scholar Chris Finley of the Colville Confederated Tribes observes that this queering move reveals that "all sexualization of Native peoples constructs them as incapable of self-governance without a heteropatriarchal influence that Native peoples do not 'naturally' possess."[70] Their non-normativity therefore justifies their being controlled or eliminated by the settler order.

It might be tempting to dismiss the myth of the sq*aw as outdated, but the eroticized Indigenous woman is still very much a part of contemporary US rape culture. As Hunt explains, part of the work of settler rape culture is to "naturalize sexual assault [particularly of Indigenous persons] as occurring 'out there' or 'back then,'"[71] even though Indigenous people are still disproportionately targeted with sexual violence. Visual representations of Indigenous women in the United States are still highly sexualized,[72] evinced in the ubiquitous "sexy Indian" costumes that appear each Halloween and in the "tribalization" or "Indianification" of lingerie at four (!) Victoria's Secret fashion shows in the past decade alone.[73] And a video game from the 1980s, *Custer's Revenge*, allowed players, in the visage of Custer, to rape an Indigenous woman tied to a post to win the game: "when you score, you score."[74]

To dismiss the myth of the sq*aw as "no longer relevant" thus replicates the colonial move to claim ignorance to justify inaction ("no one knows") and ignores the ways in which the myth still shapes the lived experiences of Indigenous women. In her 1996 memoir *I Am Woman*, Stó:lō scholar and writer Lee Maracle describes growing up as an Indigenous girl and experiencing the violence of the myth of the sq*aw as she contended with settler and lateral violence (violence against members within one's own community as a learned response to settler violence and internalized colonialism),[75] both of which reflect settler, heteropatriarchal control of the household, community, and economy.[76] Maracle discusses her struggles against the idea of the disposable Indigenous woman: "I, too, have had to fight over and over for my womanhood. After thirteen short years, I learned that the world hates women and 'squ[*]ws' do not even qualify as women."[77] If some men hate women enough to rape them, Maracle asks, how much do they hate the sq*aw?

As long as they represent political or sexual autonomy that challenges white heteropatriarchy, Indigenous people will be neither protected nor grieved by the settler state. Drawing on philosopher Judith Butler's work, Hunt observes that "even raising the missing women into public discourse fails to trigger a change in the normalization of violence against Indigenous women, because Indigenous women and sex workers are categories of belonging predetermined by colonial power relations."[78] Women are only grievable, Hunt notes, if they can be placed into categories that the white heteropatriarchal settler state recognizes as grievable: "mother, sister friend" but not, say, "sex worker, drug user, and Indigenous woman."[79] A 2011 qualitative study of Indigenous women in Minnesota found that, among respondents who were engaged in commercial sex work, "62% saw a connection between prostitution and colonization, and explained that the devaluation of women in prostitution was identical to the colonizing devaluation of Native people."[80] Thus, the myth of the sq∗aw renders Indigenous persons ungrievable because the sq∗aw is never figured as a mother, an assimilable "princess," or anyone else worthy of white strongman protection.

As Audra Simpson notes, even in rare instances when Indigenous women are grieved—as when Loretta Saunders, a 26-year-old Inuk woman, was found murdered in New Brunswick in 2014—it is not because her death is horrible, or even that, because she looks white, "she is [presumed to be] more precious than the darker ones among us" but because "her death demonstrates that *no one* is safe"[81] from sexual violence, dispossession, or murder. Loretta Saunders became grievable because she stood in for "every woman," including (or perhaps especially) the white, middle- and upper-class exemplars of heteropatriarchal normativity whose bodies require protection by white settlers.

In *Wind River*, sympathy is cultivated for the victim, Natalie Hanson, a young Arapaho woman, because she is recognizable in the settler culture as a "good girl": a sister, daughter, friend, and girlfriend worthy of settler protection. The scene just before she is raped by a group of oil workers depicts her in a loving, caring relationship with another white oil worker (a security guard named Matt) as they plan for a future in a quiet town like Ojai, California (1:14:08). She is not a prostitute or a victim of sex trafficking; she is a young Indigenous woman in love with a white man and, perhaps, with settler culture. The vicious men who beat her boyfriend to death and rape her are portrayed as savage, ostensibly distinguishable from most white men on the Bakken. They fulfill the "bad man rapist" myth: they are racist animals (before they enter the trailer, they are heard outside howling like wild animals) (1:14:22) and one of the men castigates Matt for "acting like a pussy for this prairie n*gger"[82] (1:16:48), a statement that both emasculates Matt for caring for his girlfriend and emphasizes the rapists' dehumanizing racialization of Natalie which, to borrow a term from philosopher Charles Mills, renders Natalie a "sub-person." The film contrasts Natalie's innocence and goodness (she was the best friend of the protagonist's murdered daughter) with the vicious, inexplicable irrationality of her white assailants. The screenplay describes the scene as "a drunken, feral orgy of no reason,"[83] which suggests the screenwriter imagines this moment as almost unintelligible. Given that the film purportedly intends to highlight MMIW, it is remarkable that the rapists are characterized as if their perpetration of sexual violence would be exceptional and inexplicable rather than commonplace and *normal*. Even in this narrative attempt to tell the story of gendered violence and MMIW with care and respect, the victim is portrayed in terms that are legible to the settler audience, and her white male assailants are only legible to the settler audience *as assailants* if they are virtually inhuman. This approach subtly reinforces the characterization of brutish or savage (non-white) men as likely rape perpetrators and of white men as unlikely to rape. Natalie's aspirations (if not her skin) may be white, and her death—perhaps like that of Loretta Saunders—convinces the audience of a contradiction: because "no one is safe" from the inevitable violence of white settler heteropatriarchy, white settler protection is always necessary.

Finally, although this chapter concentrates on the relationship between sexual violence and extractive practices, the cultural representation of Indigenous people as sexually violable extends to those who live far from wastelanded places. Indigenous research groups like the UIHI, the Sovereign

Bodies Institute, and the Brave Heart Society have undertaken independent studies and found vastly higher rates of MMIW than are disclosed in state and federal crime statistics and high rates of male, non-Native perpetrators.[84] High rates of sex trafficking are associated with Indigenous women and girls[85] but are not limited to reservations or reservation border towns.[86] A 2016 UIHI study of seventy-one urban areas across the United States found that MMIW who live in urban areas often have limited access to culturally safe resources and support.[87] Violent crimes against Indigenous persons in both rural and urban areas go uncounted and unaddressed, further supporting the argument that settler culture regards Indigenous women and children as expendable.

In US rape culture, the myth of the sq*aw persists to assert the values of heteropatriarchal settler culture over Indigenous cultures that provide critical sociopolitical alternatives to the rape culture. This myth, contrasted with the Indian princess, perpetuates the eroticization of Indians in popular culture and the construction of Indigenous bodies as hypersexualized, non-normative, and dirty. Because these bodies are not considered worthy of protection or care, there is a sense that they can be treated in violent and sexually violent ways. The minority of Indigenous persons who are afforded care in US rape culture either approximate whiteness or further the narrative of white settler innocence. But for the most part, like the landscapes in which they dwell, Indigenous persons (particularly Indigenous women, queer, and two-spirit persons) are considered wasted and wastable.

"They treat Mother Earth like they treat women"

I have never been to Fort Berthold and cannot claim to have a relationship with this place and certainly could never experience something like a "grounded normativity" in relation to it (as Glen Coulthard and L. B. Simpson describe the concept and which I discuss below). At the same time, as a settler, I think it is important to challenge my "ungrounded normativity" by making a point to bring the land into my thinking; to treat it as a source of life, relationship, and reciprocity; and to acknowledge that the settler state regards it as an object to dominate and subdue via violence. I begin this section by drawing on local accounts, photographs, and histories to offer a brief account of the landscape and what it might mean for those who dwell there, live in relationship with it, and certainly do not regard it as a wasteland.

The part of the homelands stewarded by the affiliated tribes of the Mandan, Hidatsa, and Arikara (Sahnish) Nations, known now as the Fort Berthold Indian Reservation, follows the Missouri River through North Dakota. The landscape features striated buttes of sepia and sage, rolling grasses, badlands, and the expansive river. It is home to abundant wildlife including bighorn sheep, elk, deer, and mountain lions.[88] For centuries, many of the Mandan and Hidatsa people were farmers who lived in villages along the river; others lived in woodlands nearby.[89] The Arikara (Sahnish) migrated westward later than the Mandan and Hidatsa and eventually settled along the river as well.[90]

In the 1950s, the US government dammed the river as part of a flood abatement project, flooding the villages of the three affiliated tribes, which contained the richest farmland along the riverbed; the project created a reservoir called Lake Sakawakea, now the largest lake in North Dakota. More than three-quarters (80%) of the tribal membership (325 families)[91] were forced to relocate to new towns and farms on less fertile land.[92] Communities on either side of the river that had once interacted regularly were suddenly divided by an enormous reservoir.

Yet despite the changes brought "when the waters came"[93] and through decades of booms and busts, Fort Berthold remains a beautiful, austere place. Sometimes the landscape is glazed with hoar frost, and sometimes the grasses roll like waves onto shore; winters can be bitterly cold, while summers can be warm and sun baked.[94] Today (as in the past), the settler state does not honor or recognize the homelands of the three affiliated tribes—what is sometimes called "flyover" land or "wasted" land—as a place of fertile soil, diverse wildlife, a generous river, rich communities, and inspiring vistas. It is instead valued for what lies 2 miles below it: a concentration of oil shale known as the Bakken oil formation, which is routinely fractured by explosives so that oil and gas can be extracted and snaked through the Dakota Access Pipeline across the Standing Rock Indian Reservation to Patoka, Illinois, and then on to Nederland, Texas.

Valuing land entails committing to a particular relationship with it based on whether anything can be gotten from it (especially anything that can satisfy US consumer capitalist and geopolitical interests). For understandable reasons, some Indigenous people relate to this idea of "valuing" the land. For them, extracting resources from the land might produce wealth to serve their communities, which had been impoverished by relocation, dispossession, and other US federal policies. For those people, "the saving power of wealth" seemed to promise health and safety for the community and deliverance from poverty.[95]

Yet Glen Coulthard and L. B. Simpson challenge this value orientation and explore alternative ontologies. They argue that relationships—developed in and with specific places, fostered in light of enduring histories—can inform, reaffirm, or inspire different practices of knowing and being. They call this approach *grounded normativity*.[96] From their respective traditions, Coulthard and Simpson share stories of reciprocity between the plant, (non-human) animal, and human worlds that are mutually beneficial, without romanticizing these forms of reciprocity as if they do not require loss or sacrifice. In Nishnaabeg thought, as I understand it, the relationships of a grounded normativity are rooted in "deep, reciprocal, consensual attachment,"[97] unlike the possessive normativity of settler colonialism. Coulthard explains that grounded normativity informs Indigenous political struggles about land, which are "*for* land, but also deeply *informed* by what the land as a node of reciprocal *relationship* (which is itself informed by place-based practices and associated forms of knowledge) ought to teach us about living our lives in relation to one another and our surroundings in a respectful, nondominating and nonexploitative way."[98] I understand Simpson and Coulthard to be saying that grounded normativity teaches that the natural world can be understood as an entwinement of relationships of (and in) *place*: "a way of knowing, of experience and relation to the world and with others."[99] This entwinement can be addressed by knowing and practicing mutual dependency, reciprocity, and care for a particular place and all its relations, rooted in a deep and shared history. By contrast, the settler colonial approach seeks to possess and extract value from the land, without regard for its histories or relationships.

In contrast to the grounded normativity that Coulthard and Simpson describe and that the earliest settlers must have encountered, the modern European tradition asserts a counter-ontology centered on land possession that informs the practices of free market capitalism and motivates the extraction projects of the US settler state. This counter-ontology makes three significant presumptions: (1) land *becomes* valuable through private ownership and development using non-reciprocal human practices of claim, enclosure, cultivation, and extraction; (2) because its value is bound to its cultivation, relatively little energy is devoted to repairing or replenishing land once it has been used; and (3) human history is a story of progression and improvement driven largely by European innovation and insight.

According to Coulthard and Simpson, these assumptions bind capitalism with colonialism by requiring the continuous "improvement" of land and resources through human cultivation and capitalization. This is only tenable, they argue, through a dispossessive process.[100] Because enclosure and elimination are ongoing and shift in form, dispossession is also ongoing.[101] Coulthard draws critically on Marx's account of "primitive accumulation"—an imagined, singular moment of pre-capitalist violence that is necessary to transition European society out of a feudal order and into a cycle of capital accumulation.[102] Coulthard argues that Marx understates the way in which land dispossession renews and refigures social relations of production through shifting (and always violent) practices of extraction, enclosure, and elimination.[103] Like labor, when land is exhausted through extractive processes, new sites and resources must be found; new social relations of production must sometimes also arise. Therefore, a singular violent moment of primitive accumulation cannot sustain the promise of perpetual human progress and indefinite (or even infinite) economic growth: capitalists must continue to exploit and dispossess people and land in order to facilitate ongoing capital accumulation. Instead, dispossession is "recursive": originary property ownership in the United States had to be assigned to Indigenous persons *retroactively* to justify present-day dispossession.[104]

The assumption that European settlers are uniquely capable of making good on the promise of resource extraction and economic growth is built into the logic of private property itself. For example, John Locke offers an influential articulation of this view that land must be *improved* by human intervention: "Land that is left wholly to Nature, that hath no improvement of Pasturage, Tillage, or Planting is called, as indeed it is, *wast*."[105] His account, rooted in the Book of Genesis, grants humans dominion over land: "God and his Reason commanded [humans] to subdue the Earth";[106] the "Industrious and Rational" are invited to draw conveniences from the land that are not possible if it remains "uncultivated."[107]

Indigenous activists all over the world argue that extraction is undergirded by an ideological commitment to *extractivism*, which Naomi Klein defines as "a nonreciprocal, dominance-based relationship with the earth, one purely of taking. . . . It is the reduction of life into objects for the use of others, giving them no integrity or value of their own."[108] From the vantage point of grounded normativity, which recognizes that relationships of domination and exploitation over land redound to human relationships, the link between extractivism and sexual violence cannot be dismissed as merely metaphorical. White Earth Ojibwe scholar and activist Lisa Brunner says "they [extractive industries] treat Mother Earth like they treat women."[109] Although the practices and discourses of fossil fuel extraction may seem distantly related to US rape culture, Indigenous scholars like Brunner see a clear relationship between them, and understand that the high rates of sexual violence among those who live in the Bakken region,[110] and especially of Indigenous persons, are facilitated (if not required) by a settler discourse and practice of resource extraction that (1) emphasizes the power of the white (male) extractor over nature, (2) denies the mutuality and relationality of all living creatures and the land, and (3) reduces people to mere objects that can be used and discarded, as extracts from natural spaces whose raw inputs fuel capitalist consumption and growth. A related insight is that land is often "used" by the settler state to achieve both its economic and geopolitical goals. For example, fracking is often justified via the promise of "fossil fuel independence," and as Hawaiian scholar and activist Haulani-Kay Trask notes, maintaining the US empire and the related processes of securitization have justified the extraction, exploitation, and occupation of Indigenous lands, such as Hawaii.[111]

In US rape culture, extractivism is both a practice and a discourse that enables sexual violence. Resource extraction is often analogized as a mode of domination over nature that is akin to male sexual domination over women. Carolyn Merchant argues that Francis Bacon, writing in a period when English families were "becoming more patriarchal and authoritarian,"[112] justified men's mechanistic control over nature through rape and other gender-violent metaphors.[113] Bacon's metaphors are replicated in subsequent philosophical investigations of science, technology, and progress, as well as the emerging commercial society which presumed that human dominion over nature is necessary for human progress.[114]

Literary scholar Deborah Saidero makes the case that this analogy between land cultivation and sexual violence pervades colonial narratives: "the metaphorical envisioning of conquering a virgin land as an act of sexual penetration is used to justify colonial expansion and the exploitation of the land."[115] Political science and comparative women's studies scholar Kristen Abatsis McHenry notes that colonizer metaphors have extended to the fracking industry: fracking sites are often described as the "Wild West" or as a virgin landscape to be (re)conquered.[116] McHenry also observes that both pro- and anti-fracking activists use the word "frack," with its proximity to "fuck," to associate fracking with violent sex[117]—which she calls eco-misogyny, "a logic of masculine domination, implying that the earth is a mother and that the act of fracking is best understood as a sexual act against women."[118] Studies of fracking discourse and imagery often associate fracking (or oil drilling more generally) with sexual violence, domination, penetration, and conquest.[119]

The common phrase "rape and pillage" explicitly pairs sexual violence with extraction in historical reimaginings of colonial invasion. The trope of the raping and pillaging Viking represents an expression of masculinity that is meant to be both savage and alluring, though it is largely a construct of nineteenth- and twentieth-century Anglo-American colonial/conquest narratives, not an accurate depiction of Viking practices.[120] This trope embodies a colonizer masculine ideal of a man who takes whatever he wants.[121] The association of the rapist-pillager reinforces the relationship between places and people as objects whose use-value can be extracted. These discourses analogize rape and extraction: "women's bodies [are] presented as a form of material booty,"[122] just another object for the colonizer's taking.

Finally, many clichés in US popular discourse describe heterosexual sex as an extracted or extractable resource. They associate female sexuality with objects of consumption (in limited supply but high demand) that men labor to obtain. For example, women are assured that men won't "buy the cow" if they can "get the milk for free." Women "give it up" while men "get some." Women who are undesirable or are not virgins are "damaged goods." Pure women "save" themselves until they "lose" their virginity to the men who "take" it. This discourse treats feminized bodies as objects to be *given* to or *taken* by men. These pervasive clichés reflect the logic of conquest and extraction rather than an imagined ideal of egalitarian, voluntary sexual consent. Political theorist Anne Phillips suggests this discourse around sexual consent has contributed to a peculiar kind of commodification that does not result in voluntary exchange for mutual benefit.[123] She argues that this framework is so difficult to escape that even the discourse of bodily integrity, which defines violation and infiltration in terms of boundaries or borders, contributes to the understanding that some bodies are territories that must resist being conquered.[124] And, just as consent is violated in the "trust" relationship with Indigenous persons and disregarded when it imperils the impulses of the settler state, sexual consent is violated in sexual relations that are similarly understood via a discourse of extraction.

Beyond these discourses—which reinforce the notion that male violence, enacted on women, feminized people, and a feminized landscape, is somehow both natural and justifiable—extraction is often predicated on a practice of eliminating people, cultures, and wildlife whose presence interferes with settler control of extractable resources. As Native feminist theorists Maile Arvin (Kanaka Maoli), Eve Tuck (Aleut Community of St. Paul Island, Alaska), and Angie Morrill (Klamath Tribes) put it, "In order for settlers to usurp the land and extract its value, Indigenous people must be destroyed, removed, and made into ghosts."[125] (One example of this removal was dramatized in the 2023 movie *Killers of the Flower Moon*, which details the murder of dozens of members of the Osage by white men in the 1920s who wanted to gain access to Osage oil "headrights.") Indigenous elimination is pursued through violence, murder, assimilation, blood quantum (a controversial settler state invention that renders Indigenous tribal membership contingent upon an individual possessing a certain fraction of Indigenous blood[126]), and various forms of sexual violence, which echoes abolition scholar Ruth Wilson Gilmore's definition of racism as "the state-sanctioned or extralegal production and exploitation of group-differentiated vulnerability to premature death."[127]

In the United States, rape has been used as a genocidal practice: racialized sexual violence has facilitated the dispossession of Indigenous persons by "diluting" blood quantum and enabling the transfer of land titles.[128] As I noted above, the destruction of alternative sexualities and genders was central to the construction of the Indian princess or sq*aw, two female figures whose value to the settler state is wholly dependent on the ways in which they serve white settlers. Involuntary and non-consensual sterilization was another avenue of sexual violence against Indigenous women and girls designed to curb Indigenous reproduction.[129] Intergenerational trauma, including the "normal" trauma of sexual violence, contributes to stress and other health problems that lead to the untimely deaths of Indigenous persons. According to a Centers for Disease Control report from 2023, life expectancy for Indigenous persons in 2022 was 67.9 years, the lowest for all reported groups (compared to 84.5 for Asians, the group with the highest life expectancy).[130] Thus, rape, the threat of rape, and the presumption of other forms of sexual domination over Indigenous women serve the settler extractive project by contributing to the project of eliminating Indigenous persons from the landscape.

Fracking itself is a violent extractive practice of drilling, flooding, toxification, and removal that materially separates Indigenous people from their relationships with the natural world, both disconnecting them from grounded normativities and contributing to cultural alienation and genocide.[131] Guatemalan activist and politician Sandra Morán argues that "resource extraction projects destroy the land and social fabric, and both are fundamental for the lives of women and communities. The land is history, identity, beauty, culture, and life, and the social fabric is relations, history, future, heritage, culture, and identities."[132] In other words, by disrupting Indigenous relationships with the land and destroying the landscape, extractivism can adversely impact whether (and how) communities are able to sustain their own relations, values, and systems of self-governing. Extraction serves not only as a claim to land and resources but as an attempt (not always successful) to disrupt the relationships and practices of Indigenous, land-based ontologies. When settlers treat places as "wastelands" and leave them damaged, drilled, mined, fracked, and toxified, the people who live in reciprocal relationship with that land are being treated as "wastelands," too.

In *Yellow Bird: Oil, Murder, and a Woman's Search for Justice in Indian Country*, journalist Sierra Crane Murdoch details Lissa Yellow Bird's (Arikara) months-long search for bodies in Fort Berthold. From Yellow Bird's observations, Murdoch describes how the land has been impacted by the fracking boom:

> Marks of the boom were everywhere. Even land that remained intact was on its surface changed: creeks and sloughs sucked dry, the water purchased or stolen; the prairie littered with food wrappers, plastic bottles, scraps of carpet, aluminum flashing, jerricans, busted work boots, bullet casings, oil rags, electronics, cigarette cartons, and empty tins of chewing tobacco; and a dense smog overlaying it all.[133]

Murdoch links this wasting landscape to the wastelanding of people. She speaks with Sadie Young Bird, the director of Three Affiliated Tribes Victim Services at the MHA Nation, who daily witnesses rampant drug use and related domestic and sexual assault: "'When the boom's over, what's it going to be like here? . . . They're not going to take their trailers with them. It'll just be deserted, with a lot of broken people.'"[134]

Oil companies don't promise a broken landscape or broken people, of course. They promise that the oil wells of the Bakken will be operable for twenty to forty years before they are sucked dry of oil and gas and capped. At that point, a Marathon Oil promotional film cheerfully promises, "the land can then be used again by the landowner for other activities, and there will be virtually no visual signs that a well was once there" (5:35–6:05).[135] The desire not to see what was once there—and what is *still there*—ensures plausible deniability for those who benefit from the sacrifice of land and people in order to fuel life in the capitalist settler state. Naomi Klein explains: "the people reaping the bulk of the benefits of extractivism pretend not to see the costs of that comfort so long as the sacrifice zones are kept safely out of view."[136] The drilling and fracking also represent a twenty- to forty-year disruption (at least!) in reciprocal and non-dominating relationships between the people and the land, a disruption that permits violence against people and places in order to extract what settlers and the settler state deem valuable. The discourse and practice of extraction lay an ideological foundation that makes it possible for the temporary workers in the Bakken region to engage in violence. These interlopers have come to understand extraction as a mode of domination writ large, which they have the power to wield in order to extract value from people and places that they will leave behind, and leave to waste.

"To *wield* . . . and *exceed* the law": Frontier Masculinity and Violence

The film *Wind River* depicts two types of white men: the good white guys, who are caring, hardworking, and protective of their families and loved ones (including their Indigenous loved ones), and the bad white guys, who are feral, dangerous, and unpredictable. The contrast between the two is clearest in the film's rape scene, when Matt—a good guy and Natalie's "knight in shining armor" (1:11:25)—has been knocked unconscious while Pete beats and rapes Natalie as his friends look on, eager for their turn. Life in the camps has dehumanized these bad men: Pete is so desperate for sex he claims he can smell it when he invades Matt's room (1:14:54); when Natalie covers her nearly naked body, the screenplay notes, "the look on the men's faces turns from humor to hunger in an instant."[137] These men, some of whom are security guards hired to maintain safety in the camp, have harassed Matt and Natalie before. The film suggests it is all entirely predictable: in the isolation and desolation of the oil patch, these men become so crazed for sex and violence that they lose any capacity for reason or moral judgment. Matt defends Natalie valiantly, but he is no match for the wild men who beat him to death as Natalie runs away, into the frigid Wyoming night.

The characters of Matt and Pete represent the twin sides of a hegemonic frontier masculinity. Connell and Messerschmidt define hegemonic masculinity (in general) as a "pattern of practice (i.e., things done, not just a set of role expectations or an identity) that [has] allowed men's dominance over women to continue"[138] and note that hegemonic masculinities are plural, normative, and adaptive.[139] What Connell calls *frontier* masculinity involves two figures: "the brawling single frontiersman and the settled married pioneer."[140] In the US popular imagination, while both are necessary to the settler project (and both are white), they are entirely different people: the violent trailblazer dominates his way through an untamed landscape while the settled pioneer domesticates it with help from his family. The settler project requires both to impose their values on the frontier. Yet I contend that these masculine figures are not, and should not be imagined as, distinctive people because this imagined distinction creates an interpretive lens that suggests the evil rapist is easily distinguishable from the innocent "good guy." In fact, they are one and the same figure: a man who uses violence to *dominate* and *domesticate* the bodies and lands of the frontier and who later uses violence to *dominate* and *protect* his home life.

As Leann Simpson explains, survival on the land requires diversity and fluidity. Yet, when confronted by the gender fluidities and grounded normativities of Indigenous life and culture, settlers asserted white supremacist heteropatriarchal, middle-class (and perhaps specifically Christian) values by relegating men and women to discrete gender roles and spheres of life.[141] This binary could not support the settler project because, to survive on the frontier, settlers needed diverse emotional, physical, and intellectual resources, not only the ones relegated to heteropatriarchal manhood or womanhood (in their "separate spheres"). Simpson makes clear that sex binaries that distance some people from the tasks of domesticity, care, and family life while distancing others from hunting, trapping, farming, or other means of subsistence created entire communities of people who were not, individually or collectively, self-sufficient.[142] Lisa Brooks makes a related observation in her analysis of Mary Rowlandson's "captivity narrative"—that Rowlandson's confinement as a Puritan woman in a domestic space contributed to her suffering while in captivity, since she was unaccustomed to walking long distances or carrying supplies.[143] In short, settler culture might insist on a clear sex binary, but the demands of self-sufficiency and survival on the land required much more fluid understandings of tasks and capabilities.

Yet on the lawless frontier, the settler man wielded violence according to his own inclinations while fostering (at least the illusion of) the judicious application of violence, as befitting a civilized man. Frontier masculinity normalizes a man who can dwell outside of the law while also embodying it, depending on whether he must be a violent aggressor against the forces of wildness and savagery or a strongman protector who preserves domestic tranquility via heteropatriarchal control.[144] Settler masculinity sustains white heteropatriarchy by putting white men in the position of executing or ignoring the law in order to protect "their" people and property. Political theorist Cristina Beltrán argues that in the "frontier," white settler men could "both *wield* the law and *exceed* the law.[145] Likewise, when confronted with a lawless and dangerous frontier that must be tamed, settler men can wield righteous violence to protect "their" people and property and to dominate (and domesticate) the frontier.

The frontier man is also sexually insatiable. Untethered to family, working and living hard, and with ostensibly "natural" sexual appetites, he turns to local women.[146] As Barman argues in her history of aboriginal sexuality in British Columbia, the brawling frontiersman satisfies his sexual appetites through encounters with Indigenous women (perhaps both consensual and non-consensual) until or unless his family joins him, at which point he is expected to become a good pioneering patriarch. This figure who reverts to "natural" and uncivilized behavior when on the frontier is observable on the Bakken where, despite their declaration of filial duty, married oil workers often engage in sex and sexual violence.

Frontier masculinity persists in US rape culture partly through the imagined dichotomy of the vicious rapist and the strongman protector. As I note in Chapter Two, the strongman protector is revered for the righteous ends he achieves, even if he uses condemnable means. The empowerment of settler men to use violence fosters a contradiction at the heart of frontier masculinity: US rape culture suggests that it is easy to distinguish between good men and bad men *and* that good men must sometimes be bad. This implies a stark distinction between dangerous and protective men. Yet rape culture actually sustains an ambivalence that enables settler men to act with impunity and then be forgiven or exonerated for the violence they commit. The judgment is that violence is bad when done by bad men, but when it is done by good men, it is acceptable.

Wind River demonstrates the complication of the civilized protector who is allowed to wield extra-legal violence by suggesting that justice is only possible when a good white man takes the law into his own hands. Cory Lambert, the protagonist, represents frontier masculinity in a way that renders his ultimate use of lawless violence justifiable and righteous. Cory is a white man with deep roots in the local Shoshone and Arapaho community: "Indian enough to do favors, but not enough to pull a check."[147] He is a tracker with the US Fish and Wildlife Service who hunts and destroys wild animals that prey on local livestock. In one subplot, Cory tracks and kills a mountain lion—a judicious use of violence that is necessary to preserve life on the frontier.

Although he is a government official, Cory engages in both legal and extralegal violence.[148] The film depicts the challenges of jurisdiction in "Indian country" and how jurisdictional competition limits the responsiveness of tribal, federal, and state law enforcement agencies. This may be why, when Pete (the last surviving rapist) runs away—the other bad guys have died in a good, old-fashioned Western shoot-out at the man camp—FBI Agent Jane Banner entreats Cory to "go get him." "I won't bring him back," Cory says, "you have to know that." "I do. Go get him," Banner replies, empowering Cory to enact frontier justice, even though he is not a law enforcement agent.[149] Cory tracks Pete into the wild and forces him to run. He doesn't need to use a bullet to kill Pete because he knows that, as Pete runs into the frigid winter cold, he will asphyxiate on his own blood and die the same miserable death that Natalie did. He thus facilitates justice by enabling Pete's "natural" death because the law is powerless to do the right thing. At the end of the film, Cory sits with Natalie's father and Cory's old friend, Martin, who is deep in mourning. Martin says he has heard that one of Natalie's rapists got away and is still missing. "No. . . . No one's missing," Cory says, matter of factly. "How'd he go out?" Martin asks. "With a whimper," Cory replies. Martin emits the smallest sigh of relief in his grief, which assures the audience that Cory did the right thing.[150] Settler order has been restored, ironically, because the pioneer sidestepped the rule of law to deliver justice.

Like the man camps in and around the Wind River Reservation, the Bakken is a site of frontier masculinity, where the discourses and practices of this form of hegemonic masculinity have indelibly altered the homelands of the MHA Nation, polluting the land and cultivating unsafety. It is perhaps not surprising that oil workers liken the Bakken to the "Wild West" as they live with and through precarities and violence,[151] though Fort Berthold and the cities and towns in the Bakken region are not "frontiers," and it is strange to treat a place with a Walmart like it is untamed wilderness. Still, oil work is dangerous work, undertaken by men who see the job as an opportunity to finally "get ahead" as precarious workers in the US economy. The payoff comes at a great risk: in 2012, North Dakota workers died "at a rate four times the national average."[152] The overwhelming majority of men who come to work on the Bakken are white and non-local (though, given the homogeneity of the local population, it is also likely that the influx of Bakken workers temporarily increases racial diversity in the region).[153] Workers are embedded, in both their housing and work sites, in a "male-centric industry culture" that, coupled with its rural location, "may contribute to increased levels of interpersonal violence" outside of work.[154]

Perhaps not surprisingly, some workers express a sense of relative powerlessness in the Bakken. In *Yellow Bird*, Murdoch writes that "men were pushed to work so fast that inevitably they made mistakes." Rick, a white roughneck doing temporary work, describes his feeling of helplessness to Murdoch: "'I got to thinking,' he said. 'The middle class, we don't run shit, we're just herded around like a bunch of cattle, and the powers that be, the people running this country, they're not doing anything to stop it.'"[155] Rick's understanding of himself as middle class may well be accurate, although in the early years of the Bakken boom, wages in the oil-producing counties of North Dakota increased by 100% (compared to a national average wage increase of 8.1% during the same period),[156] which is likely what made workers willing to move so far from home. The point is not that Rick was wealthy but rather that he understood himself and his fellow workers as relatively powerless against the forces of real wealth. In a context where workers are subjected to danger and precarity for temporary work, their attempts to assert control through settler violence might be entirely predictable (even if also despicable).

The terrible working and living conditions in the fracking industry contribute to a culture of hypermasculinity that has dangerous consequences for Indigenous people. The Secwepemcul'ecw Assembly, which convened in 2017 to stop the Kinder Morgan TransMountain pipeline in British Columbia, explained:

> "Camp culture" has been reported to exacerbate isolation, mental illness, drug and alcohol abuse, violence, misogyny, and racism among the men living there. Away from family, friends, and social supports, these men face stressful, difficult, and potentially dangerous working conditions, including long hours, shift work, and "two-week in, two-week out"

> work schedules. In this environment, and with heightened disposable incomes, increased substance abuse is "well documented." Amidst a culture of "hyper-masculinity, sexism, and apathy towards self-care" direct and indirect impacts shift onto women, children, and two-spirit people.[157]

The assembly's statement links the horrible working conditions to stress, isolation, and substance abuse, while noting that the hypermasculine culture in the camps is not confined to the camps: it extends outward, visiting oppressive violence and abuse on the local population, and especially on Indigenous women, girls, and two-spirit people.

The "man camps"—which are typically temporary structures that house thousands of oilfield workers who have traveled for short-term work—represent a site of both domesticated control and lawlessness. In their ethnographic work of Bakken man camps, Caraher et al. describe it as a new housing form, an impermanent structure that exists "outside the gaze, jurisdiction and living space of the established economic and political order."[158] Although some man camps include women and children (either as residents or as guests), most residents are men. Life in these camps can be difficult, especially in the frigid North Dakota and Montana winters. Archbold et al. find that police in the Bakken describe a "'bachelor culture' reminiscent of the California gold rush that embodie[s] a hegemonic masculine standard of risk taking, excessive alcohol use, financial greed, and sexual conquests."[159]

Oddly, despite this bachelor culture, Caraher and his colleagues describe a landscape that replicates a suburbia: residents enclose their "lots," construct "mud rooms" outside their trailers, insulate them against the frigid winters, and build patios that they adorn with objects, planters, American flags, barbell racks, and grills.[160] In these temporary camps, sexual conquest and violence intermingle with the settler-capitalist values of enclosure and home ownership, just as they do in "settled and civilized" places.

Many of the Bakken oil workers act in ways that reflect their investment in heteropatriarchy. As Caraher et al. observe, the residents of man camps often replicate a "traditional" home life, sometimes literally enclosed by white picket fences.[161] Filteau notes that the respondents in his study believed "safe work practices promote[d] hegemonic masculinity in the domestic sphere through breadwinning."[162] He recalled, "Every participant (even unmarried men) stated that being a man meant fulfilling one's responsibility to provide for themselves and/or their family members."[163] These men, even unmarried or childless ones, understand themselves as breadwinners and protectors of their (eventual) families. Yet they do not have to act like breadwinners or protectors while they are living on the Bakken, as befits the frontier man.

Increases in crime in the Bakken are well documented, from property crimes to violent assaults to sexual violence.[164] Women in the Bakken avoid certain places (like the infamous local Walmart) where they experience harassment and believe "men [wait] to rape unaccompanied women."[165] For most women, life in the Bakken boom feels insecure and unsafe: "victim agency data for North Dakota" reveals "statistically significant increases in the average number of sexual assault clients served in Bakken victim assistance programs" from 2002 to 2014, though there is no comparable increase in reports of sexual assaults to law enforcement agencies.[166] For many, feeling unsafe at home is a direct result of changes brought by the Bakken oil boom—particularly from the temporary workers.

The documentary short film *Nuuca* depicts the everyday effects of settler masculinity in and around Fort Berthold. The 2018 film, directed by Michelle Latimer, juxtaposes images and sounds of the area's quiet, peaceful, natural spaces with the jarring horns, glugging motors, and moaning derricks of industry. The narrator—a young, local Indigenous woman—describes a place that was once "more lively with nature" (1:50) but since the boom has become marked by a "dullness . . . [that] just kind of drooped over . . . this area" (4:36). She recounts feelings of constant discomfort and unsafety in a place that once felt safe and secure. The narrator describes being a runner in high school but says she stopped running after the boom began because she was harassed in the street by a man at a local motel. While the narrator had not been sexually assaulted herself, she describes women who have been chased, catcalled, and terrorized. She knows danger is all around her, ever since the man camps "took over" (7:12): "the women here, they're being taken. They're being raped. They're being sold. In the beginning it was a big shocker, but . . . it's just kind of like the norm now" (07:30–08:15). Her new "normal"—and the normal of other young Indigenous women like her—includes living within a changing natural landscape and an increasingly unsafe community.

Even many of the temporary workers perceive the Bakken as a lawless place. In *Yellow Bird*, journalist Murdoch reports that tribal officers told her that non-Native workers in the Bakken acted with impunity because they knew tribal law enforcement had limited jurisdictional authority.[167] Yet, rates of gendered violence increased at Fort Berthold from the beginning of the boom in 2008. "In 2012, the tribal police reported more fatal accidents, sexual assaults, domestic disputes, gun threats, and human trafficking incidents among tribal members than in any year prior."[168] Drug-related crimes also increased, and the domestic violence unit "counsel[led] more victims in 2013 than in any year prior. Ninety-six percent of these cases would involve alcohol and drugs," according to its director.[169] For at least some of the men who move there temporarily, in the Bakken it is acceptable to be violent and lawless.

During the Bakken boom, frontier masculinity has fostered violence and a sense of unsafety for residents that, in turn, replicates heteropatriarchal control of women and children among long-term residents and contributes to the discourse (outlined in Chapter Two) that women are weak and need male protection. To defend "their" women against the temporary workers, some local men have reasserted themselves as chivalrous wielders of righteous violence.[170] They exhibit frontier masculinity by accompanying "their" women everywhere as reflected in discursive shifts in which men detail what they will "let" their wives or daughters do.[171] These pioneering men reassert themselves as strongman protectors and promote a common trope that local men are good and outsiders are bad to distinguish themselves from their violent frontier counterparts. Sociologists Pippert and Zimmer Schneider reported that locals "called attention to the fact that they needed to defend their wives, girlfriends, and daughters from the migrants. This competition was naturalized when the local men continually spoke about men's sexual aggression as intrinsic to manhood and therefore the primary reason women needed protection."[172] In this rendering, the strongman protector is a virile man whose violent aggression in defense of his wife mirrors his aggressive sexual appetite. Far from providing protection against sexual violence, this hegemonic masculine figure of protection is reinforced in the Bakken, where (like other rural areas in the United States) rates of sexual violence are higher than average even when there is not a fracking boom, partly due to widespread acceptance of heteropatriarchal values and economic arrangements.[173]

Frontier masculinity also perpetuates a myth that "real men" cannot be raped, which reinforces female victimization and obscures male victimization. Male sexual assault has increased on the Bakken since the start of the boom. Grace Her Many Horses, a former Rosebud Sioux tribal police chief, described the sexual assaults of women and young children on Fort Berthold (noting that some, including a 4-year-old child, have been trafficked). She also noted that men are at risk of sexual assault; they are told "Don't get drunk and pass out. Because you're going to get raped."[174] Inhabitants of the area have observed an increase in sexual violence against men since the oil boom.[175] They also noted that resources for male victims are rare: in many cases, the medical professionals who are trained to complete a forensic medical exam on a male victim are more than 100 miles away.[176] Yet local residents express the importance of protecting women and girls (but not boys) from temporary residents.[177] This denial that men or boys could be at risk of sexual violence reflects the hegemonic masculinity that characterizes much of the settler culture (of both long- and short-term residents) in the Bakken.

Amidst all this, white women and Indigenous men may seek to secure some benefits from the heteropatriarchal order even though it subordinates them: the former due to their *racial* privilege and the latter due to their *gender* privilege. Settler women, perhaps in response to their gender subjugation, have often used their racial privilege to uphold white heteropatriarchy by subjugating non-white marginalized others and calling on white men to exert violence to protect whiteness (embodied in form of the white female).[178] Long-term residents have expressed concerns about their safety during the boom, and many women have described altering their behavior to avoid risk. But they often also enlist their heteropatriarchal protectors to ensure their safety, sometimes by suggesting their male aggressors are non-white even though oil workers in the Bakken are far more likely to be white.[179]

Violence (including sexual violence) has long been a part of life on the "frontier," but the temporary workers have reasserted a frontier masculinity in the Bakken through their violence. In the US popular imagination, frontier masculinity requires two settler figures: the violent man to tame the unknown landscape and a civilizing pioneer to domesticate it. Yet in US rape culture, these two masculine figures overlap in a way that obscures our collective ability to condemn dangerous, violent, unethical behavior by excusing some perpetrators as "good men," even when they engage in violence and sexual assault, while suggesting that some people—such as Indigenous and other non-white persons, queer people, and poor people—are always predatory, dangerous, and irredeemably bad.

Conclusion

Leann calls heteropatriarchy "a *foundational dispossessive force* because it is a direct attack on Indigenous bodies as political orders, thought, agency, self-determination, and freedom."[180] Lee Maracle declares "racism is recent; patriarchy is old."[181] The sexual violence in the Bakken and the systematic interracial violence perpetrated against Indigenous women, queer, and two-spirit people are part of the ongoing history of gendered and racialized settler violence, made worse by the temporary influx of young, usually white, men onto Indigenous land to satisfy the settler culture's thirst for oil and natural gas. This history of the "American West" and "the frontier" has been sustained by legal and extra-legal enactments of "justice" and through white lawlessness, enacted with impunity.

Sexual violence is a central part of the settler project, and on the Bakken and in other wastelanded spaces, violence and sexual violence increase with the influx of temporary workers. I have argued that US rape culture creates a context in which this kind of sexual violence is excused and justified. Through the myth of the sq*aw, the discourses and practices of extraction, and the practices of frontier masculinity, Indigenous persons and lands are wastelanded and settler men are granted impunity to act violently, at least much of the time. The normative masculinity of temporary workers in the Bakken reflects normative masculinity further afield, where the broader settler culture is similarly willing to draw a bright line between good and bad men. In *Wind River*, in the face of undeniable injustice, a white frontiersman restores a life of domesticity on and near the reservation, which is still wild and untamed by the bad guys who live there. He is able to enact justice through his selective mastery of violence, which only he—and others who share his position—are empowered to exert.

Chapter Four
There's an App for That
Sexual Consent by Contract

Introduction

In 2013, CNN contributor Roxanne Jones wrote an op-ed detailing the advice she had given her son as he left for college.[1] She told him to work hard, have fun, and be safe. But amid increasing news media coverage of sexual assault on college campuses, she worried that she had "left out one important piece of advice that is a must-do today: Never have sex with a girl unless she's sent you a text that proves the sexual relationship is consensual beforehand. And it's a good idea to even follow up any sexual encounter with a tasteful text message saying how you both enjoyed being with one another—even if you never plan on hooking up again."[2]

Understandably, Jones wanted to protect her son—a young African American man—from false rape allegations, which have been used in the United States to control Black men's bodies for centuries. Jones's advice suggests that she believes protection from such allegations requires written evidence of consent, a belief almost certainly informed by the fact that some of the most sensational stories of sexual violence in the United States since Reconstruction have involved white women falsely accusing Black men of rape or sexual misconduct, including Emmett Till, the Scottsboro Boys, and the Central Park Five.[3] Seen in this light, Jones's advice to obtain proof of consent in the form of a documented agreement (like a text message) makes a certain amount of sense: ensure that your partner has consented before sex and then ask them to communicate their agreement directly.

In US rape culture, we collectively imagine that consent unequivocally distinguishes rape from sex and that, as if by discursive magic,[4] consent is therefore the solution to the problem of rape. In its ideal form, sexual consent asserts equal agency between partners and is taken as proof of a mutual and voluntary agreement to have sex. And mutually agreed-upon sex cannot, by definition, be rape.[5] Yet any account of the promise of consent must confront the ways in which this concept has been deployed to reinforce the long-standing myth of the false rape allegation, while it also asserts that all members of society are in a position to freely give or withhold consent. As I argued in Chapter Two, in US rape culture, efforts that seem to be designed to prevent sexual violence are often contorted to facilitate it instead. This is how the well-meaning advice of a concerned Black mother can mirror that of a misogynistic commentator in the "manosphere" who unapologetically asserts male entitlement to sex and counsels his readers on how to get laid while avoiding false rape allegations.

The manosphere is a network of blogs, Reddit and subreddit boards, 4chan channels, and other online forums that are frequented by self-described men's rights activists (MRAs), pick-up artists (PUAs), involuntary celibates (incels), "Men Go Their Own Way," and other groups which claim to have an interest in "men's issues." These forums lament a "crisis" of masculinity resulting from the emasculation of men.[6] The manosphere is largely anti-feminist and misogynist[7] and has been increasingly linked to the alt-right.[8] Traffic on these sites has increased since 2016, and the content has become "more toxic and misogynistic."[9] There are also indications that internet traffic migrates from the manosphere to the more explicitly white supremacist, Islamophobic, anti-Semitic content of the alt-right.[10]

This community believes false rape allegations are "extremely common" and endanger men.[11] To protect against them, MRA sites are replete with advice for using technology to "prove" that sex was consensual, from sending text messages to clandestinely recording audio and video to prove it was mutually desired. They interpret this "proof" as incontrovertible and irrevocable, like a contract. Like Jones's desire for her son, MRAs seek evidence of consent via text to avoid false rape accusations; yet unlike Jones's intentions, these activists recommend using these tools to avoid such accusations while they engage in (often violent) sexual activity to which they feel a deep, even brutal, sense of entitlement.

In this chapter, I argue that new technological interventions—apps, text messages, photographs, and video recordings—are variations on an increasingly *documented* and *contractualized* model of sexual consent which presupposes that, since partners cannot trust one another and have few incentives to behave trustfully toward one another, the terms of any sexual agreement must be meticulously documented. In order to document those terms, sexual consent must be distilled into *a precise moment* when participants enter into a binding agreement—a moment that is knowable, recordable, and preservable. New technologies facilitate this shift in the articulation of sexual consent: the birth of the smartphone means that people now carry devices that connect, record, and upload; and the emergence of surveillance capitalism normalizes the use of technologies that "[intensify] . . . the means of behavioral modification and the gathering might of instrumentarian power."[12] Yet rather than serve as a source of protection that could disclose the private realm (the site of most sexual violence) in a way that has never been possible before, these apps deploy smartphone technology to preempt allegations of rape by binding individuals through consensual "contracts" to engage in sexual activity. These efforts evince a desire to prevent sexual assault *allegations* but not sexual assault itself.

This chapter focuses on what the practice of recording sexual consent as if it were a contract tells us about US rape culture.[13] Many who are concerned they will be accused of sexual violence turn to contracts as a form of criminal indemnification. I conclude that consent contracts, recordings, text messages, and other such technologies foster a surveillance ethos and entrench transactional, indemnifying practices to protect perpetrators from accusations of sexual assault. Yet these practices do not—and cannot—protect potential victims from sexual assault. In what follows, I recount the history of the myth of the false accuser and the discourse of the social contract to illuminate how sexual consent is evolving into a practice of contractualization that preserves white heteropatriarchal power in the United States. While the contractualization of consent may *appear* to be a positive anti-rape effort that strengthens mechanisms for consent, it actually enables potential perpetrators to easily co-opt the notion of consent: they use the logic of contracts to perpetuate the myth of the false accuser and facilitate sexual violence, while indemnifying themselves against rape accusations.

I am skeptical about sexual consent and how it is (and can be) *practiced* in a context structured by multiple systems of domination, but my skepticism motivates a critique of consent that is advanced from a solidly anti-rape position. I do *not* argue that perpetrators of rape should be given a break simply because "sex is complicated." Instead, I maintain that the concept of consent itself performs a discursive function that allows victims to continue to be blamed for their own assaults and permits rapists to continue to shield themselves using techniques of indemnification. I advance this argument cautiously as I am aware it could easily be misread or misused to argue that desire, agreement, and mutuality are not important in sexual engagements. I believe they are *essential*, but what we call "consent" is no guarantee of them. Rapists have long wielded the tool of consent (or, in some cases, the claim that there was no clear *refusal* of consent) to protect themselves. Because it is constructed as if it were so simple, the concept of consent makes it difficult for victims to protect themselves, which allows us to (collectively) assign the cruelest kind of blame to them when they come forward. Consent alone is not sufficient to transform the problem of rape into the promise of mutually desirable sex, and as it is used in US rape culture today, the concept of sexual consent supports the conditions for victim blaming and perpetrator indemnification that allow sexual violence to persist.

The Myth of the False Accuser

The discourse of victim blaming and the myth of the false rape accuser coincide in US rape culture because they are both motivated by the assumption that women (and other feminized people) are manipulative and dishonest. Victim blaming implies that a rape occurred but that it was the victim's fault, while the myth of the false rape accuser presupposes there was no rape at all. Together, these ideas are mutually sustaining: if potential victims can prevent themselves from being raped, then they must either be lying about getting raped or responsible for it. Either way, perpetrators escape blame and consequence. In US rape culture, the myth of the false rape accuser protects the beneficiaries of white heteropatriarchy by portraying accusers as schemers and manipulators who scapegoat innocent men (who happen to be sexually voracious by nature). Yet the myth has also been used to punish some (such as Black men [Chapter One] or trans people [Chapter Two]) who threaten the political order; it declares them sexual threats.

Although some studies have shown that false rape allegations in the United States occur at higher rates than false allegations for other violent crimes such as murder, they are still quite rare (around 5% of all rape allegations compared to around 1% for most other violent crimes).[14] What "counts" as a false allegation is a crucial question: in some cases, law enforcement officers have judged allegations to be false due to their perception of a lack of evidence or a perception that the victim was not traumatized enough to be believed; in others, accusers admit they have fabricated their stories. At the same time, the tendency for rape victims to choose not to report their rapes to law enforcement is well documented,[15] and the recent Netflix documentary *Victim/Suspect* details cases in which victims report their rapes to law enforcement only to be charged with making false reports that were not, in fact, false. Unfortunately, there are also high-profile instances of rape accusations that turn out to be false (such as the 2014 *Rolling Stone* story depicting a rape at the University of Virginia), which are accepted as generalizable proof that most rape accusers are liars. Indeed, some MRA sites claim the rate of false rape accusations is as high as 40%–50%.[16] We need to grapple with the ways that rape accusations are withheld, wielded, and disregarded to cast doubt on rape victims and insist on the innocence of perpetrators.

To understand how victim blaming and false rape accusations shape US rape culture, we must view the false rape accusation through an intersectional lens, which can uncover when and how one individual might accuse another of rape to assert dominance and/or to counteract their own marginalization. To wield a false rape accusation in the context of a rape culture may, for some, be an exercise in what Christine Keating calls "compensatory domination,"[17] wherein an accuser (for example, a white, female, cisgender accuser) might marshal the power of white supremacy to protect herself against patriarchal rule. False rape accusations, which some women might make to protect themselves from patriarchal rule, can in fact insulate patriarchal rule by confirming the myth of the false rape accuser and fostering disbelief of rape victims.

In US rape culture, the myth of the false rape accuser presumes female deceit and (white) male innocence. Here, I use feminine pronouns as a matter of historical accuracy about who was considered a potential victim. While a central claim of this book is that anyone who threatens the existing order can be a victim of rape, regardless of their gender, there are particular invocations of gender, race, class, and other structures of domination which manifest in distinct ways in US rape culture. The mythic figure of the false accuser is a dissembling, seducing, teasing opportunist—always a woman, frequently a white one—who willingly engages in sex but later accuses her partner of rape to secure gains (or stave off losses) in reputation, fame, or money. The mythic figure of the falsely accused is a white man with a healthy sexual drive who is doing what men naturally do by enthusiastically pursuing a sexual encounter (because "boys will be boys"), only to be condemned for it later. In the myth of the false rape accusation, the accuser acts with impunity when she accuses her partner of rape, leaving the accused (who is innocent) to face severe, unjust consequences[18] that one contributor to the MRA site *Return of Kings* describes as "at least as severe of a crime as rape itself":

> [A] false rape accusation is not merely an attack on a man's character. It is an attempt to kidnap, imprison, torture, and perhaps murder an innocent man. It is a profoundly evil act, and yet there are often no consequences for women who make false rape accusations.[19]

Feminist scholar Amia Srinivasan observes that the myth of the false rape accuser is "a predominantly wealthy white male preoccupation."[20] Relatedly, the ostensible prevalence of false rape accusations is considered convincing evidence of the "masculinity crisis" for those who participate in the manosphere.

Disentangling the myth of the false rape accuser, the false rape accusation, and the problem of compensatory domination requires identifying who benefits from *both* the myth *and* the reality. The myth of the false rape accuser disciplines accusers and normalizes disbelief of rape victims, which benefits those who feel entitled to sex. The white woman's false rape accusation disciplines both Black men and Black women (the latter, by complicating their means of self-protection against sexual violence)[21] but also disciplines individuals from other marginalized groups, such as immigrants and queer, trans, and non-binary persons, by threatening them with vigilante or state-enacted "justice" carried out by those who feel entitled to dominate. It further conditions women to believe that their protectors are men: as I note in Chapter Two, these are the very men who feel entitled to dominate anyone who challenges the white heteropatriarchal order. Here, I am mostly talking about a "protector" dynamic between white, cisgender, heterosexual men and women since that dynamic is at the root of most racialized false rape accusations in the United States. However, non-white persons are not immune from patriarchy and misogyny: they can also be conditioned to believe their only protection comes from cisgender and heterosexual men. In short, the myth of the false accuser and the myth of the false rape allegation both preserve the white heteropatriarchal sociopolitical order, albeit in different ways.

Since its earliest history, the crime of *raptus* has been shaped by class motivations to protect male property ownership and by misogyny to safeguard men from the manipulative wiles of untrustworthy women. Rape has been a plot point in many myths in the European context, including ancient Greek or Roman ones that involved rape and, in some cases, consent.[22] Some early Christian writers characterized women as sex-obsessed manipulators of men.[23] In a history of rape in the medieval period, historian Caroline Dunn writes: "Medieval religious precepts considered women's default position to be a sexualised temptress in the model of Eve. Women could hope to change their behaviour and follow the model of the converted prostitute Mary Magdalene, but their fundamental nature, according to many male theorists, remained unchanged and susceptible to sex."[24] Historian Shani D'Cruze argues that during the Victorian period, "feminine sexual attractiveness was seen as provoking potentially uncontrolled male desire, and hence, in effect, female victims were assumed to have caused the violence they experienced. The rapist became represented as monstrous and therefore different from respectable men; by the later nineteenth century he was a marginal, working-class deviant."[25] In each of these periods, women were presumed to be at least partially responsible for being raped unless the man in question was deemed unrespectable.

Moreover, rape was not always criminalized. The crime of *raptus* (qua crime) arose with the ancient Romans,[26] seemingly in response to the adverse risks it posed to men's property claims (the wives who would bear them male heirs or the daughters who could be exchanged through marriage for goods, status, or alliances).[27] As a property crime, *raptus* pertained particularly to the property-owning classes.[28] Upper-class or free Roman women were the most likely to be taken seriously as rape victims,[29] while lower-class women were often dismissed as non-credible accusers because "credibility depended on social status and . . . unequal social status frequently legitimated the use of force."[30]

Yet in Rome, *raptus* was limited to the abduction of women, and the household (not the woman) was considered its primary victim,[31] a notion that was replicated in Mosaic law and, centuries later, in medieval English law.[32] In Mosaic law, victimhood was more explicitly associated with the property owner; compensation for damages was thus often paid to the father of the victim.[33] In the Christian medieval period, the association of rape as a property crime became more muddled. Dunn (2012) and historian Emma Hawkes (1995) both challenge Susan Brownmiller's polemical claim that all rape was treated as a property crime because all women had the status of chattel; their more nuanced assertion is that most rape entailed a property element but that high-status women had certain protections that elevated them above the status of mere property.[34] Dunn notes that, irrespective of the status of some women, rape laws focused on "familial consequences rather than the individual female perspective."[35] Thus, although there is variation across time and place, there is a relatively stable history here: rape law centers men of relative power (property owners and members of the ruling classes) as the primary victims of rape, rather than the people who have actually been assaulted.

Over time, *raptus* was understood as a crime not only of forced abduction but also of sexual assault, which shifted the calculus of criminal responsibility. By the end of the eleventh century BCE, abductees in some jurisdictions were presumed to have been sexually assaulted when they were kidnapped.[36] A 1382 British statute on rape reform explicitly distinguished rape (forced sex) from ravishment (forced abduction of a woman that did not involve forced sex).[37] Yet both crimes were typically still considered crimes against the husband or father.[38] The woman was not the victim and may even have been the instigator. When a woman was forcibly kidnapped from her home, it was relatively easy to prove the crime of *raptus*. But when sex entered the equation, the courts struggled to determine whether a woman had been sexually assaulted: had this pure, innocent woman relented to a suggestive gaze or gallant gesture, had she been forced into sex, or had she, in fact, done the seducing? In this new schema, the only way a victim could establish that she had been raped was to prove she had actively resisted her assault and that she had been raped "against her will." The question of victim complicity in *raptus* evolved into an expectation that a potential victim could have prevented her own rape and thus bore some responsibility for it.

Medieval legal historian James A. Brundage argues that by the fourteenth and fifteenth centuries in Europe, "treatment of rape and related crimes depended greatly on the victim's resistance to the advances of the offender."[39] To prove she had been raped, a victim would have to establish "[that] she had protested, that she had attempted to escape, and that her abductor had threatened her life or the lives of members of her family."[40] At various points throughout history, including the medieval period, it was presumed that "a woman who was abducted and ravished against her will . . . should have prevented the incident altogether by more vigorous resistance" and was therefore punished (albeit less severely than her abductor), on the grounds that she was an accomplice to the crime.[41] During the Victorian period (though not only this period), victims were presumed to have invited their own assaults by inspiring uncontrolled sexual urges in men.[42] As a matter of historical practice, then, even when there was evidence of a refusal of consent, rape has long been presumed to be a crime for which the victim is responsible because she did not protest ardently enough, secretly wanted to have sex, or provoked her assailant to rape her.

It might be tempting to dismiss this ancient history as . . . ancient history. And certainly, there have been important disruptions and shifts over time. Yet the myth of the false rape accuser endures in present-day US rape culture. For example, beginning in the nineteenth century and extending through most of the twentieth, the US legal standard for non-consent was "utmost resistance."[43] Philosopher Joan McGregor argues that this standard "reflect[ed] the belief that a woman should protect her chastity with her life" because, particularly for an upper-class white woman in the eighteenth- or nineteenth-century United States, her chastity *was* her social worth. McGregor explains: "female chastity was worth a lot to fathers interested in marrying off their daughters and to husbands wishing to ensure that children were biologically theirs."[44] Thus, "utmost resistance" was expected of those whose chastity was considered worth protecting but not required if the veracity of the victim's testimony was *not* in doubt, as when she was accusing a Black man of raping her.[45] The "utmost resistance" standard did not apply to white men accused of raping Black women because white men had what Davis calls "an incontestable right of access to black women's bodies,"[46] so the degree of Black women's resistance was irrelevant. Legal scholar Susan Estrich details several other cases in which a victim's resistance, while emphatic, did not rise to "utmost resistance." She observes: "rape is most assuredly not the only crime for which consent is a defense; but it is the only crime that has required the victim to resist physically in order to establish consent."[47]

This legal standard corresponded to nineteenth-century criminal seduction laws that protected the chastity of white women. Because these laws did not typically extend to non-white women, stereotypes about Black persons' sexual promiscuity "[led] southern courts to assume that African American women did not have the moral standing to protect their own chastity."[48] The utmost resistance standard required *proof* that rape victims had resisted their assaults to the "utmost." To hold victims of crime to this standard assumes they cannot be trusted, so their resistance should not be trusted either unless it was emphatic and corroborated.

Although it is no longer enshrined in law, the "utmost resistance" standard lingers in the practice of US rape law. In 2021, Madison Smith invoked an obscure Kansas law to convene a grand jury in her own rape case after the local prosecutor, Gregory Benefiel, opted not to bring rape charges against her assailant on the grounds that the assailant had no way to know that Smith had withdrawn her consent to sex. Smith acknowledged that she had initially consented to sex with her assailant, Jared Stolzenburg, but noted that she was unable to withdraw consent because she was being strangled at the time and could not speak, a claim that was substantiated by bruising discovered during her forensic medical exam (a.k.a. a rape kit). Instead, the prosecutor brought charges of aggravated battery, to which Stolzenburg pleaded guilty.[49] The remarkable aspect of the prosecutor's enactment of the law here is that it reflects the expectation that, no matter the circumstances (and even with corroborating evidence), the burden still falls on the potential victim to prevent her own rape. In this case, the expectation was that Smith would have to *withdraw* consent, even while Stolzenburg was strangling her, rather than that he should be obligated to ensure that consent was ongoing.

In the face of this virtually unsatisfiable and still implicit legal standard, some white women clearly conclude that being occasionally protected by white heteropatriarchy is better than not being protected at all. Yet this determination is misguided. Angela Y. Davis explains that racism and sexism "nourish" each other[50] and are used with and against each other to normalize sexual violence, against which no marginalized person is really immune. In a rape culture, the interlocking logics of systems of domination[51] evolve and expand to preserve the existing power structure and to normalize (and minimize) sexual violence by dictating who can be a victim and who cannot. Thus, in US rape culture, the white upper-class woman-as-property nourishes the doubly "propertified" Black woman (in chattel slavery and its afterlives, as well as in patriarchy) whose rape is rendered inconsequential by her marginalized status; at the same time, the mythic jezebel is restyled into the figure of the white female tease who is "asking for it" and should not be believed.[52] As Srinivasan notes, while the exhortation to "believe all women" pushes back against the myth of the false rape accuser, it is a dangerous universalism in a context where the words of white women are sometimes used to discipline Black men and women via false rape accusations.[53]

US rape culture places distinct normative expectations on women of different races or ethnicities, classes, and sexualities, which locate women in competing myths and discourses that distinguish those who will be trusted and believed from those who will not. The myth of the false rape accuser renders all women untrustworthy but uses race, class, and sexuality to render them untrustworthy for different reasons, in different contexts. These reasons are *internally* contradictory: white women are disciplined to be chaste virgins in public but whores in the bedroom;[54] Asian American and Pacific

Islander women are depicted as simultaneously exotic (powerfully magical) and submissive;[55] Black women are both hypersexualized as promiscuous jezebels and asexualized as nurturing mammies.[56] The contradictions are slippery and evasive, they are virtually impossible to satisfy, and each helps buttress patriarchal justifications for political and sexual domination by portraying women as always simultaneously weak *and* powerful, innocent *and* guilty. At the same time, these contradictions may seem to provide a safe haven for some women who hope that if *they* can be seen as trustworthy, they might be safe. But this is a false hope—one that reinforces, rather than undermines, the trap of the contradictions.

The mutual reinforcement of racism and sexism does *not* mean that some women are sexualized while others are not but does mean that women (and other persons who are feminized as weak) can be sexualized and targeted in different ways based on their race, class, sexuality, and ability. In their 2008 psychology study, Settles, Pratt-Hyatt, and Buchanan found that both Black and white women experienced gender discrimination in the workplace and expressed concerns about sexual violence. In the study, respondents from both groups reported being harassed or groped by strangers; white women reported being groped or harassed by acquaintances as well.[57] Settles et al. attribute these differences to racialized narratives about what kind of woman (and sexual actor) a member of each racial group is expected to be and how, when, where, and by whom they are sexualized. This difference may also be a function of the fact that Black women carry the added burden of protecting their harassers, especially if they are also Black, from the US criminal justice system.

In a related large-*N* study of experiences of sexual harassment among female military personnel, Buchanan, Settles, and Woods found that race–gender dynamics explain qualitative differences in the treatment of Black and white women. They find that "[w]hite women reported higher rates of gender harassment, and Black women reported higher rates of unwanted sexual attention and sexual coercion."[58] They attribute these differences to the warring myths of the "cult of true womanhood," which portrays white women as domestic, innocent, and in need of protection (and therefore transgressing gender boundaries when they appear in military uniform) and the jezebel, which depicts Black women as sexually promiscuous (and therefore inviting sexual attention in any context).[59] The misogynistic discourses that flow from these myths impose distinct expectations about normative behavior on white and Black women that, in turn, determine their blameworthiness should they be harassed or assaulted and the extent to which popular culture decries their harassment or assault.

Taken together, the myth of the false rape accuser and the reality of false rape accusations conspire to sustain a rape culture that renders accusers simultaneously unbelievable and deserving of the violence visited upon them. At the heart of the myth of the false accuser and the fact of the false rape accusation seems to be a *trust of women* problem. But in fact, this mistrust extends to anyone who challenges the white, settler capitalist, heteropatriarchal order.

The Discursive Magic of Consent

Drawing on the liberal tradition of political consent, sexual consent assumes that individuals are equal agents who—by virtue of granting or refusing consent—have the power to simply accept or reject sex. In US rape culture, sexual consent *seems* to distinguish sex from rape. But in the struggle over consent—whether it is given, implied, or denied; whether a denial is real or "a tease"—the potential victim is culturally confirmed as both the *object* of the uncontrollable desire essential to passionate sex and the *agent* who has the power to reject unwanted sex.

The notion of consent appears to offer "a definition of [sexual] violence beyond the vagaries of interpretation."[60] Yet sexual consent, like political consent, is limited by the context in which it is given, a context characterized by systems of domination and oppression such as heteropatriarchy, white supremacy, settler colonialism, and capitalist exploitation.[61] When it occurs within contexts of inequality, consent does *not* affirm the equal power of consenters but reveals (and sometimes further entrenches) relations of subordination. Consent presumes an equality between parties that, as Carole Pateman and Charles Mills have made clear, simply does not exist. Wendy Brown makes the similar point that consent never actually involves *sharing* power but always requires one party to relinquish something to another—whether one relinquishes one's right to be judge, jury, and executioner of the law of nature or decides to "give it up" to a sexual partner: "Insofar as consent involves agreeing to something the terms of which one does not determine, consent marks the subordinate status of the consenting party."[62] Therefore, consent cannot be egalitarian and cannot live up to its promise as a panacea for sexual violence.

The consent framework fosters inequality in three ways: (1) by insisting on equality between agents, (2) by amplifying a logic of reciprocal exchange, and (3) by creating conditions to indemnify perpetrators against prosecution. First, the association of sexual consent with the social contract tradition leads those who invoke sexual consent to assume that consenting individuals are equal agents who can agree to (and withdraw from) the social contract as they wish. Pateman and Mills have argued that vulnerable bodies are created and re-created through expressions of consent, which some *choose* to grant but others are *forced* to grant. Those who are forced to consent are rendered what Mills calls "sub persons," who are both persons and non-persons at the same time.[63] Historically, for example, women were (and, in some contexts, still are) sub persons with respect to the marriage contract: they are expected to utter "I do" (as a person) as if they had agency to choose otherwise, even when they have no actual right to refuse to consent to the marriage (as a non-person). The incoherence of such contracts makes it "possible [for persons] to get away with doing things to sub persons that one could not do to persons, because [sub persons] do not have the same rights as persons."[64] The result is that "sub persons" are held responsible for many of the things that happen to them on the grounds that they had consented all along.[65]

Mills's formulation of the racial contract is complicated by the myths, discourses, and practices that facilitate sexual violence. Which persons can be subject to victimization depends very much on which persons are doing the victimizing. According to Mills's account, persons can "get away with doing things"; sub persons, by contrast, are not allowed to get away with anything. Carolyn Bryant's husband had a right to rape her because she had no right to refuse to consent to sex with him in Mississippi in 1955. Yet the possibility that a Black child like Emmett Till had flirted with or whistled at Bryant, a white woman, justified Till's brutal murder and his killers' acquittal.[66]

To further complicate matters, sub persons are sometimes conceived as persons *relative* to other sub persons. In interactions between individuals, multiple, simultaneous structures can shift relations of dominability. Relative to her husband, Carolyn Bryant (later, Donham) was a sub person who had no right to refuse to consent to sex and no way to assert that she needed protection from her own (white) husband's violence; yet relative to Emmett Till, she was a white woman who was deemed worthy of protection by the white heteropatriarchal order. The interaction of accuser and accused is also evident in the different reactions to Anita Hill's accusations against US Supreme Court nominee Clarence Thomas, who is Black, in 1991 and Christine Blasey Ford's accusations 28 years later against nominee Brett Kavanaugh, who is white, even if the outcome (the Senate Judiciary Committee's general disregard for both claims, the cynical politicization of each, and the confirmation of both men as justices) was similar. One can imagine how differently each hearing would have progressed if Thomas's accuser had been white or Kavanaugh's had been Black. Kavanaugh would likely have been confirmed in either case, but Thomas—a Black man having been accused of threatening white femininity—almost surely would not have been.

As I discuss in Chapter Six, through the interaction of race and gender, Thomas's confirmation hearing revealed the relativity of sub personhood in three ways. In turns, it erased Hill's Blackness or womanhood in the face of Thomas's insistence that he was a victim of racism;[67] it reinforced the myth of the Black woman as hypersexual and therefore perpetually the agent of the violence committed against her, as opposed to the sanctified white woman;[68] and it diminished Black women's claims to agency, autonomy, or safety when such claims compete with those of Black men.[69] I believe it is central to Mills's argument that the problem with historical liberalism's conception of personhood is not only that it denies personhood to some but that it strategically uses claims of personhood to protect *white* personhood, even (or especially) if that means protecting the personhood of white women (who are conceived, in other contexts, as sub persons).[70]

Victims of sexual violence are sub persons in that they, too, are treated as both persons and non-persons at the same time. For example, US laws long presumed that white women were both *persons* who should not be sexually violated but who bore responsibility for ensuring that they remained unviolated and *objects* (non-persons) with no legal or political claim to bodily integrity. Of course, this object status was determined not only by gender but by race, class, sexuality, and other categories of domination as well. Certain "irresistible" white women apparently have the agency to "tease" white men into a state of powerlessness, which is why white men who "can't help themselves" will be forgiven for their overzealous, and often violent, sexual attention. By contrast, Black women in America are often objectified and are not imagined to be rapeable precisely because they are structured at times as *persons* who are imagined to be agents of their own, overripe sexuality (the jezebel).[71] Finally, in one remarkable 2012 Connecticut Supreme Court decision, a man was found not guilty of assault on the grounds that a physically and intellectually disabled woman he was alleged to have assaulted (who does not speak) had the capacity to kick. She therefore was not "helpless" to resist sexual assault as the statute required.[72] As scholars Joseph Fischel and Hilary O'Connell put it, "Resistance, in this instance, is proof not of *nonconsent*, but of *capacity to consent*."[73] In these cases, the victim is construed as an agent who always has the power to resist. If they do not exercise such resistance, they must be consenting.

In terms of the perpetuation of rape culture, the power that matters in any given situation depends very much on the race, gender, class, sexuality, or ability of the perpetrator, the victim, and the observer who interprets the scene. A rape culture identifies how—and to whom—to assign responsibility, blame, and care in each context. The discursive magic of consent is that it promises to distinguish sex from rape by helping us determine who is responsible for the encounter. It promises clarity and simplicity to onlookers in the broad, cultural context who desire to know, beyond the "vagaries of interpretation," how to read their world. In that sense, the promise of consent is not a guarantee of mutually desired sex but the promise that observers in the broader culture can definitively determine whether it was sex or rape—and who to blame for it.

The possibility of rape is the reason for the articulation of consent. To be able to consent (or to have consented) is to be able to determine whether a sexual encounter was rape or not. *To have consented* is an utterance that changes everything. This may be why consent is so rarely expressed in the present progressive tense ("I am consenting" or "my partner is consenting"). This alternative framing would suggest an ongoing-ness to the communication around a sexual encounter, during which consent could always be withdrawn or reconfigured. I believe the discourse of consent is rarely expressed in this way because such reconfiguring is incompatible with the simplifying promise of consent. Instead, it is typically expressed as a simple present- or past-tense declaration ("I consent/I consented" or "my partner consents/my partner consented"). In this way, the moment of consent—like a contractual commitment—transforms a potential rape into sex in a way that is supposed to be final, complete, and uncomplicated.

The second way the consent framework fosters inequality is by amplifying a logic of reciprocal exchange. By the nineteenth century in the United States, legal and popular understandings of consent to sex reflected an emerging logic of free market exchange, in which trading sex for economic goods was evidence of reciprocal, voluntary (and therefore uncoerced) sex.

During this period, a "contract, as the social act or enactment of laissez-faire ideals, constituted legitimate social relations"[74] and was considered a pinnacle expression of individual freedom, irrespective of the context in which the contract was made.[75] Within the exchange logic, sex came to be seen as a service that single, working poor women could trade to avoid adverse consequences (such as job loss) or to secure advantage (such as the promise of marriage or a job).[76] These kinds of exchanges may have been a matter of survival for many single, immigrant, and/or working-class women; but there was an apparent (inaccurate) consensus that they were making uncoerced choices, a question which I will take up in more detail in Chapter Five. The point here is that logic of exchange became so central to distinguishing consensual sex from rape that economic gain came to be regarded as *proof* of sexual consent.[77] If a woman stood to gain economically from a sexual encounter, according to this perspective, she must have been participating in a voluntary exchange as a free individual—and was therefore not a victim. This new consent-as-exchange discourse portrayed women as free, contracting individuals who orchestrated their economic destinies by exchanging economic advantage for sex.[78] When paired with the long-standing myth of the false rape accuser that casts doubt on women's claims to have refused consent, this discourse offered yet another calculus for assessing who was the seducer and who was the victim: given their nature as scheming manipulators, women used sex to achieve economic gains or even independence. When need be, they used the false rape accusation to achieve economic gain as well.

The third way the consent framework fosters inequality is by creating the discursive conditions for indemnification: potential victimizers seek the certainty that consent ostensibly provides in order to indemnify themselves against accusations of rape. The concept of sexual consent originated in an attempt to distinguish forced abduction (*raptus*) from women's trickery and manipulation.[79] The burden was on the ostensible victim to prove sufficient refusal of consent. The anxiety underlying the use of consent was motivated not necessarily by the protection of the woman but by the protection of the property of the man (the father or husband) to whom she belonged. In the US context, consent—or the absence of it—protected white men's control over their property and secured the integrity of their lineage. Today, the anxiety manifests as a different mode of self-protection of the perpetrator: protection against false accusations from unpredictable and unreliable (female) victims. The desire for certainty is not motivated primarily by a wish to avoid committing rape or other form of sexual violence but by a desire to avoid being raped or being accused of it. Consent seems to provide that certainty.

Consent protects potential victimizers in two paradoxical ways. First, the consent framework (in cultural terms, if not legal ones) allows for *implied consent*, the ambiguity of which grants a kind of protection to potential perpetrators by virtue of the lack of certainty about whether consent was granted. In the best-case scenario, the most consent can do is to clarify whether partners have said or implied that sex could occur at some point. But because consent need not be explicitly granted, even the unequivocal act of "saying no" can be (and has been) construed as "meaning yes." The potential rapist can exploit this feature of implied consent: a victim's non-refusal is sufficient to avoid a rape accusation. The second paradoxical way in which the concept of consent may protect victimizers is that (contrary to the ambiguity consent provides around implicit agreements), the consent framework also appears to be absolute and irrevocable: once consent is established, it seems, sex *must* happen. The notion that sexual consent is irrevocable is likely to affirm a potential perpetrator's entitlement to sex, irrespective of the experience and desires of their sexual partner. For example, former Canadian Broadcast Company radio host Jian Ghomeshi was acquitted of rape charges in 2014 by relying on the assumption that consent to sex is irrevocable. Ghomeshi's accusers had expressed interest in a sexual relationship with him via text messages but not in the kinds of intensive and violent sexual encounters that were in line with his sexual preferences. The court apparently concluded that even if Ghomeshi and his accusers were "consenting" to different things, they were consenting to *something*, so Ghomeshi could not be found guilty of rape.[80]

Conceptually and discursively, sexual consent promises to distinguish sex from rape and victims from perpetrators. When victims or potential victims of rape cling optimistically to this promise, they do so because they believe consent can protect them from rape. Yet Pateman and Mills have noted that consent is already inscribed by subordination through white, settler capitalist heteropatriarchy; thus, it tends to replicate, rather than undermine, those structures. Victims are refigured as agents who could have prevented their own rapes, while perpetrators are refigured as victims who were manipulated or misunderstood. In the context of sexual consent, even ambiguity is presumed to mean certainty. The possibility that consent is implied unless expressly retracted undergirds the attachment to certainty that perpetrators can assume themselves blameless most of the time. The protective power of consent is used to safeguard would-be assailants, who use the specter of implied consent to sex when none was expressly granted in order to dominate via sex. Sexual consent is not a contract, but would-be assailants want to act as if it were. As I detail in the next section, when sexual consent is protected via contractualization, potential perpetrators can indemnify themselves against rape accusations.

There's an App for That: The New Contractualization of Sexual Consent

Almost since its earliest conception, rape could only be "proven" when the victim could demonstrate that she resisted loudly, publicly, and ceaselessly. If a victim did not resist her rape strenuously enough, judges and juries would conclude that she had participated willingly. As I have shown, a grounding assumption of US rape culture is *still* that consent is implied until expressly denied. Unless victims can prove their dissent—and most of the time, such proof is limited to bruises and wounds—how is a man to know that his female partner is not a willing participant?

In recent years, a so-called affirmative consent standard has emerged in response to the presumption of implied consent. The reason that the affirmative consent (or "yes means yes") standard is so appealing to some—and so controversial to others—is that it reveals that the negative consent standard assumes consent has been implicitly granted and must be expressly rescinded. If negative consent didn't always imply consent, the affirmative standard wouldn't make sense. In other words, affirmative consent is a necessary counter-framework precisely because the overwhelming assumption is that women are always tacitly agreeing to sex by what they wear, what they say (even when what they say is "no"), who they are (poor, a person of color, a sex worker, a tease, for example), and how they behave.

The "negative consent" framework—which insists that a victim must unequivocally refuse sex—has a long history: as I detail above, only the strongest evidence that a would-be victim had actively and publicly refused to consent to sexual intercourse would suffice to prove rape. Legal minds have imagined all kinds of evidence that consent to sex had been granted. In the twelfth century, the canon law scholar Johannes Teutonicus argued that a woman's silence signified consent.[81] There is evidence from the medieval period, from the legal statutes of the Massachusetts colony, and even from remarks made by a 2012 Missouri congressional candidate that many believe(d) a resulting pregnancy indicated consent to sex.[82] In the nineteenth-century United States, a woman could not be raped unless she was a virgin as there would otherwise be no loss (of property value).[83] And historian Joanna Bourke notes that proving rape required evidence of physical harm: "In rape discourse the penis most typically became a weapon, but (the logic goes) since weapons leave wounds, if there is no wound, there is no rape."[84] In other words, the proof of rape rested with the victim, whose word was doubted much more often than it was believed.

Since rape often occurred in concealed places, and since rape accusations pitted a man's word against a woman's, victims have historically struggled to prove they refused. Women, especially lower-status women, would not have been believed on their own; their accusations would often have to be corroborated by someone else, even though there was likely no witness to the rape. Dunn notes that, "[w]hen raising the hue and cry, the woman was required to document the event by showing any wounds and her torn and bloodstained clothes to the local bailiff, sergeant or coroner. With a crime that usually had no witnesses, this rapid publicity of the offence was, as today, an essential step in the prosecution."[85] "Rapid publicity" required immediate action on the part of the victim, who had to marshal witnesses almost from the moment her rape was over. Yet since victims were often alone with their assailants in open fields or other sequestered places, publicity was hard to come by.[86] The legal requirement of public, third-party corroboration of consent *refusal* hindered successful rape prosecution, serving instead as an effective strategy of indemnification for rapists, which is reflected in contemporary legal standards like the "utmost resistance" standard.

Today, however, mobile devices have transformed the private realm: what was once a space that concealed (and therefore enabled) *raptus* is now always, potentially, a disclosable and surveillable space. This shift might have been a boon for sexual violence prevention, but instead, technologies are being used to blame victims and indemnify assailants against accusations. In an essay for the *New Yorker* about the 2012 Steubenville, Ohio, rape case, Ariel Levy describes how the shifting terrain of surveillance exposed the rape of a teen girl: "Fifteen years ago, [accused Steubenville students] Richmond and Mays would have escaped suspicion: before smartphones and Twitter, rumors floated around high schools and then dissipated, often before adults knew what was real and what was adolescent imagination.

As it was, the evidence was limited to tweets, the photograph of Richmond and Mays carrying the girl, and a cell-phone video recorded late on the night of the parties and then uploaded to YouTube."[87] The case made national headlines precisely because these new technologies allowed people to photograph, videorecord, upload, tweet, and comment on what was happening in real time. The victim, who was unconscious and had no memory of the events, only became aware of having been raped because of the digital traces her assailants and bystanders left behind.

One might assume that the emergence of new technologies that permit the surveillance and disclosure of private spaces would protect those who might otherwise be subjected to sexual violence in private. Instead, a new strategy of indemnification has emerged that uses mobile device capabilities to preempt accusations of sexual assault. This new strategy involves "contractualizing" sexual consent. I use the term "contractualize" to identify a set of practices and discourses that partners employ to indicate a desire to have sex or affirm that they participated willingly. These include text messages; apps that document, timestamp, and store data about sexual encounters; right swipes on Tinder or Grindr; or digitally signed "smart contracts" via blockchain technology. These documentation practices are presumed to prove consent, protect both parties, and internalize obligations. Proponents of contractualization defend these new technologies on the grounds that they can document clear communication between sexual partners, yet their rhetoric reveals a more troubling motive: to indemnify potential perpetrators against rape allegations. A contract to sexual consent offers little protection to marginalized individuals who are already at higher risk of sexual violence and assault. It offers substantially more protection to potential perpetrators who fear they will be accused of sexual assault.

In the liberal tradition, the social contract represents a voluntary agreement between persons in order to maximize individuals' freedom of choice.[88] Today, individuals use contracts to codify legal obligations to other people, particularly in a free market economy. Contracts are intended to create reciprocal obligations and facilitate free movement in a context that would otherwise (it is presumed) be governed by individuals' worst tendencies for self-interest. Although there is ongoing philosophical and legal debate about what a contract is,[89] the widely referenced treatise *Restatement (Second) of Contracts* defines it as "a promise or a set of promises for the breach of which the law gives a remedy, or the performance of which the law in some way recognizes as a duty."[90] In its ideal form, a contract is a formal, mutual obligation characterized by *consent*[91] and *reciprocity*.[92] It documents a promise—which is recognized and enforced by the state—that obligates parties to one another. State enforcement of contracts overcomes two problems: (1) it gives individuals "confidence" that their agreements with each other will be upheld[93] and (2) it prevents them from enforcing their contracts on their own terms, which could result in vigilantism or self-help.[94] The promise of state enforcement allows contracts to foster a kind of trust between individuals who might otherwise distrust each other.[95] Finally, particularly in its free market instantiations, contract discourse identifies *exchange* as the principal mode of *voluntary* and *reciprocal* agreement.[96] In this discourse, the contract resolves problems associated with trade and helps make the free market more efficient.[97]

Consent, reciprocity, and exchange are essential to free contract relations; but the concept of consent in sexual relations predates the contractarian thinking of the early modern period. There is evidence that consent was a core aspect of prosecuting *raptus* by at least the eleventh and twelfth centuries BCE in Europe.[98] The earliest instantiations of sexual consent (often phrased as "assent" or—in inverted form—as not being forced to have sex "against one's will") did not presume that women had an equal and unequivocal right to refuse consent. The language of sexual consent did not become entwined with the social contract until the seventeenth century. At that point, historian Julia Rudolph argues, British contract theorists began to draw an analogy between tyranny and rape to explain violations of natural law.[99] But this analogy only went so far: these theorists could not bring themselves to argue that women had a political right to resist *tyranny*, even though they agreed that women had a right to resist *rape*.[100] And while these theorists did not question whether political resisters knew tyranny when they saw it, they tended to agree that women often lie about having granted sexual consent.[101] Thus, sexual consent as political consent was an imperfect analogy that did not reflect the egalitarianism that the social contract reserved for men.

Since then, the allure of the contract ideal has extended to sexual consent. For example, when Roxanne Jones counseled her son not to have sex without a text confirming consent in advance,[102] she implicitly suggested that a text message, received *before* engaging in sex, creates a mutual obligation to sex and therefore can prove the sex was consensual. Yet her column functions in two registers. First, she offers advice that all parents of college-bound offspring (irrespective of race, it seems, since her analysis does not mention it)[103] might share with their sons. She reinforces a gendered formulation of sexual consent informed by the myth of the false rape *accuser* when she tells her son to "watch out for the stupid girls"—"the party girls who thrive on attention."[104] In the second register, Jones, as a Black mother, shares the advice she wishes she had given her Black son. This advice is structured by the history of the false rape *accusation* that has been consistently wielded against young Black men in the United States. For Jones and for many other parents in US rape culture, the intersecting structures of political domination and mistrust suggest that the only context in which one should be comfortable having sex is after having documented "proof" of consent "[b]ecause just as damning text messages and Facebook posts helped convict the high-schoolers in Steubenville of rape, technology can also be used to prove innocence."[105] Given this context, Jones entreats young men to use their phones to safeguard themselves.

Jones's advice is not unusual. In many personal and professional contexts, I have heard parents of boys and young men express a similar sentiment to me, certainly because they do not want their sons to commit sexual violence but also because they understand that consent is not clear-cut. But the move to contractualization—that is, to obtaining an exonerating text message *beforehand*—does not resolve the problem of unclear consent, nor does it improve communication about sex. In the context of US rape culture, the need for proof is often predicated on an assumption that women are either untrustworthy narrators or false rape accusers. Based on such an assumption, "proof" of consent does not protect rape victims; instead, it indemnifies those who might otherwise be accused of rape.

In a similar vein to those well-meaning parents, but with very different motives, commentators in the manosphere encourage one another to collect "evidence" to protect innocent PUAs and "alphas" from feminist social justice warriors who frustrate male entitlement to sex. MRA/PUA commentators (some of whom admit they have been accused more than once of rape) also encourage men to use their mobile devices to surveil and document to protect themselves. For example, a 2016 post on the MRA blog *Return of Kings* (ROK) about how to avoid a false rape accusation included the advice to "Delete NOTHING":

> Nowadays, there's an avalanche of evidence to be found in our phones. Snapchat, Facebook, SMS, text messages, Tinder, and the list goes on and on. If she won't stop flirting with you via Facebook, take a screenshot and

> save the images. If she sexts you on Tinder, screenshot and save the images. And if she sends you nudes on Snapchat? Screenshot the shit out of them.[106]

Certainly, this "avalanche of evidence" might not satisfy evidentiary standards of legal consent to sex and does not amount to a contract. Yet it is still accumulated as "proof" that might protect sexually appetitive men from manipulative teases who will exploit the male weakness for sex to gratify their own desires for power, money, reputation, or revenge through false rape accusations. For this commentator's audience—like "the men of ROK" who believe they are entitled to dominate women—documentation (including, ironically, surreptitious and non-consensual videorecording) protects against female dissembling and manipulation. Viewed through this lens, a sext or Tinder swipe proves a woman's consent to sex, which she may later deny. Given the female penchant for manipulation and dissembling, these men assert, they have no choice but to protect themselves by recording women without their consent.[107] This kind of "documentation" has been successfully amassed as evidence to challenge rape accusations. As I noted above, Jian Ghomeshi's acquittal was partly based on text messages that were considered proof of consent to sex, even though his accusers suggested that the sex they had consented to was not the violent sex they experienced. Like Madison Smith, the young woman who was strangled by her sexual partner, Ghomeshi's accusers bore the burden of proving they had withdrawn consent as they were being strangled or subjected to other (non-consensual) violence. In these cases, documentation was treated *not* as a contract but as proof of intention, a strategy that a potential rapist can use to indemnify himself against a false rape accusation.

If a text or screenshot counts as evidence, what is it supposed to be evidence *of*? To satisfy the legal standard that sex must be consensual, these digital engagements would have to be interpreted as evidence of sexual consent; this is certainly what Roxanne Jones hopes. But there is a qualitative difference between a parent's advice to get a preemptive consent text and an MRA/PUA's admonishment to "delete NOTHING": the former is understood as evidence of consent, while the latter is interpreted as authorizing male entitlement to sex by proving that she was "asking for it." According to this latter misogynistic (and decidedly inegalitarian) view, consent is neither relevant nor necessary. Here, the move to document is nothing more or less than an unfortunate necessity in a world of feminist killjoys and widespread false rape accusations and is deployed as an explicit strategy of indemnification.

Even Jones's earnest desire to document consent is corrupted in a rape culture where parents are always already convinced of the innocence of their offspring. For example, her advice to her son includes a troubling addendum: "it's a good idea to even follow up any sexual encounter with a tasteful text message saying how you both enjoyed being with one another—even if you never plan on hooking up again."[108] Though the first piece of advice Jones offers her son is to get proof of consent beforehand, this second strategy approaches gaslighting. The presumed interpretation (taken for granted by Jones as appropriate general advice, no matter the circumstance) is that the male enjoyed his encounter but also that the enjoyment was mutual—"you both enjoyed being with one another"—an attempt to (tastefully) quash any narrative to the contrary.

Drawing on philosopher Kate Abramson's account, I argue that Jones's advice lays the groundwork for a gaslighting campaign, even if it does not rise to the level of gaslighting on its own. Certainly, the tasteful next-day text Jones describes could be construed as encouraging young women to doubt their own judgments about sex—or anything else. But as Abramson explains, gaslighters "don't just need the world to appear to themselves to be a certain way—they need *you*, the target, to see it that way."[109] A gaslighter needs to "destroy even the possibility of disagreement . . . [such that] his sense of the world [is] not merely confirmed, but placed beyond dispute."[110] Jones's day-after text does not go so far as to destroy the possibility of disagreement, even though it certainly aims to shape the narrative by drawing on other sexist patterns of socialization and doubt to assert the male's interpretation of events. Thus, even under the most generous interpretation, this parental advice is comparable to the gaslighting "day-after" text advocated by MRAs and PUAs, who are convinced that women use false rape allegations to hurt men and help themselves. The aim of such texts is to document exculpatory evidence of a consensual encounter rather than to express care for one's partner.

While text messages are not contracts, when they are construed as "proof" of consent, they fall on the spectrum of the contractualization of sexual consent. Consent apps are a newer approach to documenting consent. They are designed explicitly with the documentation purpose in mind and are a step further toward contractualization. They are marketed as tools for communication (such as Good2Go and We-Consent) or as self-protection (such as SaSie and LegalFling). Yet in a context that presumes distrust between sexual partners, the self-protective consent apps adopt the explicit language of contracts as a way to cultivate safe, consensual sex.

LegalFling, a consent app developed in 2018, promises worry-free hookups. Yet it seems clearly focused on preventing rape accusations by documenting consent. LegalFling differs from other consent apps because it utilizes blockchain technology to create and preserve what it calls a "legally binding" and secure "live contract"[111] that articulates the terms of agreement to sex between people who wish to hook up but who may not know each other very well. LegalFling claims that any departure from such an agreement amounts to a "breach of contract."[112]

One common critique of treating sexual consent like a contract is that, unlike standard contracts, sexual consent is supposed to be revocable at any time. A consent contract (or app) may not allow individuals to withdraw consent, no matter the circumstance. To address this problem, an early version of the LegalFling FAQ explained how the app *could* be used to revoke consent:

> Can I still change my mind? Absolutely. "No" means "no" at any time. Being passed out means "no" at any time. This is explicitly described in the agreement. *Additionally, you can withdraw consent going forward through the LegalFling app with a single click.*[113]

Yet, remarkably, only a few months later, once the app was available for download, LegalFling could no longer be used to withdraw consent. The updated FAQ now read:

> Can I still change my mind? **Absolutely.** "No" means "no" at any time. Being passed out means "no" at any time. Revoking consent is always done verbally at any time and without giving a reason. *You never use the app to revoke consent.* In case the rules of consent were not honered [*sic*], the app can be used afterwards to secure a statement and get professional help.[114]

In other words, LegalFling's developers determined that it would be better for the app *not* to allow parties to revoke sexual consent. Because a blockchain is effectively a digital ledger, it is not clear—as either a technical or legal matter—why a line of code could not be added to reflect a change in contractual status. But as the website notes, all that is stored in the LegalFling ledger as evidence of consent is the transaction hash and timestamp. Revoking consent would require a new transaction, a new timestamp, and an indication of revocation.

Without a formal process through which to revoke consent they had already expressly given, victims would be in precisely the same situation earlier rape victims found themselves: they would need to amass evidence to prove they had been raped. If two individuals enter into a LegalFling consent contract and Individual A later verbally withdraws this consent (perhaps because they are feeling unsafe, uncomfortable, or uninterested), Individual B may not understand (or may choose not to understand) this verbal withdrawal as superseding the earlier contract and may thus not cease sexual activity. Individual A is then left to advance a rape accusation in a context in which the only incontrovertible evidence is the original "contract" that both parties agreed to at some point. This evidence protects Individual B, while Individual A is left to deal with the consequences (personal, psychological, legal) of an assault. At best, consent via contract binds individuals to unstipulated but ostensibly consensual sex. At worst, it indemnifies assailants against legal action by formalizing consent to sex without providing a formal avenue via which to withdraw it.

In a culture that normalizes sexual violence, the contractualization of sexual consent imposes the added burden of a *contractual* obligation on parties who may have already internalized a sense of obligation to relent to sex. The theory of contract law considers contracts useful legal tools because they are "pseudo self-enforcing"[115] in the sense that they rarely require state enforcement. Once they are contractually obligated, people feel a strong sense that they must fulfill their end of the bargain. Marginalized persons often internalize an obligation to have sex, and this sense of obligation may intensify under a logic of contractualization of sexual consent that formalizes it. Participants may believe that they have entered into ironclad agreements that entitle their partner(s) to sex; that the contract indemnifies their partners against rape allegations, so there is no use in leveling one; or that, once "contracted," sexual partners have no grounds on which to assert their evolving desires, preferences, and limits. US rape culture maintains that assault victims are more likely to be accused of "crying rape" than of being the victim of a violent crime; in this context, if a person believes they have entered a legal binding sexual consent "contract," they are likely to think they are irrevocably bound by it.

In a rape culture, discourses about sex shape the extent to which individuals feel they can refuse consent. For example, the discourses of male sexual gratification and female sexual compliance, taken together, prioritize male sexual desire and impress expectations on both male and female sexual partners about what constitutes desirous sex. Srinivasan describes the discourse of male sexual gratification as one that can "make men want to have sex with women who don't really want it, or make them feel that it's their job to overcome a woman's resistance, and . . . make women feel they must have sex with men when they don't want to."[116] Kate Manne adds that these discourses, coupled with the long-standing practice of disbelieving rape accusers, condition women to believe they are better off avoiding the repercussions of accusing someone of rape, even if the accusation is true.[117] In the context of these discourses, a contractualized form of sexual consent may inspire a sense that any agreement to sex—now formalized in a text, app notification, or contract—is legally binding and irrevocable. Those who accept a discourse of male entitlement to sex may, with a "contract" in hand, feel no obligation to respond to their partners' shifting preferences; those who accept it may feel no power to express their own preferences, much less to withdraw consent. In the context of a rape culture that structures a woman's refusal as a signal of her desire and as an obstacle for a male to overcome, it is possible—perhaps even likely—that a male sexual partner would be sexually emboldened by a post-contract refusal of consent. Rather than foster healthy communication about sex and consent, introducing a consent "contract" could intensify the terms of male domination and control over sex. Counterintuitive as it may seem, the contractualization of consent may be more likely to facilitate than prevent sexual violence.

Another app, called SaSie, is marketed as an "affirmative consent app" and treats the internalization of obligation to others as a feature, rather than a bug, of its contract application. SaSie was developed in 2016 as an alternative to earlier consent apps like Good2Go. It produces "a digitally signed, and legally binding contract between two adults" that in turn serves as "a legally binding modicum of evidence for students, and adjudicators, too."[118] Unlike earlier consent apps that aim to serve educative or communicative purposes, SaSie's developers presume that the contract language will inspire stronger obligations on parties than the mere language of consent. What distinguishes SaSie from earlier consent apps is that, rather than an impulsive "click" to consent, the SaSie contract is meant to be completed prior to a sexual relationship and later rescinded via a "termination sequence" once the relationship has ended.[119] The problem with most consent today, SaSie's developers surmise, is that sex and consent are treated too casually (particularly among college students) and that "pretending that sex is anything other than a contract already between students also does them a major disservice."[120] The developers believe that formalizing sex in a contract will cultivate more intentional commitments to sex and consent and that, by formalizing the contract, it will "put students on **equal** legal footing."[121]

Curiously, SaSie's consent framework is structured around ensuring student compliance with university codes of conduct, even though it promises students legal recourse through civil proceedings in lieu of criminal or student conduct proceedings. It presumes that students will wish to "be in compliance with their school's ethos and policies regarding affirmative consent,"[122] perhaps because a contract that is out of compliance with existing requirements and standards might not be enough to absolve an accused person of guilt (or, in the student conduct context, of responsibility).

Yet, as with any contract, the SaSie contract is not immune to pressure, power, control, and dominance, particularly as these are mediated through sex. Such contracts are developed in a context shaped by both hidden and manifest structures of domination that promise equality to relatively powerless parties to the contract while simultaneously stimulating their sense of obligation to male entitlement to sex. But even beyond those external structures, the app fosters inegalitarian relations, to the benefit of the person who is *not* withdrawing consent. For example, the developers explain that the "termination sequence" "obligates your partner to confirm" that you have withdrawn consent, which grants final authorizing power to the person who has not initiated termination.[123] Even if the app "obligates" confirmation somehow, this move, in a rape culture where stalking and intimate partner violence are common, bolsters the dominance of the more powerful actor, who may simply refuse to accept termination or may harass the terminating party into rescinding the termination sequence. The developers of the app believe that a contract can overcome the lack of clarity around consent that causes sexual violence. However, the contractualization of sexual consent may, in many cases, reinscribe the very myths, discourses, and practices that normalize it.

The contractualization of sexual consent rests on faulty premises of voluntarism, mutuality, and exchange. Yet US rape culture conditions marginalized persons to internalize obligations to the more powerful, sustains the myth that many women falsely accuse men of raping them, and prioritizes indemnifying men from rape accusations. Thus, such contracts do little to address sexual violence. If anything, the contractualization of sexual consent is an attempt to preempt the disclosive power of mobile technologies and to reinforce victim blaming and victim distrust.

Conclusion

In her expansive history of rape since 1860, historian Joanna Bourke explains that rape myths are stories that "survive as fragments"[124] and that the fragmented nature of a rape myth allows it to flex but not break—even when confronted with contradicting narratives.[125] The myth of the false accuser exists in uneasy tension with the myths of the Black male rapist and the unrapeable body (often a racially marginalized woman). Yet the history of *raptus* also reveals a rupture (or potential rupture) born of new technologies—particularly the surveillance capabilities of the smartphone, which have changed the nature of publicity with respect to public declarations of a withdrawal of consent. Into this rupture, some have imagined the liberatory possibilities of contractualizing sexual consent. Yet, in the context of US rape culture, this potential is limited because contractualization is enlisted to indemnify potential perpetrators against sexual assault allegations. The contractualization of sexual consent thus prevents rape *allegations* but not rape.

In US rape culture, where the myth of the false rape accuser persists and is even amplified by the grievance and entitlement of the manosphere, the contractualization of consent to sex might seem very compelling. Yet the motivation to contractualize sexual consent seems to come—whether from a concerned parent, a nervous sexual partner, or a PUA—from a desire to protect potential perpetrators from manipulative women, who cannot be counted on to be honest about their desires or experiences. Potential perpetrators turn to contracts, which they can use to secure and sustain their power. Consent contracts are *not* tools of liberation from systemic domination but rather are tools that those in power use to hold onto that power. Consent via contract cannot distinguish sex from rape in the context of a popular culture that consistently uses such contracts to preserve white supremacist, heteropatriarchal, classist, and ableist structures of personal and political power.

Chapter Five

The Customer is Always Right

Intimacy on Demand

Introduction

During the 2020–22 COVID lockdowns, when people were unable to spend much time outside their homes, subscriptions to the online web platform OnlyFans increased by 500%.[1] The *New York Times Magazine* reported that "In 2019, there were reportedly 120,000 content creators using the platform; by December 2020, that number had risen to more than a million."[2] The shift to OnlyFans made good sense for content creators because the emergence of direct-to-subscriber platforms gave them greater independence in precarious economic conditions.[3] But why would consumers opt to visit a subscriber-based platform when they could have found erotic content for free on PornHub instead? According to the *New York Times Magazine*, OnlyFans offered something that PornHub did not: "Many creators on the site aren't just posting nudes. The real product is relationships. Money from subscriptions can be trivial compared with the profits earned by selling custom videos, sexting sessions and other forms of fan interaction that require more concerted engagement than simply posting to a feed. . . . OnlyFans works because people pay for a connection that feels deeper than porn."[4]

The connection that consumers feel, one that is "deeper than porn," comes from the "normal," "accessible," and "attainable" content that a creator can make in their own home using little more than a webcam, a ring light, and some editing software.[5] Consumers connect with the everyday intimacy of those they follow or subscribe to, and because the content on OnlyFans and other direct-to-subscriber platforms is typically purchased directly from the creator, consumers feel they are participating in a more ethical exchange than they would at mainstream "tube sites" like PornHub.[6] As one writer concluded in 2020, "for the time being, the rise of . . . subscription-based platforms has made it easier than ever to find and directly support quality, ethical erotic content created by consenting adult sex workers who are earning money for their work."[7]

Yet by 2022, OnlyFans content creators were increasingly relying on specialized marketing firms to help them grow their subscriber bases—which a *New York Times Magazine* article described as *awkward* "because OnlyFans markets itself as providing the infrastructure for authentic, personal connections between creators and their fans" and *inevitable* since such platforms "naturally encourage businesses to scale up, maximizing profits through growth however they can find it."[8] In other words, marketing an OnlyFans performer involves attracting more and more subscribers, yet subscribers are seeking personal attention and connections. The problem becomes obvious: to remain competitive and profitable, content creators must provide intimacy that is both available *on demand* and replicable *at scale.* To scale up a commodity that is valued because it is intimate, personal, and authentic, creators (and their firms) have to find a way to standardize their product. I argue that standardization often requires replicating mythic characters and discourses from US rape culture, from the "wide-eyed ingenue" to the "MILF." Additionally, the promise of immediate and personalized attention can reinforce or even intensify the discourses and practices of male entitlement to emotional attention and sexual attention without expectations of reciprocity or mutual care. While it may be true that "not all pornography is exchanged within a capitalist frame,"[9] I argue that when ethical porn is mediated through a capitalist frame, this strains its potential to be or remain ethical.

This chapter explores how direct-to-subscriber services like OnlyFans, when mediated through neoliberal capitalism, contribute to US rape culture. I focus on the pressures and mechanisms of such services, which are likely liberating to content creators in many respects. I do not claim that porn is bad or that it cannot be empowering. My argument is that, within the exploitative context of neoliberal capitalism, even a move toward ethical porn is likely to be co-opted in ways that create new avenues of exploitation. This is part of the work of US rape culture and its entwinement with capitalism.

I explore the implications of scaling up these direct-to-subscriber services in three parts. First, I discuss the promise of ethical porn and the distinctive consequences of trying to scale up within a neoliberal free market in which the producer is also the product. Second, I describe how the myths and discourses of rape culture are reinforced when competing content creators try to attract subscribers and keep their followers engaged with promises of 24/7 availability. Third, I argue that when intimacy, authenticity, and accessibility are mediated through direct-to-subscriber services like OnlyFans, they produce a unique form of intimacy that must be made available *on demand.* Intimacy on demand reinforces male entitlement to non-reciprocal care and sexual attention—a form of entitlement that can encourage sexual violence by affirming (if not intensifying) male entitlement to unreciprocated care, sexual attention, and sex. I conclude the chapter by reflecting on how the emergence of AI chatbots could further intensify the demand for male entitlement to sex that is intrinsic to US rape culture.

At its best, performer-created ethical porn and sex-positive content might seem to promise an important shift in rape culture, especially when direct-to-subscriber platforms offer performers a comparatively safe way to generate income through creative, sexual explorations that many find fun and rewarding.[10] Yet, even if direct-to-subscriber services like OnlyFans help foster an ethical and sex-positive porn industry, as long as the market is structured by the neoliberal capitalist technologies of social media, the imperative to scale up will pressure content creators to replicate the myths and discourses of US rape culture and reinforce the practices of male entitlement that enable sexual violence. Rather than creating a vehicle for sexual liberation, these market imperatives perpetuate ongoing exploitation and violence against the subordinates of US rape culture.

Scaling up Ethical Porn in a Free Market

Many feminists have tried and failed to resolve a contradiction inherent in the porn industry—that porn work might be liberating for some and exploitative for others. Feminist scholar Heather Berg encourages a different approach: to think about this contradiction "as a resource rather than a limitation."[11] I aim to adopt Berg's approach in my critical analysis. For example, while some types of porn are a reaction against "misogynistic aesthetics and exploitative working conditions,"[12] we can also ask how (or whether or when) "sexually dissident styles reproduce relations of domination" and consider "how these practices operate in a system of racist and capitalist social relations."[13] I do not argue that ethical porn is impossible or that all porn is necessarily exploitative or even capitalist. Instead, I approach the question of the liberatory potential of ethical porn by embracing this irresolvable contradiction, which allows us to see that porn can be at once *both* liberating *and* exploitative and that our analysis should focus on what kinds of contexts and practices contribute to exploitation.[14]

What follows is not a critique of porn, then, but an argument based on the presumption that we should be skeptical of the liberatory and ethical horizons of *any* capitalist industry, including porn. I suspect that the promise of the ethical and liberatory potential of erotic content has helped OnlyFans become a site of neoliberal capitalist co-optation. This is not to say that it will *always* or *necessarily* be a site of co-optation but only to suggest that the structures and incentives that drive the profitability of OnlyFans, which was designed to generate profit (and not to foster ethical forms of capitalism), will impede its liberatory potential. No one knows this better, it seems, than the content creators who understand the flux and precarity of the porn market. The purpose of this chapter is to explore how and when the imperatives of US rape culture, when filtered through the profit motives of neoliberal capitalism, will undermine the possibility of pornography that is ethical, consensual, diverse, imaginative, non-exploitative, and liberatory.

When porn companies market "ethical porn," they adopt a common practice of co-opting values to fold them into a brand. Similar practices, like "rainbow washing" or "greenwashing," assert forms of allyship or environmental sustainability without attending to (much less challenging) the conditions that necessitate queer and trans liberation or environmental sustainability in the first place. Sex educator and founder of Velvet Tip studio Lola Jean recently warned that "'ethical porn' has become a new marketing term. . . . Any porn company can say they are ethical, but it doesn't mean that all of their practices are."[15] In fact, the market for ethical porn has expanded so much that Ethical Capital Partners, a Canadian private equity firm that seeks to invest in "industries that require principled ethical leadership," acquired PornHub (one of the largest free porn sites in the world) in March 2023.[16] Clearly, there is a market for ethical porn.

The notion of ethical porn appeals to creators and consumers who recognize that the "mainstream" porn industry is exploitative,[17] yet they disagree over what constitutes ethical porn. Some say it is porn you pay for,[18] while according to others it centers the welfare and sexual expression of the performer.[19] Lola Jean suggests that the hallmarks of ethical porn are that it "is shot by women or queer people, prioritizes consent, and pays performers fair wages."[20] Decaro et al. suggest that while the ethical porn industry is less likely than mainstream porn to replicate heteronormativity and cisnormativity or gender binaries, people also tend to assume it is created by amateurs, rather than professionals.[21] Feminist scholar Eleanor Wilkinson cautions against conflating mainstream pornography with unethical porn and "alternative" pornography with ethical porn;[22] efforts at ethical porn can be co-opted, just as commercial or mainstream porn could be less exploitative of performers at times.

One demanding standard of ethical porn would require that (1) it is not economically exploitative, and performers are paid directly for their work and content; (2) performers give consent; and (3) the industry supports a plurality of sexual experiences that are safe for those who perform.[23] In this section, I discuss these three interrelated criteria as they relate to direct-to-subscriber platforms like OnlyFans to explore how this technology, mediated through the imperative of neoliberal capitalism and informed by US rape culture, can provide some independence for content creators and still be co-opted by the porn industry in ways that undermine ethical intentions and contribute to a culture of sexual violence.

First, one clear advantage of OnlyFans and similar platforms is that they offer performers a way to maintain economic control over the content they create. OnlyFans is a social media platform that works in tandem with an individual's other platforms, like Instagram and X (formerly Twitter). It allows content producers to "monetize their influence"[24] by producing special content that their fans might be willing to pay for[25] but that they would not be able sell on other social media platforms. For example, a creator might invite their Instagram or TikTok followers to "find workouts on my OnlyFans page that you can't find anywhere else!" Because OnlyFans is not a searchable site itself, to be successful, a content creator must attract people to their OnlyFans page from other social media and engage with them enough to convince them to subscribe and pay for exclusive content. Creators can make money by selling subscriptions, creating and selling custom content, earning tips for personal attention or performances, and charging for one-on-one chats. Until creators reach a higher level of subscriber engagement, they often try to balance providing free and paid content to entice their fans to subscribe. And although content creators can use their OnlyFans pages to sell any kind of exclusive content, from special workouts to home improvement videos, the platform's biggest growth—by far—has been sexual content.[26]

Unlike other social media platforms like Instagram or TikTok, OnlyFans allows content creators to process payments. It arguably offers creators little else. Danielle Blunt, a researcher, organizer, and sex worker, calls it "a glorified payment processor. . . . It's being celebrated for putting more money back into performers' hands and creating a space where performers can own and distribute their own content, but they're taking a predatory cut."[27] Only-Fans maintains that its 20% cut reflects the security and privacy costs it must absorb to host erotic content online.[28] In return, OnlyFans gives content creators control over what they produce and whom they engage.

OnlyFans promises a niche approach to porn, but, as in any free market, creators of erotic content still need to sell content that others want to buy. Consumers seem to appreciate that ethical porn performers—with whom they may have a personal relationship—are not exploited. Yet there is a tension here: in order to attract consumers, at least some content creators feel pressure to portray themselves as living lives of luxury in order to appear unexploited, even when they are not economically secure. In an interview with Berg, Shane writes,

> "[The] empowerment narrative of the 2020s isn't sex positivity . . ." but rather "raking it in," and escorts in particular project a life characterized by luxurious travel, designer clothes and other forms of conspicuous consumption. This is old-fashioned marketing, undertaken to convince clients that the service provider is worth the price they've set. It's also a marginalized population's bid for social respectability. "How can I not take a job that pays this much?" implies every posted screenshot of an OnlyFans cash-out—or, as Berg put it, "If I'm so exploited, why am I making more than you?" But above all, she said, it's a form of protection. When clients see economical vulnerability, they're more likely to push boundaries, haggle rates and behave in otherwise exploitative and abusive ways.[29]

Content creators must sell the fantasy (to consumers and perhaps to critics) that they are successful capitalists, that they are in demand, and that they are worth the prices they charge. Berg suggests that performers are also selling an image of easy sexuality unencumbered by economic need. At the same time, content creators wish to project images of luxury and wealth because hints of their own vulnerability suggest that their content can be obtained at a discount.[30] Images of luxury thus perform double duty: they soothe the consciences of consumers who profess a desire to purchase ethical porn and want to feel reassured that they are not contributing to exploitation, and they insulate content creators from those who would exploit their apparent vulnerability. Based on this logic, if the lives consumers see in the images and videos appear safe and secure, then consumers need not concern themselves with other difficulties in the lives of the performers they follow.

And even if OnlyFans creates more opportunities for economic independence, the technologies and private spaces that allow people to generate content on a platform like OnlyFans are not equally available to all. Activists and scholars observe that white, middle-class workers are more likely to have the resources and skills to participate in the creator economy,[31] while those without such access may continue to experience exploitation, violence, and insecurity doing in-person sex work or non-ethical porn.[32]

The second criterion of ethical porn is that performers consent to everything they do. On this score, OnlyFans may seem to live up to its promise because there is no director, producer, or other person making demands on the performers, who are instead free to create what they want and say no to what they don't. Recent studies report that many content creators feel empowered and enthusiastic about their work and supported by other content creators in their community.[33] Yet, as I argue in Chapter Four, the discourse of consent often conceals the exploitation of marginalized people. Obviously, I think it is important for those who engage in sex work to do so for their own reasons, without being coerced. But there are limits to consent if people are making decisions from positions of persistent inequality, exploitation, and marginalization. At the same time, I think we should be skeptical of political discourses (feminist or otherwise) that diagnose "false consciousness" and presume that no unexploited person would ever choose to participate in the ethical creation of erotic content. Therefore, we should consider the *context* in which the proclamation of consensual (and therefore ethical) porn is created and consumed to identify the boundaries of consent and highlight where it fails to live up to its liberatory promise.

Today, "ethical porn" is created and consumed on OnlyFans in a context of neoliberal capitalism, which compels creators to build a brand and scale it up. There is a danger that the market imperative will supersede the ethical one and that, despite certain important elements of consent, content creators will feel the pressure of subtle and not-so-subtle coercive forces to change what they create and how they create it. Even if direct-to-subscriber services offer more diverse and personalized erotic content, the market metric—accumulation of followers and subscribers—encourages standardization, rather than variation and dispersal. In other words, to generate sustainable revenue, producers must create products that are in high demand and therefore worth their cost. Such products might often build upon the mythic figures, discourses, and practices of US sexual culture, which includes rape culture.

While the production of porn via online platforms allows creators to develop content in the safety of their own spaces and can foster liberation from troubling sexual mores, the logic of human capital appreciation works against this liberating function. Human capital appreciation requires that, when in competition with other "human capitals," a producer will feel pressure to generate content that is legibly "popular" in order to compete, generate livable wages, and maintain their product's market value. By fostering the need to continue to grow a brand, often by standardizing content, neoliberal capitalism undercuts the liberatory promise of consent and limits the representations of potential sexual pluralities.

The third criterion of ethical porn is that it supports a plurality of sexual experiences. But the "creator economy" is not as expansively creative as one might imagine. The emergence of new social media platforms and the growth of direct-to-subscriber services like OnlyFans may indeed foster pluralism and niche sexualities, but these services also subject *everything* to commodification, such that "every aspect of human existence is produced as an entrepreneurial one,"[34] and every creator becomes "an entrepreneur *of himself*."[35] Technology interfaces with this creator economy through processes of quantification and scale that create incentives for entrepreneurs to sell themselves far and wide (or hire marketing firms to do so) in order to increase their value and "influence" and boost their chances of being found online by new consumers.

The creator economy has altered the dynamics of capitalist production and consumption. Karl Marx argued that the owners of the means of production in industrial capitalism are the exploiters because they extract surplus value from workers in order to generate profits for themselves. In a creator economy, however, the producer is the product—or, as Berg puts it, the creator must appropriate their own surplus labor.[36] In this version of capitalism, a "human capital" appreciates its own value by competing against other human capitals for consumers' attention to build a more valuable "brand." A creator economy mediated by social media measures value in followers, retweets, subscribers, and other metrics that signal the potential for the appreciation of brand value.[37] The imperative to constantly boost the value of the brand creates powerful incentives for content producers to appeal to consumers whose preferences are easily discernible, even when the producers might prefer to create unique, countercultural content. At the same time, competition requires content creators to grow their following so that they appear to be in demand. They must therefore scale up and outcompete others who are vying for the attention of a relatively homogenous audience that will purchase what they have to sell: "the typical OnlyFans user could be described as male (63.1%), white (68.9%), married (89.5%), and either heterosexual (59%) or bisexual/pansexual (37.8%)."[38] Human capitals will likely have to appeal to this audience in some way if they want to grow their brands.

New technologies also help creators find fans in niche online communities that are broadly accessible. The wide distribution of the means of online content production facilitates specialization in erotic content production, which in turn changes the structure of the relationship between consumers and producers.[39] The mainstream porn industry tends to produce content that has broad appeal because its "agents and established directors tend to have narrower visions of what sells than what the realities of the market bear out."[40] By contrast, decentralized platforms like OnlyFans have hosted erotic content that is more niche, diverse, or representative.[41] Even so, Berg observes that some content creators replicate familiar representations of mainstream porn.[42] Because profit is generated on OnlyFans through perpetual effort to build and maintain a fan base, some creators are likely to develop ever more creative or alternative representations of sex while others replicate "familiar" sexualized character types that are guaranteed to sell.

This market imperative to scale up a fan base undermines the potential to represent plural sexualities. The technologies that enable many more producers to create and sell their own content—which can, in some cases, undermine the economic exploitation integral to capitalism—can also discipline content producers and undercut the liberatory potential of direct-to-subscriber ethical content. For example, to outcompete other producers, OnlyFans content creators must sell what customers want: individualized, emotional care; access to intimate and personalized content; the promise of personal relationships; and a departure from the depersonalization of mainstream porn (where materials were distributed in theaters and video stores).[43] In other words, customers want 24/7 access to their sexual fantasies.

Customer engagement is demanding work, particularly when it comes to building relationships with new people. Through personal exchanges over social media, creators build relationships with potential subscribers, negotiate the terms of specific content, and persuade people to subscribe. Personal relationships are the bread and butter of the OnlyFans model, particularly when it comes to erotic content. Jayson Rosero, the owner of an

OnlyFans marketing firm and self-described "e-pimp," attributes the success of OnlyFans to its ability to foster personal connections that are "deeper than porn."[44] A post on his firm's website is less generous: "Hustling simps has been an art since the beginning of time!"[45] Because content creators typically direct people to their OnlyFans sites via other social media platforms, like TikTok, X, and Instagram, what they are trying to sell is exclusive content. For consumers, the allure is that the content on OnlyFans is unavailable on the performer's other social media outlets: they are getting something that is exclusive to only one or a few.

Content creators spend hours every day trying to maintain a semblance of deep personal connections to their subscribers, particularly as they try to grow their subscriber base. As Marcus explains, it is not subscriptions per se that drive a profitable Only Fans site, but one-on-one engagements:

> Money from subscriptions can be trivial compared with the profits earned by selling custom videos, sexting sessions and other forms of fan interaction that require more concerted engagement than simply posting to a feed. This can be extremely time-consuming: In an interview with this magazine last year, an OnlyFans creator said she spends six hours a day just sexting with subscribers. But these relationships are important to cultivate. In a blog post on its website, OnlyFans encourages creators to cater to their "superfans," who pay for custom content and will "give more if they feel they're getting something special."[46]

For many performers, even those who enjoy their work, the time investment is greater than they anticipated when they started.[47] In 2021, according to one study by the Avery Center, the average OnlyFans content producer made about $1,111 per month.[48] Another commentator noted that "if 10 percent of site creators earn $1,000 a month or more, 90 percent of creators take home less than $12,000 a year for what can amount to a full-time job."[49] Many performers, even those who enjoy their work, end up spending more time than they anticipated when they started,[50] often trying to draw in paid subscribers through long direct-message exchanges for which they are not paid. OnlyFans marketing and advice resources even contain recommendations for dealing with such time wasters. Well-established content creators are eventually able to charge for personal chats, but for many, this is unpaid work, performed as a "freemium" (an investment in a future subscription or other revenue).[51]

The time needed to grow a brand on a platform like OnlyFans may become unsustainable for one person alone. According to "camming"[52] model agency owner Justin Dallas, "most OnlyFans models with large followings have some kind of team in their corner. 'It becomes overwhelming consistently creating content, promoting and maintaining 20, 30, 50+ conversations daily,' [Dallas] wrote."[53] Many content creators hire "chatters" to impersonate them in online chats with subscribers.[54] OnlyFans marketing firms like Rosero's outsource the direct-message labor to chatters around the globe (often English speakers who reside in Asia and are paid meager wages), who can spend hours with clients in a way that the performer/creator cannot. In order to make a convincing case that the hired chatter is the "real thing," Rosero instructs his hired chatters to replicate specific types: "'An 18-year-old girl . . . texts different than a 25-year-old girl, you know, or an older lady. An older lady won't use emojis; she'll use, like, a semicolon and parentheses for a winky face, when a younger girl will actually use a winky emoji.'"[55] A training manual for hired chatters at Ekko DM, a social media "marketing" firm, "explained in granular detail how money is earned. 'Every page needs to have an established back story to make the person seem more believable.'"[56] As long as the performers can be marketed as reliable, sexualized characters with clear back stories, chatters can convincingly impersonate them.

To ensure that his chatters can engage consumers, Rosero typecasts his clients, often as recognizable sexual figures. Thus, rather than fostering an expansive and creative counterculture, certain market imperatives are likely to reproduce the mythic figures, discourses, and practices of US rape culture. Rosero describes his process:

> "This girl we literally just started yesterday," he said. "She started with eight subscribers. OK, now she's got 108 subscribers. You know, an older lady. But the thing is that, look, since she's blond and white skin, bro, it's easier to market her, because all over the world, they like blond girls with white skin." Rosero tries to position OnlyFans pages in line with archetypes familiar to habitual porn viewers. A model this age could be marketed as a "MILF"; someone younger, a "barely legal" teenager, or a relatable girl-next-door type.[57]

This approach makes sense in a neoliberal capitalist context in which the number of subscriptions determines the brand value. To charge higher prices and signal higher demand, content creators must scale up; by driving up subscriptions, they can charge a premium for their content. The well-known, stereotyped, racialized figures of US rape culture are easy to sell, particularly to clients who do not already have a connection to the performer. They are also easy to impersonate.

"Marketable" figures like the MILF or the "girl next door" are sexualized according to how men understand them. The MILF—a "mother I'd like to fuck"—is typically a white middle-class mother in her 30s or 40s who, as one analysis puts it, "frequent[s] malls, schools, and daycares."[58] The term "MILF," unlike other sexualized archetypes such as "cougars" or "pumas," is objectifying in the distinct sense that a MILF is the object of another's sexual desire—the "I" who has deemed her fuckable. It doesn't denote a "mother who likes to fuck" but one who is a desirable object to be fucked. As a porn archetype,[59] the appeal of the MILF is revealing since she is typically represented in a context "devoid of actual children."[60] So why might one seek a MILF rather than a woman who is DTF ("down to fuck"), for example? Unlike sexually expressive women who threaten the heteropatriarchal order, MILFs are "expected to be insatiable in the bedroom, but selfless mothers outside of it. MILF, in its marriage of 'good' motherhood with sexual objectification, thus becomes a short hand for the only acceptable, normative way to incorporate sex into motherhood."[61] I discuss male entitlement to care in the next section, but it is worth noting here that the MILF as *mother*—with all those Oedipal intimations—centralizes the woman's role as both the object of sex (who someone else would like to fuck) and the caregiver (who offers selfless attention).[62] The paradoxical appeal of the MILF is that she is hot enough to be fuckable but prioritizes the care of others and does not center her own desires (sexual or otherwise). This kind of mythic figure and imagined archetype is an easy sell to potential subscribers who recognize her and feel empowered by what she offers: simultaneous access to sexual satisfaction and selfless care.

Despite the imperative to standardize characters in order to scale up, some performers are still able to build followings by creating a distinctive "brand." Direct-to-subscriber services are more likely than the mainstream commercial porn industry to support niche sexual explorations. Yet, the broadest markets, whether in the mainstream or in the creator economy, are accessible to those who replicate widespread expectations of beauty and sexuality. Those who are "conventionally" beautiful—young, white, cisgender women or men—tend to find work that is more profitable and safer than those who are marginalized by the mainstream porn industry (and often by popular culture).[63] For influencers who share selfies, "conformance to heteronormative prescriptions of attractiveness and femininity is fundamental to gaining attention."[64] In a study of trans porn performers, anthropologist Sophie Pezzutto observes the persistence of porn aesthetics that incentivize "cis-passability" and "cis-normativity" among trans content creators.[65] Trans performers and escorts share that the camming industry is characterized more often than not by "cissexism, transmisogyny, and racism."[66] It is also overwhelmingly structured around a gender binary: many sites primarily support content from cisgender female performers,[67] even if the amateur porn industry sometimes challenges these norms.[68]

In another study, content creators on OnlyFans "suggested that white women or those with an existing audience tend to have an easier time on OnlyFans, whereas fat, disabled and racialized performers as well as straight men might have greater struggles building a following on OnlyFans and making ends meet."[69] Those who are marginalized in the mainstream industry may be willing to work for lower wages or may, instead, "manipulate racialized markers"[70] or find other ways to change their looks[71] in order to draw higher fees. Not only do these marketing approaches rely on and replicate existing tropes, discourses, and forms of marginalization; they also reveal the precarity of content creators, who may feel pressure to conform to existing sexualized norms and tropes even as they are striving to act as their own agents.

The structures of social media marketing discipline content creators even when they are selective about their working conditions and only do what they feel comfortable doing. Regardless of their preferences, creators still need to build up likes, views, and subscribers to remain competitive in the direct-to-subscriber market. One suggestive 2019 study[72] classified Instagram influencers as either established (those who had monetized their brand) or aspiring (those who had not). All of the influencers they studied presented a "porn chic aesthetic" while performing distinctive forms of emotional, sexualized, or other labor but responded differently to "sexually suggestive or aggressive" fan comments on their feeds. None of the workers deleted aggressive fan comments, which tend to drive traffic up. However, the aspiring influencers seemed to feel pressured to engage publicly with aggressive commenters, while the established influencers did not. The study suggests that content creators sometimes feel pressure to respond in ways they might otherwise avoid when they are trying to build up a following.

Others who are marginalized by the mainstream porn industry may experience adverse consequences as they try to scale up a marketable brand, especially when they are pressured to present a normatively desirable product. In her 2019 study, Pezzutto describes the tension experienced by trans performers whose economic stability in the industry often depends on their ability to conform to what Pezzutto calls its "powerful aesthetic-erotic hierarchy."[73] Because a social media influencer/gig economy requires creators to sell themselves, the self becomes the brand—thus the individual must reflect what is marketable, not necessarily what is sincere to them. For example, despite being motivated to participate in sex work to pay for gender-affirming health care that is not covered by insurance, some of Pezzutto's interviewees recounted that they opted not to undergo such care due to fears that they will not be booked or viewed. Because the most marketable trans performers have both breasts and a penis,[74] some report foregoing vaginoplasty (even if they want the procedure) for fear they will not be able to get work without a penis.[75] Some who take hormone replacement treatments reported intermittently skipping them, at risk to their personal (mental and physical) health, so that they could maintain an erection or achieve orgasm. One respondent discussed using medical means (plastic surgery) to achieve transition, while another underwent a breast augmentation that they did not want in order to be more marketable.[76] In these cases, the pressure to generate market demand and foster economic security can imperil creators' chances of obtaining a secure, gender-affirming life. Given the precarity of trans life in the United States, it is understandable that one might, having found a profession that affords them some basic security that they have struggled to find otherwise, seek to maintain it. But at the confluence of the precarity of trans life and the precarity of labor in the "gig economy," individuals' "free" choices are structured by the need for likes, follows, bookings, and subscriptions and sometimes come at great personal costs.[77]

Ultimately, the imperative to scale up via social media can discipline workers in three ways: by incentivizing them to create marketable "personas," many of which will evoke the mythic figures of rape culture; by requiring intensive one-on-one engagement that demands time and energy; and by creating pressure to grow one's brand, even at great personal cost. Although many content creators find ways to express themselves, enjoy their work, and generate income, competition for subscribers will likely drive them to at least one of these disciplining practices in order to "grow" their brand.

Unfortunately, each of these practices has the potential to reinforce the myths, discourses, and practices of rape culture.

The Customer Is Always Right: Care and Intimacy on Demand

The rapid growth of OnlyFans suggests there is a market for erotic content that feels personal and intimate. It is possible that porn consumers have always wanted this, but technology has only recently been capable of supporting it. It could also be a new market demand created by new sociocultural circumstances. Some evidence suggests that some forms of social media use may exacerbate feelings of loneliness.[78] Isolation during the COVID-19 pandemic encouraged people to use devices and social media to connect with people in new ways, though the mental health effects of these forms of sociality, especially if they replace in-person connections, are still not clear.[79] The rapid rise of OnlyFans during a global pandemic may suggest that consumers were drawn to the platform and willing to pay for content because it promised direct, individualized engagement between fans and content creators;[80] as Marcus put it, "What people really want, in the end, is someone they can imagine talking to in real life."[81] Recent studies seem to confirm that the desire for connection was a main reason that consumers flocked to the site.[82]

In many ways, the desire for personal and human relationships is a positive development for sex work and has driven many fans away from the free, uncompensated, and often non-consensual porn that is also available on the internet. Paying creators directly for labor that has historically been unremunerated[83] represents an important shift from unpaid labor to exchange. Of course, being paid for one's labor is better than not being paid at all, but in both instances, heteropatriarchal and white supremacist frameworks dictate whose labor is valuable and what work is worth paying for—and, crucially, what expectations accompany compensation.

In a free market, exchange relationships are understood to be reciprocal in the sense that each side fulfills the terms laid out in their negotiation (another form of contract). Yet reciprocity does not confer mutual care or shared obligation; as I note in Chapter Four, it can also replicate systematic inequality. Like most other kinds of relationships, those between fans and performers feature power imbalances. Performers seek subscribers, followers, likes, and revenue and often reserve the right to turn away customers who harass or bother them (one study found that content creators say they are more able to draw boundaries on OnlyFans than on other social media platforms).[84] Fans seek attention and care, but they reserve the right to walk away from performers whose content becomes unappealing or whose care is not forthcoming.

These relational imbalances make creators and consumers vulnerable to one another, but content creators disproportionately bear the imbalance in at least one important sense, even when they enjoy their interactions with fans. As in other "creator economy" industries, performers must position themselves "to strengthen [their] competitive positioning and appreciate [their] value, rather than [act] as a figure of exchange or interest."[85] In the direct-to-subscriber milieu, they can do this by fostering close relationships with fans and by promising more engagement and better content than their competitors—sometimes offering these things for free to draw new customers to their sites.[86] Yet this work imposes uncompensated costs on creators. Bonofacio et al. conclude that direct-to-subscriber services like OnlyFans differ from other forms of commerce in consumers' expectations of "constant accessibility and intimate self-disclosure" from performers.[87] Several recent studies of erotic content creation cite Arlie Russell Hochschild's work on emotional labor to explain that the preponderance of emotional work is done by performers.[88] And since online access is a 24/7 proposition, content creators may feel pressured to be accessible on social media all the time to avoid losing customers.

The same customers who seek "a connection deeper than porn" bear no reciprocal emotional burden: they can easily unsubscribe with no regard for the consequences. This dynamic reinforces the idea of "intimacy on demand" that is mediated by a free market and hypermobile technologies. Customers seek access to performers' emotional and sexual availability 24/7 and may expect their emotional and sexual whims to be addressed immediately, irrespective of the needs of the other person in the relationship, because the reciprocity is presumed to be granted by payment rather than mutual care. The promise of intimacy on demand can entrench consumers' sense of entitlement to unreciprocated care, foster the unrealistic expectation that being in a relationship means that one's emotional and sexual needs will always be met, and confirm that when one's needs are unmet, they can walk away and find another relationship.

In his 2019 study of gay sex workers on OnlyFans, film studies scholar Daniel Laurin coins the term "subscription intimacy" to refer to the "new forms of performer engagement and emotional labour [which become] yet another social media presence for [performers] to manage and further taxing adult performers who must always appear 'on' and accessible in order to maximize their earning potential in a rapidly changing adult industry."[89] As the term suggests, "subscription intimacy" is a paid, free market relationship facilitated by social media. Because fans are directed to OnlyFans from other platforms, they are likely to already have a sense of a relationship with content creators who have shared their travels, diet and fitness tips, flirty photos, or other content on social media. To many fans, sexual intimacy might thus seem like a natural extension of a developing personal relationship (which often includes one-on-one chats). Yet "subscription intimacy" is structured by the pressures of free market competition and the mechanisms of social media. This form of intimacy, rooted in exchange, presumes that fans can expect what they pay for, which they are paying for because it is not available for free elsewhere. They want to have relationships with the performers they subscribe to, and they expect these performers to be emotionally and sexually available to them. The "customer is always right," and they set the terms of customer satisfaction.

Neither Laurin nor I are suggesting that "subscription intimacy" is fake intimacy. Instead, it is a form of intimacy circumscribed by what sociologist Elizabeth Bernstein calls "bounded authenticity."[90] The belief that performers are sincere about their lives, experiences, and desires is important for customers who not only want personal interaction but also want relationships that are special, authentic, and (in some senses) real. For example, in a comparison of PornHub and OnlyFans on Medium.com, one user professes to prefer "OnlyFans for its more intimate connection with creators, 'the enthusiasm that someone puts into recording themselves getting off and then sharing it is just as exciting to me as the recording itself' he also added that 'famous porn stars are kind of scary looking' and that he looks for creators who 'genuinely enjoy it. That's what I'm personally interested in, and that's why I use OnlyFans as much as I do.'"[91] Unlike professional porn productions, this user seeks a connection that feels more amateur, and therefore more sincere and less "scary." One performer observes what he presumes is the appeal of OnlyFans compared to other sites: "Tumblr was filled with the most extreme sexual experiences you could see. . . . And I think a lot of people were turned off by that. It's not what they're looking for. They want more intimate experiences. They want a boyfriend experience. They want to fantasize about someone that they want to have sex with and not feel disgusted by it."[92] That is, the desire expressed here is for an authentic connection but without mutual obligation. The difference between having a boyfriend and having a "boyfriend experience" is in the expectation of obligation and who is obligated: with the "experience," one gets the (admittedly temporary) benefit of an intimate connection driven by one's own wants and needs without the emotional or sexual cost of tending to or fulfilling a partner's needs.

As Bernstein notes, for those who seek it, the appeal of the boyfriend/girlfriend experience is *bounded* in the sense that it is sequestered from the rest of one's life and, one assumes, from the obligations of "real life." These can be intimate and authentic connections, but they are "bounded" by time and space; and both parties will eventually walk away from them.[93] As Bernstein's 2007 study makes clear, the desire for "bounded authenticity" is transforming sex workers' relationships with their clients. What is different about online direct-to-subscriber services involving erotic content (and not necessarily physical contact) is that technology now permits, and the imperatives of free market competition require, this kind of intimacy to occur *on demand*.

As many scholars, activists, and sex workers point out, there is nothing exceptional about porn work when it comes to the maneuvers and adjustments that workers must make to survive precarious economic conditions.[94] The "gig economy" promises consumers that they can get anything, anytime, anywhere: whether it is a ride, same-day grocery delivery, or online therapy.[95] Service providers therefore feel pressure to be available 24/7 so that they don't lose out on revenue. In this regard, porn is like any other industry.[96] This hyper-individuated economy allows us to get exactly what we want, when we want, on our own terms. But when the product being sold is 24/7 access to a hyper-personalized, non-reciprocal, intimate relationship, more than the creator's subscriber base is being scaled up: a discourse and practice of male entitlement to sex is also being scaled up. This is intimacy *on demand*, without obligation to others.

Feminist philosopher Kate Manne's concept of entitlement highlights the consequences of an expanding expectation of intimacy on demand. Manne focuses on male entitlement, which she describes as a dynamic in which "women are expected to *give* traditionally feminine goods (such as sex, care, nurturing, and reproductive labor) to designated, often more privileged men, and to refrain from taking traditionally masculine goods (such as power, authority, and claims to knowledge) away from them. These goods can in turn be understood as those to which privileged men are tacitly deemed *entitled*."[97] Male entitlement is often paired with another form of entitlement: "white entitlement."[98] Entitlement is an assumption that one is *owed* certain kinds of support and goods from others and that one is entitled to claim them, through violent means if necessary. It is also a marker of political power: those who feel a sense of entitlement do so because they already occupy a dominant position in social hierarchies structured by race, class, and gender and expect those who are subordinate to them in these hierarchies to support them.

Manne cautions that male entitlement has real and material consequences for those who are expected to extend unreciprocated care, power, sex, or other resources to men. Building on Manne's work, I argue that in US rape culture, male entitlement contributes to sexual violence because it is a central mechanism through which gendered violence and discrimination manifests. Manne conceptualizes misogyny as a related, intersectional phenomenon that is expressed differently across groups.[99] For example, feminist scholar Moya Bailey defines misogynoir as "the uniquely co-constitutive racialized and sexist violence that befalls Black women as a result of their simultaneous and interlocking oppression at the intersection of racial and gender marginalization."[100] Activist Julia Serano defines trans-misogyny as a form of discrimination in which "a trans person is ridiculed or dismissed not merely for failing to live up to gender norms, but for their expressions of femaleness or femininity."[101] Each form of misogyny operates as a policing of bodies that dictates what those bodies should and should not do, where, and with whom; and each reflects different aspects of male entitlement.

In US rape culture, entitlement to care and sex often looks like the prioritization of the care and sexual needs of men.[102] Often, it is justified via the discourse of heteropatriarchal protection I identified in Chapter Two: men provide physical protection to women and girls (against the violence enabled by white heteropatriarchal capitalism), and in return they are entitled to certain kinds of care, including sexual attention. One insidious aspect of the discourse of male entitlement is that it tells women and girls that prioritizing and providing care to men is the way to be(come) a good woman (and, as I also note in Chapter Two, a good woman is one who serves heteropatriarchy as a wife, mother, sister, or daughter). It holds women responsible for the emotional health of men (as when, in an example I'll detail below, a prominent social influencer takes it upon herself to "cure loneliness" among her predominantly male fanbase),[103] provides countless popular cultural examples of women as helpmates to men who don't get or need credit for their efforts, and encourages women to set their own needs aside to prioritize giving men what they are entitled to. Moreover, women are expected to be grateful for the protection against heteropatriarchal violence that men provide—through heteropatriarchal violence.

Male entitlement is also reproduced through heteronormative practices like the extension of "himpathy" to perpetrators of sexual violence and the "herasure" of victims from their own stories (such as prioritizing concern for Brock Turner at the expense of Chanel Miller, as discussed in Chapter One).[104] Victim blaming is another practice of entitlement, according to Manne, because their ostensibly insatiable, uncontrollable, natural sexual aggressiveness entitles men to sex but holds the feminized objects of male desire responsible for preventing sexual violence.[105] Similarly, the assumption that consent is implied unless expressly rescinded or denied and many women's tendency to "go along" rather than endanger themselves in precarious sexual situations are the result of male entitlement to sex.[106]

The expectation of male entitlement to emotional support and care on demand requires women, girls, and other feminized persons to satisfy the wants, needs, and emotional health of entitled men *at the expense of* their own wants, needs, and emotional health. Certainly, people tend to the wants, needs, and emotional health of their loved ones all the time—and sometimes set aside their own needs to do so—but male entitlement to care is different because of the expectation that, as a rule, men are entitled to unreciprocated care.

The 24/7, on-demand intimacy afforded by direct-to-subscriber platforms like OnlyFans encourages content creators to prioritize customers' emotional and sexual needs as a market imperative. The expectation that the customer's needs take priority over those of others is central to any claim of entitlement to emotional and sexual care. The new market and technological mechanisms of direct-to-subscriber services for erotic content cultivate this expectation of emotional and sexual care. For example, while many consumers of OnlyFans feel obligated to pay for content, some take advantage of performers' sense that they need to show care in order to earn revenue (rather than to get paid first and then provide the service of care). Some performers are willing to engage with fans before they are compensated, but some fans make payment contingent on interacting with performers first:

> Sex buyers expect personalized interactions on OnlyFans and social media before purchasing content. One content creator elaborated to sex buyers on

> the discussion forum about the expectations for emotional labor: "I had a free Snapchat for a few weeks. All I got were gents thinking they could chat endlessly with me with no intent to ever book." *Buyers confirmed this, giving advice to content creators relating to emotional laboring*: "Spend a lot of time building up fans on Twitter etc. Pics get the eyeballs, interactions gets [sic] the credit card though."[107]

Content creators must engage in unpaid labor in hopes of being paid, but there is no guarantee that they will. The fact that buyers were offering advice along these lines suggests a curious relationship: at once an intimate relationship in which one participant offers friendly advice to another and a consumer relationship in which one only pays when one wishes.

Performers must also *appear* to be interested even when they are not: they must be warm, engaging, and kind to give customers the boyfriend or girlfriend experience they seek.[108] Maintaining the new forms and levels of personal interactions with fans that are required from direct-to-subscriber services can take a toll on performers,[109] who often set aside their own exhaustion to keep customers engaged. The expectation of intimacy, emotional labor, and constant access is tiring, even when they enjoy their fan interactions.

In some cases, subscribers' expectations of unfettered virtual access to care and sex may translate into expectations about real-life access and sexual assault. Since OnlyFans is a subscription service, content producers must draw followers from other social media platforms. Therefore, some subscribers may know the producer personally or live in the same location. One performer shared that she developed a justifiable fear that her subscribers might come to expect to be able to assault her:

> [Her] posts started innocently enough: A shot in her underwear or in a bikini wouldn't hurt anyone, she thought, right? The pictures weren't far off from what she was already posting on Instagram. But it wasn't long before she realized that being on OnlyFans would bring consequences, some of them disturbing. She sighs as she recounts how men who recognized her from the site tried to grope her in public. She became afraid that being on the site would make strangers feel that they had the right to assault her.[110]

For this content creator, the expectation of access—to her care, her attention, and eventually, her body—was likely nurtured by the subscriber intimacy of OnlyFans, where at least one of her subscribers developed a sense of entitlement to sex.

Another performer reported something common to many erotic performers: a fan will steal screenshots of erotic content and then sell or distribute them without consent or payment. A content creator named Claudia "discovered that one of her main 'clients' had made a pornographic meme out of one of her topless photographs and posted it on a porn site. 'He actually sent it to me, all proud. I tried to complain to [OnlyFans] but I never heard from them. I emailed them five times. In the end I gave up and deleted my account.'"[111] Some subscribers come to perceive entitlement to sexual or financial gratification, to some form of ownership over the bodies and images of the performers they engage with, irrespective of the performers' wants and desires.

The hyper-personalization of the direct-to-subscriber porn market can reinforce expectations about entitlement to care and on-demand sexual availability, both of which are foundational practices of US rape culture. Content creators must offer intimacy, care, and sexual availability at any time of day or night. This expectation is not limited to female creators and male consumers. As I've noted throughout this chapter, qualitative studies of queer, trans, and cis heterosexual content creators suggest that, irrespective of the creator's gender, at least some consumers develop deep senses of unreciprocated entitlement to care and sexual availability; what's worse, they do so in a context that convinces them they are being *ethical*. The structure of direct-to-consumer services mediated by social media contributes to this sense of entitlement because there is virtually no expectation of reciprocity or mutual obligation beyond payment, and even that is contingent upon continued access and engagement.

The emergence of artificial intelligence (AI) technologies portends even more profound changes to gig economy work. While AI and direct-to-subscriber erotic content are not the same, both focus on hyper-personalization so that consumers get exactly what they want. For example, in May 2023, social media influencer Caryn Marjorie launched CarynAI, a "virtual girlfriend"[112] chatbot designed to mimic Marjorie's "voice, mannerisms, and personality." For a dollar a minute, Marjorie's 98% male fanbase can get "personal attention" from CarynAI, which Marjorie anticipates will help "cure loneliness" among her fans. The beta test was quite popular and reportedly earned Marjorie nearly $72,000 in its first week.[113] Forever Voices, the company that developed CarynAI using Marjorie's existing online content, describes this venture as just the beginning of a "new AI companion initiative, meant to provide users with a girlfriend-like experience that fans can emotionally bond with."[114] Upon release of the chatbot, Marjorie tweeted:

> Men are told to suppress their emotions, hide their masculinity, and to not talk about issues they are having . . . I vow to fix this with CarynAI. I have worked with the world's leading psychologists to seamlessly add [cognitive behavioral therapy] and [dialectic behavior therapy] within chats. This will help undo trauma, rebuild physical and emotional confidence, and rebuild what has been taken away by the pandemic.[115]

In other words, the new "girlfriend experience" now includes cognitive therapy, available 24/7, for only a dollar a minute.

CarynAI has been marketed as an "extension of Caryn's consciousness" that can be "accessed anytime, anywhere" and is "always here for you."[116] The chatbot is designed to "wind down" conversations after about an hour, but some users are spending hours a day on it.[117] CarynAI's accessibility and seemingly infinite responsiveness aim to center the wants and needs of the customer. Obviously, one does not need to concern oneself with mutual obligation when talking to a chatbot, but this practice of talking to someone who is not a person has real consequences. Recent studies of "personal assistant" technologies have found evidence that people feel comfortable speaking in abusive terms to them, particularly when they are gendered female. Indeed, there is preliminary evidence that people project human traits onto virtual assistants.[118] What happens when the "personal assistant" is an intimate, sexualized chatbot?[119] And what about when the AI is designed to look and act like an actual person with whom one already has a "relationship"?

Moreover, despite Marjorie's intention to "cure loneliness," it is not clear that all of CarynAI's subscribers are interested in deep conversations about their feelings. CarynAI uses end-to-end encryption, so Marjorie does not know what CarynAI tells subscribers unless the subscribers share it with her.[120] Days after the initial launch, Marjorie learned that at least some users were engaged in sexually explicit conversations with CarynAI, even though the AI had not been programmed to conduct such conversations;[121] and Marjorie has stated that she "doesn't want that to become the service's dominant feature."[122] (Replika, another AI chatbot, has also had difficulties trying to navigate users' desires for erotic engagement with their "personal assistants" while ensuring the chatbot remains safe for all users.[123]) In other words, irrespective of what the AI is trained to do, customers are seeking sexually erotic content. It is too soon to tell what will happen as these technologies are refined and, perhaps, subjected to regulation. Yet it is important to consider the consequences of made-to-order, fully customizable, AI-generated intimate relationships in a culture in which sexual violence is used to maintain the structure of domination through white supremacy, heteropatriarchy, and capitalism.

As I discuss in Chapter Four, entitlement to sex and care is already being radicalized and spread online through men's rights activist, incel, and other groups. Direct-to-subscriber porn has the potential to foster this entitlement in a new way: the veneer of ethical porn consumption will likely reinforce "everyday" expectations of 24/7 entitlement to care and sexual availability with no sense of mutual obligation or reciprocity. AI is likely to intensify the male entitlement to 24/7 care that comes from scaling up personal, unique, and intimate conversations with none of the obligation, risk, or reciprocity required of real human relationships. Such technologies may not lead directly to sexual violence, but like direct-to-subscriber services, they are likely to intensify the myths, discourses, and practices of heteropatriarchy, misogyny, and white supremacy that do. As long as creators must scale up their customer base to stay competitive, the customer will always be "right": a logic that reinforces the idea of male (heteropatriarchal) and white supremacist domination in sexual relations, which can often lead to sexual violence.

Conclusion

In US rape culture, "sex positivity" and "ethical porn" are frequently reduced to marketized proclamations of sexual liberation that often emerge out of pressure to create content that appeals to consumers. Imperatives to scale up the product and to offer intimacy on demand contribute to a deepening and widening fantasy of male sexual entitlement to care and sexual availability, which—under the guise of an "ethical" product—may convince consumers that their sense of entitlement is non-exploitative. Neoliberal, direct-to-subscriber "ethical porn" may help portray entitlement to dominate as ethical (or natural or acceptable). But this is not inevitable.

It is exciting to think that we may be on the horizon of what gender and sexual studies scholar Lynn Comella describes as "an altogether new world of sexual imaginings and possibilities."[124] Sex-positive imaginings can be a vital resource in opposing US rape culture, particularly if they emphasize practices of mutuality and reciprocity alongside creativity, generosity, and generativity. Therefore, we should not rule out the possibility that sexually dissident styles can foster sexual liberation. Since they *could* promote cultural practices as forms of political resistance against rape culture, it would be a mistake to write them off as inherently at odds with sexual liberation and the end of sexual violence.

Yet, as long as porn is co-opted by the imperatives of neoliberal capital exchange in a heteropatriarchal and white supremacist context, it has a limited ability to foster ethical, sexual emancipation. In this context, content creators are both producers and product and must compete with other "human capitals" to attract and maintain subscribers. To do this, they must often replicate the mythic figures of rape culture and provide unreciprocated care and intimacy on demand. Consumers, who may sincerely desire personal connection, become accustomed to "subscriber intimacy," in which their desires can be satisfied 24/7 somewhere on the internet without obligation to another person.

Chapter Six
"Change is relational and rarely immediate"
Dismantling Rape Culture

What Shall We Do?

Whenever I share this work, I am asked some variation of the question *What can we do about rape culture?* I understand why. I have described a pervasive phenomenon, deeply embedded in foundational structures and practices. I have explored long histories and enduring myths and shown how they adapt and persist over time. And when groups like the Alliance Defending Freedom say they seek "generational wins" for their values by stacking courts and writing ghost legislation, it is clear that they are in it for the long haul. So it is understandable that some readers would react to this book by asking what kinds of reforms we could advance to secure our own "generational wins" against rape culture and against sexual violence.

At the same time, no one who is reading this book needs a reminder that rape is *already* against the law in the United States. It is *already* widely condemned as wrong. And still it is commonplace. Legal remedies and showy condemnations of sexual violence have not prevented rape from occurring; they may not have even diminished it over time. Many efforts to prevent sexual violence, such as consent apps, actually enable sexual violence by replicating the myths, discourses, and practices of rape culture. Efforts to live beyond normativities, such as through pluralistic sexual expressions, are easily co-opted by the imperatives of neoliberal capitalism. One thing this study has made clear to me is that the standard institutional tools of political change are not up to the task of dismantling rape culture because they are precisely designed to *protect* its myths, discourses, and practices instead. How, then, can we dismantle rape culture?

In Chapter One, I discuss Sherry Ortner's "practice theory" of culture, which defines culture as a dialectical synthesis of ideas and practices. If this is right, then cultures change when adherents reflexively change their ideas and practices. Up to now, this book has focused on identifying how rape culture normalizes domination through sexual violence. In other words, it has been a call for us to change our ideas about how culture supports sexual violence. As Jacqueline Rose observes (and as I shared in Chapter One), sexual violence "relies for its persistence on a refusal to acknowledge that it is even there."[1] To me, this means that part of the ideational change we need is to insist that rape culture *is there* and to understand the complex ways it operates. Throughout the book, I have modeled an approach for how to undertake intersectional analysis about rape culture. My hope is that others will find it useful and will take up (and improve) this approach to continue to uncover the operations of rape culture. Through this critical work, we can continue to change our ideas about sexual violence and how it persists.

To change our practices *in light of those new ideas* requires that we look beyond what we do now because—as a colleague once told me—an institution is designed to get exactly the results that it gets.[2] Rape culture *is* the result that our institutions get; efforts to address rape culture through those same institutions—the ones that have deep historical roots in white supremacy, heteropatriarchy, settler colonialism, and capitalist exploitation—are very likely to be co-opted to those same ends.

This chapter explores the countercultural praxis of Indigenous and Black feminist activists as sources of inspiration for how we might collectively help dismantle US rape culture. I start by exploring how misogynoir, "the anti-Black and misogynistic representation of Black women,"[3] allows Black women to be misnamed and disregarded. I return to Anita Hill's experience at Clarence Thomas's Supreme Court confirmation hearing in 1991 because it was a watershed moment for Black feminist analysis. I revisit this moment because by understanding how these scholars' reflections changed *ideas*, we can begin to see how those ideas change and are changed by *practice*. Next, I explore four countercultural practices that have disrupted US rape culture in large and small ways: the survivor-support work represented by the Barrette Project, the Survivors' Agenda Initiative, the "red handprint," and Tarana Burke's "me too" Movement offer generative insights and inspiration for how differently marginalized people can develop their own creative challenges to US rape culture. I understand these practices (even if those who undertake them do not necessarily think of them this way) as related to and in conversation with an abolitionist political project because they recognize the limitations of institutional and state-centered reforms.

I don't present this chapter as *the* answer to the question about dismantling rape culture, in part because I doubt there is a singular answer to such a multifaceted question and in part because I am in no position to know what such an answer should be. There is no quick fix to changing an entire culture, but there is consistent, everyday praxis that invites and encourages change. We can find insights in the practices and words of survivors and their advocates, who are engaging in world-making when they tell their stories, offer their care to others, or identify the kinds of support they need. We can find particular inspiration from those whose marginalization within the dominant culture has led them to forge pathways outside it. This chapter highlights a few stars in a constellation of practices of resistance and reimagination that, through assiduous enactment and expansion, and as inspiration for other practices, may enable us to dismantle rape culture.

Multiple Misnamings: Misogynoir in US Rape Culture

Consider how two women, with the same perpetrator, have to navigate their experiences of sexual violence *and* their storytelling about it differently. In *We Need to Talk about Cosby*, documentarian and comedian W. Kamau Bell asks an African American woman named Eden Tirl, "when [Cosby] finally gets sent to prison, what did that feel like? Did it feel like a victory?" Tirl, a victim of Bill Cosby's sexual harassment, pauses, shakes her head, and says:

> It felt awful. It felt really sad. It felt like . . . I mean, look, the reality is, is that he needed to go to prison. He's a criminal. But was I at home cheering? No, I was, I was, like, this is one of the worst—uh—this is just a sad day in the history of Black culture. Actually, really more than anything what I felt sad about is what it did to Black, to our Black culture. And I said to my husband, I just said, "this sucks."[4]

The viewer feels the weight of Tirl's ambivalence as she draws her reluctant conclusion: Cosby's incarceration was a loss for Black culture. The film then cuts to another victim, a white woman named Patricia Leary Steuer, whose reaction to the same question is to express disbelief at the verdict, given her fear that Cosby's wealth and fame would ensure his exoneration: "[my husband and I] just stood there crying because neither one of us believed this would ever happen. Ever, ever, ever."[5]

Tirl and Steuer had different personal experiences with Cosby: he sexually harassed Tirl and sexually assaulted Steuer. The two women share a sense that he deserves to be called to account but also express very different reactions to the verdict: while Tirl focuses outward, on how a rape accusation will affect the health and well-being of Black culture and community, Steuer expresses her relief that a rich, powerful man was actually punished. Their reactions highlight why we must think about sexual violence and rape culture intersectionally and how individuals bear different burdens—in both their experience of sexual violence and their experience of how US rape culture will respond to how they talk about that experience. We need to be able to raise several questions all at once: how the wealth, fame, and collective adoration of a particular, exceptional Black man (who an interviewee in Bell's documentary observes was revered as "America's Dad," not "America's *Black* Dad") allowed him to victimize several dozen women over many decades; how his victims did not speak up for fear that he would wield his power and influence to punish them; how his wealth and fame could very well have resulted in his exoneration (and at least did help him secure an early release); how a white woman might consider her marginalization with respect to her gender and class; how a Black woman must also consider her race, perhaps even reading her own experience as subsidiary to the effect Cosby's incarceration will have on the broader Black culture; how so little social-level care is available for Black women, even though they experience sexual violence at disproportionately high rates in the United States; how as a Black man, Kamau Bell, is able to raise the question about Cosby without experiencing misogynoir; how white women seem to be both willfully ignorant of the ways they have historically weaponized false rape accusations against Black men and keenly aware that they are likely to be believed when they make such accusations; how Black people, deeply aware of that history, might react skeptically (and even misogynistically) to accusations against a beloved elder in the community; how white people could deploy racist rhetoric to reinforce vicious stereotypes about Black people; and how it took dozens upon dozens of credible stories of abuse before US popular culture would pay attention to the accusations against "America's Dad." This single juxtaposition reveals the myriad operations of US rape culture and the ways it reproduces white supremacy, heteropatriarchy, and class dominance as it pits marginalized and victimized persons against one another. It reveals why we need to be able to hear and learn from complex stories about sexual violence.

For a culture to change—a culture in which we are all implicated—we need to change our interpersonal practices and radically reimagine our structures. When we ask how to counteract the hegemonic stories of sexual violence that pervade US rape culture, we need to consider how to build communal practices and storytelling opportunities that support a multiplicity of voices, experiences, images, and stories that call the misapprehensions of US culture into question. Those same communal practices obligate those who have not been victims of sexual violence to hear those stories in different and complex ways and to resist easy judgments based on the myths and discourses of rape culture. Put differently, we must commit to a critical praxis that merges our critical *thinking* about rape culture with critical *action* to dismantle it.[6]

Black feminist thought has long emphasized the relationship between structural oppression and the individual experiences of those who live it. In *Intersectionality: An Intellectual History*, Ange-Marie Hancock describes phenomena such as power and gender violence as "simultaneously pervasive and highly specific in [their] enactment."[7] They are *pervasive* in the sense that they are structurally embedded and *specific* because they are individually articulated and experienced. The pairing of the pervasive with the specific is foundational to intersectional analysis, which theorizes from both locations and recognizes that distinctive knowledge emerges from each. Through analysis at the individual (or specific) level, intersectional approaches reveal the dynamics at the pervasive level which reveals that the "major systems of oppression are interlocking."[8]

One crucial insight of intersectional analysis is that, as individuals, Black women occupy multiple, simultaneous subject-positions, each of which can be marginalizing.[9] These multiple subject-positions have different resonances, and in combination they form distinctive patterns of marginalization. We cannot understand the effect of these multiple positions by simply "adding up" oppressions. Instead, we must look for patterns and relationships. Literary critic Hortense Spillers identifies a pattern of pervasive "misnamings" of Black women in the United States, which have material impacts on their lives as specific targets and victims of sexual violence and other forms of violence.[10] Spillers explains that the phrase "Black woman" can "isolate overdetermined nominative properties"[11] that are a unique inheritance of chattel slavery. By dehumanizing, ungendering, and defacing enslaved persons,[12] the agents of chattel slavery constructed a unique incoherence around the Black woman who "stands *in the flesh*, both mother and mother dispossessed."[13] They are *mothers* because they are biological reproducers of slave labor but mothers *dispossessed* both because they pass their legal dispossession on to their children through the principle of *partus sequitur ventrem* and because they have no guarantee they will be able to provide maternal care to their children since either mother or child can be sold and sent away at any time.[14]

This contradiction renders the Black enslaved woman both hypervisible and invisible in the white, slaveholding imagination: she is hypervisible as a forced reproducer of enslaved labor who stands exposed and often unclothed on an auction block but invisible as a human who has both the need and capacity to care for herself, her children, or other family members (as opposed to her white owners or employers). According to Spillers, contemporary myths of Black womanhood in US popular culture continue to render Black women simultaneously hypervisible and invisible. This practice of misogynoir situates Black women in a network of both/and, human/dehumanized, and gendered/ungendered contradictions—all at the same time.

Subsequent analyses by Black women scholars have explored these "overdetermined" inheritances of chattel slavery. Political scientist Melissa Harris-Perry details three mythic figures of the Black woman, each of which shapes collective perceptions of Black women's victimhood and believability: caregiving Mammy, hyper-sexualized Jezebel, and angry Sapphire.[15] Wahneema Lubiano, a scholar of African and African American studies and gender and queer studies, identifies two more mythic Black women: the "black lady" and the "welfare queen," both of whom are blamed (for different reasons!) for the decline of the (heteropatriarchal) African American family.[16] Today, Black women are misnamed in contradictory terms: as maternal and caregiving; conciliatory, subservient, and menial; sexless and genderless;[17] hyper-sexualized and "pornotroped";[18] bestial, ugly, and strange (though also, given her proximity to private white spaces, likely to be exposed to sexual harassment and assault);[19] traitorous to her race;[20] counterinsurgent and resistant;[21] and/or dominant, belligerent, and emasculating.[22] These misnamings form what Collins calls "a nexus of controlling images"[23] that expose Black women to "erasure and contradiction."[24]

Dr. Anita Hill's testimony at Clarence Thomas's Supreme Court nomination hearing in 1991 exemplifies Black women's subjection to multiple misnamings. Hill, a Black woman, accused Thomas, a Black man, of sexually harassing her when he was her supervisor at the Equal Employment

Opportunity Commission (EEOC). In response to this accusation, Thomas likened the hearing to a lynching—a remarkable claim, considering that lynching was a white supremacist strategy to control Black men who posed an imagined sexual threat to *white* women. Thomas deployed this powerful image in his hearing to suggest that he was victimized by the Senate Judiciary Committee's consideration of Hill's accusations, despite the fact that "allegations relating to the sexual abuse of black women have had nothing to do with the history of lynching, a tradition based upon white hysteria regarding black male access to white women."[25] The horror of the image stuck, of course, and Thomas was "deified," while Hill was "vilified."[26]

Thomas's statement only briefly mentions Hill before Thomas turns to what he calls a "second, more important point"—condemning the confirmation process as a "high tech lynching for uppity blacks." If you dare to think for yourself, he says, "you will be lynched, destroyed, caricatured by a committee of the US—US Senate, rather than hung from a tree."[27] Patricia Hill Collins observes that Thomas's suggestion that the panel of senators was responsible for this "high tech lynching" actually erased the specific racialized and gendered dynamics of the practice of lynching in the United States.[28] Thomas deploys the horrors of white supremacy (which he takes pains to deny in subsequent court decisions) to suggest that Hill is a pawn of white supremacy and therefore cannot be trusted when she says he sexually harassed her.[29] (The Moynihan Report makes the same move when it simultaneously blames Black women for the downfall of the Black community and suggests they are wholly powerless within the system.[30]) Thomas renders Hill invisible in this moment: he denies her agency, experience, and truth. Yet Hill is also rendered hypervisible throughout the hearing through contradictory characterizations that she is simultaneously an over-rational witness, an over-sexed "woman scorned," and an over-ambitious race traitor. In this context, Lubiano explains, it was Thomas, not Hill, who served white supremacy when he *chose* to act as "a minstrel—not as an unwitting or ignorant dupe but as a power figure who drew on and articulated—from behind his black skin surface—white state power."[31]

There were at least three crucial misnamings of Hill in the hearing. First, although (or because) Dr. Hill is a gifted, well-educated law professor, she was misnamed as a "Black lady." This characterization is a misnaming in the sense that it was deployed to suggest that Hill was too reserved, intelligent, and in control to be trusted.[32] In the 2016 HBO film *Confirmation* about Thomas's confirmation hearing, one scene captures a dilemma of being a "Black lady": as a group of female staffers watch Hill's testimony, one of them, a white woman, asks: "You think she should be more emotional?" Another, a Black woman, replies: "If she were, we'd be saying she should be less emotional."[33] Many professional women face the dilemma of being "just emotional enough," but only Black women face the unique risk of being misnamed as an angry Black woman (Sapphire) if they display too much emotion, passion, or intensity. Consequently, Hill had to remain unflappable.

Several decades after the Thomas hearing, a white, educated, professional woman, Dr. Christine Blasey Ford, was differently misnamed; as a white, middle-class woman, Ford was apparently too sympathetic to be written off as a false accuser of another nominee but still not compelling enough to be believed. Republicans on the Senate Judiciary Committee hired a woman, Maricopa County (AZ) prosecutor Rachel Mitchell, to question Ford during her testimony rather than question her themselves and risk appearing to harass a white female witness.[34] Later, in their rebuttal questioning of Judge Kavanaugh, the Republican committee members declared that Ford either was a helpless victim of unscrupulous Democrats[35] or had misunderstood or misremembered what had happened in the past.[36] As a white woman, Blasey Ford's testimony was dismissed on the grounds that she was a fallible or pliable witness. This is a different kind of controlling image (to use Collins's term), one rooted in the white supremacist "cult of true womanhood"[37] that renders white women weak. In contrast, as the "Black lady," Hill was too calm and collected to be believed, and (like many sexual violence survivors) she was doubted because she was too poised to convince the committee of all-white, all-male US senators that she was a sexual harassment survivor.

The second misnaming of Hill was to blame her for betraying her race in the name of personal ambition. By making public allegations against a Black man who had been nominated to the highest court in the land, many white people used her perceived "ambition at any expense" to distrust Hill's testimony as self-interested; many Black people cited it as race treachery (as if she had put her own advancement ahead of Thomas's and the Black community more generally). Similar to Eden Tirl's sense of concern about Bill Cosby's conviction, Hill was expected to bear the burden of protecting the Black community, even at her own expense. When she testified against Thomas, some in the community condemned Hill for undermining Black men in public.[38]

While Thomas presented himself as an admirable Horatio Alger figure by virtue of his educational achievement and upward class mobility,[39] these same traits rendered Hill "inauthentic."[40] Her considerable professional achievements were dismissed by white and Black observers alike as a function of affirmative action, with the implication that Hill should be blamed for taking jobs from *both* deserving white people and deserving Black men.[41] (In fact, Hill had heard this argument before, when she earned teaching positions at Oral Roberts University and the University of Oklahoma.[42]) The only explanation for her success, it was decided, must be her skill at scheming and manipulation.

The timing of Hill's testimony was also taken as evidence of her unfettered ambition and untrustworthiness. When several Republican members of the Senate Judiciary Committee asked Hill why she had not come forward earlier, Hill replied that she had never intended to come forward and only made her experiences known when approached by the committee, several years after she left the EEOC.[43] Hill had come forward reluctantly and, as she said at the time, out of a sense of duty.[44] But her words did not carry weight. The characterization of her as an over-ambitious Black women forced Hill into another impossible bind: she was so ambitious that either she chose to endure rather than leave an abusive employment situation or she was fabricating allegations now that Thomas was in the spotlight. If the former, Hill could not be trusted to tell the truth because ambitious people will say anything to get ahead; if the latter, she was an opportunist, lying for personal gain. Either way, she could not be trusted. Crenshaw observes that "anger and resentment toward Hill was reflected in opinions of commentators traversing the political spectrum *within* black political discourses. Liberal, centrist, and conservative opinion seemed to accept a view of Hill as disloyal and even treasonous."[45] And Hill herself recognized that her attempt to explain herself to Senator Arlen Specter was "useless, for whatever I said he would doubt. Even inconsequential responses met with his skepticism."[46] In other words, regardless of her self-presentation or her rationale for coming forward, Hill was going to be misnamed in a way that rendered her suspect.

Remarkably, a third misnaming was possible by virtue of the nexus of contradictory, controlling images of Black womanhood. In the exact same context in which she was criticized for being too rational, too calculating, and too unemotional, Hill was also characterized as a hyper-sexualized jezebel.[47] Some senators explicitly suggested that Hill was unbelievable because she was sex-crazed. She was accused of erotomania and delusions,[48] and Senator Howell Heflin asked her whether she was "a woman scorned."[49] This question must have left quite an impression on Hill because it is the first story she recounts in her memoir about the hearings.[50] She also noted the sexism at work in this line of questioning: while Senators Danforth and Specter raised the suggestion that she suffered from erotomania (that is, that she was harboring a delusion that Thomas was in love with her), no one insinuated the same of John Doggett, a character witness for Thomas, who testified that Hill had unrequited romantic feelings for *him* (Doggett).[51] Throughout the hearing, Hill was villainized and discounted, while Thomas proclaimed himself a victim. The confluence of misnamings imposed on Hill gave almost every audience a way to disbelieve her.

As Hill's treatment shows, within the "nexus of controlling images" that flood US popular culture, a Black woman must assume she will be misnamed. In US rape culture, these misnamings do material harm: they contribute to both pervasive and specific myths of the untrustworthiness of victims (especially if they are women; even more if they are Black women) and perpetuate broadly racist stereotypes about hyper-sexed non-white persons. The myth of the hyper-sexual Black woman even extends to Black girls. According to one 2017 study:

> [A]dults viewed Black girls "as less innocent and more adult-like than White girls of the same age, especially between 5 and 14 years old." When compared with White girls, Black girls were perceived as: needing less nurturing, protection, support and comfort; being more independent and knowing more about adult topics, including sex. Further, Black women have the second highest rate of sexual violence in the country, with 60 percent of Black girls experiencing some form of coercive sexual contact before the age of 18.[52]

Relatedly, Professor Safiya Noble finds evidence of "algorithmic oppression" not only in how search engines produce racist and sexist results but in how misogynoir manifests in the "pornification" of Black women and girls via online comments and message boards and other anti-Black forms of digital representation.[53] The harm done to Black women and girls by the misnamings they endure continues to contribute to disproportionate targeting and sexual violence.

Although Hill is a powerful example of what happens to Black women who make public allegations against Black men, her story is not new. Before emancipation, it was not a crime in the United States to rape Black enslaved women. Since that time, Black women have not fared well when they have accused white men of sexual violence. In the rare instances when Black women have achieved legal remedy, it is usually because white men have corroborated their stories. When there is no such corroboration, assailants' accounts are usually believed instead. Six white men raped Recy Taylor in 1944, but no one was ever arrested because her assailants said they had paid her for sex.[54] In contrast, in 1959, four white men raped Betty Jean Owens, but because local law enforcement had caught them in the act, they were charged and punished for their crimes.[55] Similarly, Joann Little's remarkable murder acquittal in 1975 was contingent upon the fact that she was locked in a jail cell with a police officer when she was raped and had defended herself against her assailant.[56] In each of the cases in which the courts considered Black women believable enough to convict their assailants, their word alone was not sufficient evidence of their assaults. This distrust endures: as Kimberlé Crenshaw explains, the confluence of controlling images of Black women contributes to jurors' ongoing distrust of Black women rape victims in US courtrooms.[57]

The more recent case of Oklahoma City police officer Daniel Holtzclaw reveals the treacherous consequence of the myths of Black womanhood in US rape culture today: Black women are targets of sexual violence precisely because they are always already constructed as untrustworthy. Holtzclaw targeted Black women who had had recent involvement in the criminal justice system because he was confident that they would be unlikely to report the crimes and even less likely to be believed.[58] For several months, he targeted and assaulted victims with impunity.

Despite the sheer number of accusations from Black women, many people remain unconvinced that Holtzclaw engaged in criminal behavior;[59] like Hill, these Black women were characterized as untrustworthy witnesses. Although investigators eventually found thirteen women who were willing to testify against Holtzclaw, many others were reluctant to come forward because they knew they would not be believed not only because of their own subject-positions but because Holtzclaw was a cop.[60]

It was the second accusation against Holtzclaw that inspired a larger investigation of him. This accuser was a Black woman who was described in news stories as a grandmother,[61] a quality that seemed to render her more sympathetic than the victims who were young or poor, struggled with drug addiction, or had a history with the criminal justice system. In the interpretive framework of US rape culture, Holtzclaw could be guilty only if his victim could be understood as victimizable, and everyone knows it is beyond the pale to sexually assault a grandmother. In contrast, his other victims were not described in ways that earned them the same level of care or concern. In court, many of Holtzclaw's accusers were asked about their prior encounters with the criminal justice system in an attempt to discount their testimony, despite the fact that those prior encounters were the very reason Holtzclaw had targeted them.[62]

Though Holtzclaw's conviction is an exception in the sense that it represents a rare instance of marginalized people being believed over a law enforcement officer, it also reflects a few "rules" of US rape culture. First, rape only "counts" as rape when the perpetrator can be characterized as deviant. Even when dozens of victims might come forward, the deviance of assaulting a grandmother becomes the catalyst for further investigation. Second, rape culture will still operate to exonerate white supremacy when it can. When the accusations against Holtzclaw finally became public, the news media would occasionally mention that he is mixed race (Holtzclaw is Asian and white),[63] while at other times they would omit this detail altogether. This ambiguity in reporting meant that Holtzclaw could be read as either white or non-white. His proximity to whiteness (his ability to "pass" as white) had allowed him to prey on Black women for months and escape suspicion for weeks after his accusers came forward (in fact, several webpages and social media sites still proclaim his innocence).[64] But when he was finally caught, his biraciality could be invoked to absolve white supremacy for his crimes. Holtzclaw was eventually sentenced to 263 years in prison,[65] including 30 years for each of his four first-degree rape convictions,[66] in a state where the mandatory minimum for first-degree rape is only 5 years.[67] Holtzclaw's tough sentence was meant to prove the criminal justice system could be "fair" to Black women and punish corrupt cops. Yet his convictions reaffirm the false presumption that it is primarily *non-white* men who use sexual violence to abuse their power.[68]

As I noted in Chapter Four, the myth of the false rape accuser is prevalent in US rape culture. When ascribed to a white woman, the false rape accuser is characterized as a tease, fame seeker, or feminist, all of which render her untrustworthy. It is possible for white women to be believed but only if they adhere to certain expectations about what a "good" woman is under white heteropatriarchy. By contrast, the convergence of the myths of Black womanhood makes it almost impossible for Black women to avoid being misnamed when they come forward. Among several reasons for Black women's under-disclosure of sexual violence, Tillman et al. identify three "culture-specific barriers": the prevalence of harmful cultural images of Black womanhood, past negative experiences with social or legal services, and the cultural imperative to protect Black men.[69] As some studies have shown, these pressures reveal why many Black women decide not to disclose sexual violence. Black women's "unbelievability" as rape accusers is both a cause and an effect of the multiple misnamings that Black women endure: they are often unrecognized as victims of sexual violence in the popular cultural imagination because their mistreatment fuels a strategy of self-protective silence, which historian Darlene Clark Hine describes as a "culture of dissemblance." Through this strategic dissemblance, Black women seek to protect themselves from some of the worst consequences of being misnamed, disregarded, and (re)traumatized in the US popular cultural imagination.[70]

In US rape culture, Black women are disproportionately targeted with sexual violence in both inter-racial and intra-racial contexts. According to American studies scholar Micki McElya, the contrast between the jezebel and mammy stereotypes conceals sexual violence against Black women by rendering them both "unrapeable."[71] She explains how this juxtaposition functions in inter-racial contexts:

> Presumed by many whites to be lascivious and predatory and thus supposedly not capable of being raped, black women were commonly threatened by the same white men who claimed to defend southern womanhood and civilization. The mammy figure's overdrawn maternalism and asexuality stood in opposition to this and represented a denial of sex, forced and otherwise, between white men and black women.[72]

The hyper-sexualization of Black women (via popular culture and algorithmic oppression) continues to render Black women "unrapeable" by figuring them as (1) sub-persons (in Mills's sense) who are ineligible to give or withhold consent, (2) jezebels who would never refuse to consent, or (3) mammies who are desexed, unattractive, and so undesirable that no one would deign to rape them. The ostensible contradiction between the mammy and jezebel has provided cover for white men in two ways: it enabled them to rely on Black women's domestic labor and care work to sustain white households while they maintained access to Black women's bodies after slavery was abolished,[73] and it allowed them to deny the possibility of rape on the grounds that a mammy was unrapeable because she was asexual ("de-sexed," as Collins says)[74] and undesirable.

Almost by definition, a mammy cannot be a jezebel. Yet the contrast between the opposing images is used to justify misogyny within Black communities as well. Collins explains how the mythic figure of the jezebel has been updated as the "hoochie" and observes explicit and implicit acceptance of "portrayals of Black women as 'hoochies' within Black popular culture [especially in many hip hop lyrics]" that "[make] prior portrayals of jezebel seem tame."[75] These portrayals can objectify Black women, normalize heterosexuality, and reinforce tropes of hyper-sexuality for both Black women and Black men.[76] The hoochie, like the jezebel, is unrapeable since she is, by definition, always already consenting to sex. At the same time, the contrasting tension of the mammy and jezebel can also mean that Black women risk being misnamed as race traitors if they report crimes committed by Black men. They may feel pressure to maintain a "code of silence" and not report intra-racial rape, domestic violence, or intimate partner violence.[77]

The hyper-sexualization of Black women allows white and Black people to continue to police Black women's sexual expression. The controversy around the song "WAP" by Cardi B, featuring Megan Thee Stallion, is a good example of this policing. Some Black male critics suggested that Black women should not be expressing their sexuality so publicly,[78] while conservative white critics predictably condemned the song as evidence of Black cultural inferiority and the failure of the Black family.[79] Both types of criticisms misname Black women as simultaneously the source of the decline/failure of Black culture, as hyper-sexual, and as pornographic. They aim to discipline those (like Cardi B and Megan Thee Stallion) whose expressions of sexual liberation do not comply with white heteropatriarchal notions of acceptable sexuality.

Gender-based violence also puts victims (especially racially marginalized women) at further risk of other forms of revictimization. Sexual violence creates a "school-to-prison pipeline," especially for African American, Hispanic, and Indigenous girls. According to the National Prison Rape Elimination Act (PREA) Resource Center, 86% of incarcerated women are survivors of sexual violence.[80] Communication studies scholar Moya Bailey details the adverse health outcomes that Black women experience as a result of misogynoir, including sexual violence.[81] In her recent book, Anita Hill identifies several costs of gender-based violence, including increased risks of homelessness, unemployment, suicide, post-traumatic stress disorder, and incarceration.[82] Taken together, these realities reveal that victims of sexual violence, especially Black, Hispanic, and Indigenous women and girls, are victimized in several ways, beyond the act of violence they have endured.

Yet within US rape culture, a Black woman cannot share her experience of sexual violence without the risk of being misnamed, and the misnaming places Black women at a disproportionately higher risk of sexual violence by perpetuating distrust of Black women and hyper-sexualizing them as unrapeable. In *Black Feminist Thought*, Collins argues that these convergent figures of Black womanhood in the United States all come back to sexuality.[83] They emerge out of the conditions of chattel slavery that reduced humans to property and enslaved women to forced reproducers of unpaid labor. These updated mythic figures persist in US rape culture to create a dangerous subject-position for Black women. A pervasive narrative of US rape culture says that Black women are untrustworthy. Another says they are unrapeable. What, then, are the alternative practices that could disrupt, rather than reinforce, these contradictions of US rape culture?

Praxis: Dismantling Rape Culture

As the endurance of the multiple myths of Black womanhood illustrate, the burdens of surviving sexual violence do not end with the violence itself. Victims can experience revictimization when they are disbelieved, ridiculed, threatened, blamed, shamed, or misnamed through the myths, discourses, and practices reflected in (and by) US rape culture. In this sense, rape culture serves as both a cause and an effect of victimization. It is a *cause* in the sense that it provides the interpretive framework in which perpetrators target their victims, who they already recognize as dominable. It is an *effect* in the sense that, after the violence has occurred, the myths, discourses, and practices of rape culture are invoked to perpetuate the victimization of survivors, discourage exposing perpetrators, and preserve the structures of white supremacy, heteropatriarchy, and settler capitalist exploitation. The mistreatment of victims discourages reporting, which allows sexual violence to persist.[84] The potential for revictimization is high when victims are mistreated and disbelieved. In this section, I turn to the work of those whose praxis demonstrates how to challenge rape culture both as a function of structure and as an intimate, lived experience.

The pain of sharing their stories of sexual violence is disproportionally borne by those whose embodiment and marginalization put them at highest risk of sexual violence in the first place. As anti-rape activist and scholar G. Chezia Carraway explains, "Not only do attackers rape women of color disproportionately, but women of color and poor women are uniquely situated to bear the burdens accompanying societal misunderstandings and misperceptions about rape."[85] Therefore, "taking the initiative to name for ourselves [as women of color] the violence we experience in our lives is both necessary and empowering, as well as essential to healthy survival beyond mere existence."[86] At the same time, Tarana Burke notes, "the challenges we faced as women of color to raise awareness and undo the pathologies that allowed this harm to take place were compounded by our marginalized identities and lived experiences."[87] Thus, the effort to *re*name what has been *mis*named requires support, care, and a commitment not to impose expectations about how, when, where, or for whom such initiative must be shown. While aiming to combat rape culture, it is essential that victims are not revictimized and remarginalized in the name of flooding the cultural archive with new and different stories. Yet, in order for a culture to change, its archive of images, representations, stories, and practices *must* change. We who wish to dismantle rape culture as part of the project of eliminating sexual violence must find ways to endorse and support cultural change without imposing an additional burden on its targets and victims—including taking care of ourselves, when necessary.

We can find resources for this challenging work in exemplars of intersectional praxis who model an intention to foster care and prevent harm as much as possible. In their discussion of feminist abolitionist spaces, activist-scholars Angela Y. Davis, Gina Dent, Erica R. Meiners, and Beth E. Richie boldly defend utopic visions and (as yet) unimagined horizons. At the same time, they remind us that "change is relational and rarely immediate."[88] Part of the reason transforming rape culture is so challenging is that, in order to eliminate sexual violence as a technique of domination, we must eliminate domination as a form of relationship. But another reason is that the intention to create change is fraught with unintended harm, so processes of organizing must involve trust-building work grounded in learning, unlearning, and accountability. The vision of a world without violence may be utopian, but the process of achieving it must be clear-eyed and self-critical. Through its focus on both the pervasive articulations and specific enactments of US rape culture, intersectional analysis provides a framework for a praxis of resistance and reimagination that can address (even if it could never eliminate) the problem of disproportionate burden.

In intersectional praxis, the co-locations of the pervasive and the specific correspond to different potential registers of resistance. The pervasive representations of US rape culture can be disrupted and challenged in their mythic, discursive, and practical manifestations by anyone who critically observes them. The Survivors' Agenda Initiative, a collaboration of anti-rape activist groups launched in 2017, articulates a vision for cultural change that supports survivor-led efforts to challenge and eliminate sexual violence. Their agenda identifies "cultural and narrative shift" as one core element of the project and suggests that although survivor-led initiatives are key to their efforts, "wider society" can and should take responsibility for disrupting US rape culture:

> These same systems and institutions [that shape our culture], and the wider society at large, can be a part of the solution. They can help turn the tide on sexual violence and create new narratives that support survivors and disrupt the culture of violence. We are calling for a transformation of culture that centers the experiences of all survivors; a culture that doesn't tolerate or make excuses for the abuse, violence, and harassment by those in power; a culture that encourages being active in preventing and disrupting violence when aware of harmful situations (rather than being a bystander); and a culture that is supportive of survivors of sexual violence, going beyond just "believing" survivors to actively promoting and developing a culture of prevention, accountability, and healing.[89]

Tarana Burke, whose organization, The me too Movement, is part of the Survivors' Agenda coalition, echoed this sentiment in 2019:

> As we enter the next decade, I want us to all find our place in the movement to end sexual violence, because we all have a role to play. I look forward to knowing that the movement doesn't rely on the level of celebrity and notoriety of the accused or accuser, but that it instead builds on the changed thinking, behavior and solutions created by those most impacted.[90]

These activists understand that the work of ending sexual violence is part of a larger cultural project (again, I see this also as an abolitionist project, though I do not know if all of these activists do). As I understand it, the Survivors' Agenda Initiative emphasizes that this cultural shift work should:

1. Center survivors' experiences but not shine unwelcome light on them (since only survivors can decide when, whether, or how to tell them)
2. Strictly reject abuse and violence as modes of domination and political control[91]
3. Emphasize a *praxis of disruption*, intent on challenging the content of US rape culture and intervening in the face of interpersonal violence
4. Develop survivor support in both interpersonal (specific) and cultural-institutional (pervasive) registers.

These criteria, and in particular the criterion to reject violence as a technique of domination, should guide efforts to build culturally specific and empathetic interventions to expose, challenge, and ultimately eliminate rape culture. Not surprisingly, resources and exemplars of these practices are often found within the communities of those most marginalized in US rape culture, who have been in many ways relegated outside the culture, and therefore are best situated to challenge and reimagine it.

One element of a praxis to disrupt and dismantle rape culture involves survivor-led approaches to survivor care that attend to the needs of the marginalized people they serve. Historian Darlene Clark Hine highlights the importance of protected spaces for cultivating individuals' sense of self: "in the face of the pervasive stereotypes and negative estimations of the sexuality of Black women, it was imperative that they collectively create alternative self-images and shield from scrutiny these private, empowering definitions of self."[92] "Culturally safe healing practices" emerge from a sense that that the intersecting oppressions of sexual violence yield common needs for those with similar experiences but that these needs are unlikely to be universalizable.[93] The Urban Indian Health Institute (UIHI) maintains that safe healing must be both culturally focused and safe. One example of a culturally specific healing practice is the Minnesota Indian Women's Sexual Assault Coalition's Barrette Project, which invites survivors or the loved ones of victims of sexual violence to bead a barrette, which is joined with others to form a "living memorial" for Indigenous survivors of sexual violence.[94] For many Indigenous survivors, reconnecting with cultural activities such as traditional singing and dancing, beadwork or woodwork, and participating in cultural events like the canoe journey can also foster resilience and a sense of connection.[95]

Therapeutic interventions must also feel safe—which is not a given, considering that unsafe experiences with the medical and mental health professions in the United States are common, especially for members of marginalized groups. The UIHI defines cultural safety as "a practice that moves beyond cultural awareness and cultural sensitivity and allows for a shift in the power relations of patient and provider interactions. Providers who use cultural safety also affirm that patients must have autonomy over their own care plan and wellbeing."[96] Culturally safe healing approaches can support survivors whose specific experiences of sexual violence result in their shared marginalization in US society.

Another culturally specific effort to raise awareness about the effects of US rape culture is the red handprint—a symbol of resistance that some Indigenous athletes and other public figures have used to raise awareness about missing and murdered Indigenous women (MMIW). Since Jordan Marie Brings Three White Horses Daniel (Kul Wicasa Lakota and a citizen of the Lower Brule Reservation, South Dakota), painted a red handprint over her mouth before competing in the 2018 San Diego half-marathon and the 2019 Boston Marathon, the symbol has garnered increasing attention to MMIW violence.[97] Daniel explains how she chose this symbol, which was motivated by a desire to raise awareness without claiming the work of others as her own:

> Since I was already there, a week before the race, I decided to update my racing uniform to be the color red, with the MMIW symbol and the words, "No More Stolen Sisters." But due to lack of time, we didn't hear back about being able to use the symbol I wanted until after the run. So instead, I decided to paint the red handprint over my mouth to signify breaking the silence about the violence happening with the women in our indigenous communities and raise awareness for our stolen sisters. I did research, found 26 names, and when the first mile started, I read one name out loud, said a prayer for her and her family, and tuned into the environment for the rest of that mile. I did that for 26 miles, and the last .2 to the finish, I said a prayer for my grandfather. It felt really good to end that race for him. I hope I'm making him proud, not only by crossing the finish line but also by the way I'm carrying Indian Country with me.[98]

As part of her action, Daniel made a point of individualizing and naming without publicizing the traumas of specific victims. This gesture is similar to the African American Policy Forum's "Say Her Name" initiative, which names Black women who have been killed by police violence and can no longer speak for themselves (and provides material support to victims' families).[99] The stark image of the red handprint recalls silencing and violent struggle, but it is also disruptive—a literal "in your face" proclamation that cannot be ignored by anyone who sees Daniel run. And it did garner attention: later that year, another Indigenous runner and high school student, Rosalie Fish, of the Cowlitz Tribe (Washington), asked Daniel whether she could also use the red handprint symbol.[100] Daniel encouraged her to use it, and off Fish ran.

Both runners describe feeling that they were carrying "weight" on their runs,[101] not necessarily as survivors (which neither has disclosed) but as those who choose to carry a burden to raise awareness so that others do not have to. Because Daniel and Fish run for specific individuals, each step is a commemoration and prayer to honor the victims and their experiences, families, and communities. Daniel noted the importance of taking an action that was "specifically for [victims]."[102] This approach involves Daniel and Fish picking up the weight of commemoration and awareness-building themselves, rather than burdening families. Without shining a harsh spotlight on victims, and by seeking permission before taking action, this approach centers victims and their families and perhaps helps victims restore a sense of control over their experience.

Since the red handprint first appeared, others have followed the leads of Daniel and Fish, in more and less exemplary ways. Indigenous sports teams have begun to compete with red handprints on their faces; a majority-Indigenous basketball team in Mesa, Arizona, plays with jerseys bearing the names of MMIW.[103] Indigenous artists, activists, and public figures have borrowed and adapted the approach to honor and name, to carry the weight on their own backs to alleviate the weight for victims, survivors, and their loved ones.

Yet, there are also missteps and appropriations. Some Indigenous activists have expressed concerns about how body paint is used by groups without a history of using and understanding paint. They are concerned about cultural misappropriation, even among well-meaning Indigenous activists. Even less exemplary versions of red handprint activism involve decontextualized and uninformed online activism, often by non-Indigenous people who post videos or photos of themselves with a red handprint, a practice that diminishes the disruption of the red handprint as weight-carrying and as a demand.[104] In these cases, without appropriate context, a symbol designed to raise awareness of Indigenous victims and survivors can appear to represent gender-based violence in general.

The use of the red handprint also calls into question who is in a position to "carry the weight" for a community. To claim such a position without intention, care, or permission could deepen, rather than alleviate, the burden of survivorship. Appropriation of the red handprint can also allow "the pervasive" to overrun "the specific," a consequential error that replicates, rather than challenges, US rape culture. As I detailed in Chapter Three, US rape culture disregards (or "wastelands") Indigenous victims of sexual violence and other forms of lateral and settler violence.[105] The red handprint symbol seeks to disrupt this disregard and to name and honor individual lives that may not otherwise have been "counted" (by the settler state) as lost. When some use the symbol to represent other purposes or other groups, they perpetuate the historical erasure and everyday discounting of Indigenous lives and Indigenous forms of resistance.[106]

With these considerations in mind, I have thought carefully about whether I should discuss the red handprint here. My understanding of historical trauma and grounded normativity is incomplete and inadequate. I continue to consider whether and how one who has been reared in settler values (as I have) can learn from the examples of alternative cultural practices without appropriating them. If it is possible to learn without appropriation, but with the intention to foster radical cultural change (and I believe it is), examples like the red handprint demonstrate that the ontological and epistemological practices of US rape culture must change. At the same time, this practice (and others like it) should not be taken as a blueprint for *how* to achieve that change (as if one could put a red handprint on their Instagram profile picture, et voilà, rape culture is challenged). It is tempting, especially in current US popular culture, to seek a quick and easy fix. But that is not how a culture of domination through sexual violence is eradicated. For me, witnessing and learning from countercultural practices has been essential to my ability to imagine the radical transformation of US rape culture and the end of rape itself. As Indigenous writers such as Leann Betasamosake Simpson, Audra Simpson, and Robin Wall Kimmerer note, Indigenous commitments to mutual dependence, relationality, reciprocity, stewardship, and care can offer a radical departure from the settler practices of appropriation and possession that are at the heart of settler colonialism and sexual violence. I discuss red handprint activism in the spirit of seeking sources of inspiration for resistant praxis—*not* as a recommendation or invitation for anyone (particularly non-Indigenous people) to replicate this action.

Actions that have the potential to disrupt rape culture must center survivors while taking care not to impose additional harm or burden on them. The red handprint is one example of a disruptive praxis that raises awareness of MMIW without requiring individual victims or families to detail their loss unless (or until) they wish to do so. It takes the problem of burden seriously and seeks to relieve survivors or their families and communities of its weight. Daniel and Fish displayed the red handprint with permission and intention; their private actions (such as naming and prayerfulness) reflect a depth of care for those who are missing or murdered, while the public display of the red handprint shocks viewers into awareness. The red handprint is thus an example of how to disrupt rape culture in a way that attends to both the specific lives lived and lost and the pervasive structural problems of violence (including kidnapping, assault, and murder) and sexual violence against Indigenous women and girls. It introduces an alternative narrative into the archive of US rape culture in a way that prioritizes care for victims, survivors, and their loved ones.

The "me too" Movement launched by activist Tarana Burke in 2006 suggests a second praxis to disrupt and dismantle rape culture. Unlike the Twitter (now X) #MeToo hashtag that went viral in 2018 after white actress Alyssa Milano encouraged victims to write #metoo as their social media status in response to the Harvey Weinstein scandal, the movement itself offers protected (non-public) sites for survivors to share their experiences of sexual violence without risking retraumatization and erasure. In this context, I explore what Burke calls *empowerment through empathy.*

There is a vast gulf between a hashtag that raises awareness of the scope of sexual harassment and sexual violence, on the one hand, and the set of interpersonal practices developed by Burke and Black feminists over many years of survivor support work focused on Black women and girls, on the other. When it went viral, the #metoo hashtag flooded the archives of sexual violence with stories and broadened awareness of the scope of sexual violence and harassment. People could use social media to share their experiences in public ways that might help and support others. That said, simply updating one's status cannot foster a deep interpersonal practice of "empowerment through empathy" that could support and potentially relieve some of the burdens of sexual violence survival.

In a Harvard Kennedy School case study, Burke recounts an exercise she did at a series of workshops with Black girls many years ago. After sharing several public stories of sexual assault and abuse from famous Black women like Oprah Winfrey, Gabrielle Union, and Fantasia, Burke would share her own story of assault (more recently, she has also detailed the painful effects of this kind of work on her health and resiliency).[107] At the end of each workshop, each girl was given a piece of paper and invited to write—anonymously—either three things they had learned in the workshop or the words "me too." Almost every time, nearly all of the slips of paper said "me too,"[108] which became a powerful expression to the girls in the room that they were not alone. In an interview with ESPN in 2018, Burke explained the mission of the organization that became "me too":

> When I created Me Too in 2006, it was really about the idea of empowerment through empathy, because what I realized was that it wasn't that they didn't want to talk about it—it was that nobody wants to talk about it in isolation. You don't want to be the only one that comes forward and talks about how this thing is affecting you. So, if there's somebody that you see and you trust who can empathize with you, there's power in that.[109]

This practice of empowerment through empathy focuses on what a survivor needs and how simply saying "me too" can create space for them (and others) to heal. Saying "me too" discloses the "me" but in a way that immediately puts them in community with others (those who have been victims of sexual violence "too"). When undertaken in person, this practice centers survivors in two ways: it allows them to acknowledge their victimization anonymously or semi-anonymously and locates them in an immediate community of supporters who can say "me too" to one another.

The practice of empowerment through empathy disrupts the silencing of rape culture by exposing the pervasiveness of sexual violence. The suggestion that an individual is not alone in their experience, as the #MeToo hashtag has done, attests to both the pervasive and the specific: this is a widespread problem, and you are not alone. Yet the deeper, relational practice of empowerment through empathy is *also* necessary. Even though #MeToo helps flood the archive with new (perhaps previously unheard or misunderstood) experiences of sexual violence, because it is adopted in public settings such as social media, it also risks being appropriated to reinforce US rape culture, in large part because the relational work of social media is not as deep as the in-person practice.

In the past few years, several commentators have argued that, while it did increase awareness about sexual violence and sexual harassment, #MeToo has failed. But #MeToo is a predictable cautionary tale. Professor of Chicano/Latino studies Elena Ruíz recently has argued that structural violence is self-repairing in the sense that it is "a carefully preserved social condition [such as racial inequality, which is] tied to value and its transference, garrisoned at every stage of transformation by a series of adaptive structural maneuvers thousands of years in the making."[110] The moves to appropriate a red handprint or to reduce empathic engagements to a hashtag, even when well intentioned, undermine the initial countercultural and relational energies behind these movements and invite "adaptive structural maneuvers" that aim to thwart their countercultural power. This possibility is cause for constant vigilance and ongoing self-critical reflection. It is the reason dismantling rape culture requires a community-based and self-reflective praxis.

As evidence that structural violence is "self-repairing," a new practice has emerged to discipline accusers and sustain rape culture. In 2018, emboldened by #MeToo, Amber Heard penned an op-ed for the *Washington Post* that mentioned she had been a victim of domestic abuse. Though she did not name him in the op-ed, her ex-husband Johnny Depp sued for defamation, and Heard countersued. At the conclusion of the U.S. trial, a few commentators observed that more people (like Depp) were now using defamation lawsuits to respond to public allegations of sexual violence, including intimate partner violence and sexual harassment. Legal scholar Deborah Tuerkheimer warns: "The weaponization of defamation suits is a phenomenon that extends beyond high-profile figures. Dozens of workers who have come forward with sexual harassment allegations have also been sued in recent years. Student accusers are also increasingly being sued for statements made in the course of campus disciplinary proceedings."[111] These strategic lawsuits against public participation (SLAPP) lawsuits are often undertaken with the intention of silencing or intimidating accusers. Though #MeToo seemed to usher in a new era of believing accusers, it has also fostered a new practice: individual abusers may now be able to use civil lawsuits to target and discredit accusers, even if they do not publicly name their assailants.

By contrast, the deep relational practice of the "me too" Movement exemplifies how supporting survivors requires attending to both the pervasive and the specific. Burke describes this practice as changing the nature of responding to survivors by emphasizing empathy as a mode of empowerment. For the person who speaks and the person who hears "me too," the empathic utterance can be empowering: your pain matters not because I have also suffered but because we share an experience. As observers and participants in popular culture engage in critical analysis of and challenge the myths, discourses, and practices that normalize sexual violence, the "me too" Movement offers a relational practice that centers survivors and may make it possible for them to come forward more publicly with their stories in the future.

As survivors find ways to make sense of their experiences, many of them develop practices of recovery, resilience, resistance, and reimagination. These and other survivor-led practices can inspire new creative efforts to disrupt and disassemble US rape culture and can do so in ways that are culturally specific and steeped in awareness of one's own subject-position and without appropriating the work of others in order to avoid the self-critical work that we all need to do to unlearn our own complicity in sustaining rape culture. The examples I share here emphasize deep relational work, empathy and empowerment, practices of safe healing, and, especially, autonomy over one's own story. I think any countercultural efforts must learn from and build new forms of praxis that take these points seriously. The examples also point to the practices that non-survivors must cultivate: centering survivors, carrying burdens if and when possible (given one's relationship to the burdened), and supporting survivors' safety and security. Yet these are surely not the only practices available to disrupt rape culture, and in a sense they will always be fraught because the tension at their core is that survivor-leadership imposes a burden (as does marginalization). These burdens are in some ways inescapable until people are no longer marginalized in their communities.

Cultures change through critical analysis and relational practices that challenge what we think we know about one another, about sexual violence, and about power. The relational praxis of the Barrette Project, the Survivors' Agenda Initiative, the red handprint, and the me too Movement reveals how we might undertake collective action to eliminate domination through sexual violence.

As I understand them, these kinds of approaches can be aligned with a broader abolitionist project because they recognize the confluence of structural forms of domination that are experienced differentially across society. They are also connected to abolitionist projects in the sense that, as I have argued, the resources to dismantle rape culture and eliminate sexual violence will not be found in the US carceral state, which uses laws and prisons to protect white heteropatriarchy and enable settler capitalist exploitation, the touchstones of US rape culture. Throughout this book, I have identified failures of the legal system, including those related to how prosecutors assess victims as "good" or "bad," how rape is defined and adjudicated in the courts, how some law enforcement agents commit sexual violence against incarcerated individuals with impunity, how sexual violence "pipelines" women into prisons, and how pernicious rape in prisons is. Sexual violence is part and parcel of the criminal justice system in the United States. In some ways, it keeps it in business. Until the carceral state is dismantled, I do not think US rape culture can be.

Instead, we require different critical starting points for our thinking and action. Patricia Hill Collins identified the Black feminist analysis that grew out of the Clarence Thomas confirmation hearing as one site where critical engagement and contestation openly challenged what had previously been taboo for many.[112] The multiple misnamings of Hill laid bare the impossibility of her subject-position in the context of a Supreme Court confirmation hearing and subsequently fostered complex conversations among Black feminists about sex, gender, and race that many had previously avoided (such as those who benefit from heterosexual or class privilege).[113] The kind of precise, critical, and communal analysis made possible through exploration of a specific, watershed event was able to expose how structures of oppression adapt over time.

The misogynoir of US rape culture has ensured that the lives of Black women will continue to be constricted by white capitalist heteropatriarchy. In response to this reality, a rich, counterinsurgent, and countercultural Black feminist praxis was born—counterinsurgent and countercultural because it has grown at the margins (by necessity) by those whose lives have been subjected to disregard by white capitalist heteropatriarchy. But also counterinsurgent and countercultural because it emerged from both the critical conversations of Black feminists and the everyday practice of "waywardness," of "the untiring practice of trying to live when you were never meant to survive."[114] Because chattel slavery (and its afterlives) constructed Black women as *mothers dispossessed*, Black women have at times challenged the overdeterminations of white supremacy, heteropatriarchy, and capitalist exploitation through everyday acts of refusal.[115] In her account of Black life in northern cities at the onset of the twentieth century, Hartman's archival and fabulation work rearticulates Black women's experiments in freedom. Their refusal to seek permission or approval when they raised children out of wedlock, lived with men who were not legally their husbands, supported their households financially, had (and enjoyed having) sex, or moved through public spaces was "something akin to freedom," asserted in the decades after the end of slavery.[116] Their resistant practices were not legible to the standard bearers of white respectability, for whom these acts of freedom appeared to be "no different from acting wild."[117] Yet, to those who lived these beautiful experiments, these practices were acts of refusal to be governed; refusal to contort themselves to a white, middle-class femininity that was inaccessible to them anyway; and refusal to be a "woman" as the white heteropatriarchal order understood the word.[118]

Such a praxis of refusal has the potential to dismantle the oppressive structures that enable US rape culture and to imagine (and achieve!) a world without sexual violence. As abolition feminists Angela Y. Davis, Gina Dent, Erica R. Meiners, and Beth E. Richie explain,

> [T]his is the abolition feminist imperative of the both/and: the need to rigorously pay attention to what came before but also to move expansively and generatively and be willing to learn and unlearn. The imperative to recognize that dominant power structures will attempt—often successfully—to absorb our labor and demands, and yet we still forge new language and practices, and we work, anyway. Rather than contradictory, these tensions—painful and pleasurable—*are* the work.[119]

I understand this work—collective, self-reflective, relational, critical, and creative—as the work that is necessary to dismantle rape culture.

I also hear resonances between a critical Black feminist consciousness of resistance and survival with their kinfolk—including what Angela Davis identifies as a "profound consciousness of resistance" among enslaved women[120]—and observations made by Audra Simpson and Leanne Betasamosake Simpson about how Indigenous communities challenge the heteropatriarchal, settler frame. Although the conditions of Indigenous women confronting white settlers on as-yet-unsettled land are different from those of enslaved women with white slave traders on and off slave ships, white Europeans did not recognize either group as women because they did not fit the European, "patriarchilized" notion of women.[121] In a sense, their capacity for resistance and survival makes them *not women* in the heteropatriarchal vernacular, which can only define women as conciliatory, subservient, and weak. Since Indigenous and Black enslaved women fall outside this category, at least in some senses (and even though Black enslaved women had been rendered legally subservient), the white heteropatriarchal order must either violently ungender or violently assimilate them.

Yet precisely because they are rooted in those alternative spaces and experiences, they have often found a praxis of resistance that is truly *counter* to US rape culture. Those sites of resistance include Black feminist and Indigenous feminist spaces, as I have mentioned; but there are sources of learning and inspiration in many other places as well, such as decolonial activism around the world, and in non-binary and non-normative challenges to dominant cultures. These are the sites of possibility that can inspire new and specific practices of resistance to dismantle a pervasive rape culture.

Conclusion

When Anita Hill published a memoir of her experience in the Thomas confirmation hearings, she made a point not to say more about the sexual harassment she endured than she had already said in the hearing.[122] Instead, she focused on herself—her experience, the details that made her story what it was, her actions and choices, and the impossibility of the misnaming she confronted in the hearing. She exposed the bind she was put in when she was sexually harassed by a Black man as a young professional in her mid-20s and a decade later when she spoke truth to power to the US Senate Judiciary Committee when that same man was nominated to the US Supreme Court. No matter what she said, she would be discounted and disbelieved. She said it anyway.

Hill's experience is a microcosm of US rape culture, which uses myths, discourses, and practices to sustain white heteropatriarchal rule and settler colonial–capitalist exploitation. It also reveals the nature of intersecting systems of oppression and how they work together to marginalize people. Hill was not deemed worthy of protection. She was expected to bear her victimization and protect the Black community, even at tremendous personal cost. She was treated incredulously by the all-white, male panel of senators who questioned her, as if she had equal power to challenge the sexual harassment when it happened (much less, equal power in the hearing room).

Her victimizer became the victim as she became a villain (at least to many). But as she explains in her 1997 memoir, the thousands of letters of support she received after Thomas's confirmation allowed her to heal:

> I cannot overstate the importance of these letters, notes, and other messages. They were crucial to my endurance and ultimately to my recovery.... If the hearing had left me feeling isolated and out of touch with the world, the correspondence afterward helped me to reconnect with it.[123]

Hill's tremendous burden opened up another avenue to challenge US rape culture: it allowed Black feminist activists to expose the myths that had been imposed upon her, to acknowledge tensions at the intersections of racialized and gendered discrimination, and to come to her defense publicly, as the 1,600 Black women of African American Women in Defense of Ourselves did in November 1991.[124] Her testimony allowed others to bear witness to the injustice of the hearing, to find strength to share their own stories of abuse, and to expand an alternative archive about sexual violence.

As I have argued throughout this book, rape is political in the sense that victims are "chosen" by virtue of their dominability. Thus, victims of sexual violence have already faced some form of marginalization or they could not be regarded as dominable. Speaking truth to power about that victimization in a culture that often protects perpetrators through deflection and indemnification, and targets victims as untrustworthy and/or hyper-sexualized (and therefore unrapeable), risks additional victimization.

To avert that risk, we must cultivate relationships that center survivors' needs and ask non-survivors to bear as much of the burden of flooding the archive as they can (given their relationship to those survivors), to recognize that different marginal identities may require different healing practices and care, and to build empathic and empowering survivor communities. This work must form part of a larger intersectional political project to end all systems of domination. These systems will become the next basis for sexual victimization: they will always be willing to identify new bodies that can be raped with impunity by those who claim entitlement to dominate. The Survivors' Agenda Initiative, like other abolitionist feminist-, Indigenous feminist-, and Black feminist–led movements, views the elimination of sexual violence as one part of a "complex spectrum" of concerns around white supremacy, cis heteropatriarchy, settler colonialism, and capitalist exploitation.[125] An intersectional praxis of resistance can draw inspiration from these activists who, in the face of systemic sexual violence, co-create relationships and practices that teach us important truths about sexual violence and invite resistance. This often requires confronting the false promises of protection, prevention, and imagined equality perpetuated by US rape culture—and deconstructing its associated myths, discourses, and practices. To fashion a new culture that does not need to construct mythic figures or perpetuate discourses and practices of domination, we need art, expression, engagement, and action that floods the archive with new stories, experiences, images, and practices that can provide resources for repair and resistance and for the radical imagining of a world without rape.

Notes

Chapter One

1. Parts of this chapter have been excerpted from Kessel 2022. © The Author(s), 2021. Published by Cambridge University Press on behalf of the American Political Science Association, reproduced with permission.
2. Grandoni 2014. For an analysis of misogyny in *GTA*, see Paquette 2016 and Barrett 2006. For discussion of *GTA VI*, see Moreau 2023.
3. Rockstar Games n.d.
4. Grandoni 2014.
5. Shen 2022.
6. Patel 2021.
7. Brownmiller (1993, 14–15) also maintains that rape is a political phenomenon employed in riots, pogroms, wars, slavery, colonialism, and everyday life. Yet, Brownmiller's biological framing of rape suggests it is inevitable (see discussion in Sharon Marcus in Butler and Scott 1992, 387). I agree with Marcus that this approach frames women as perpetual victims and men as perpetual rapists, and therefore support her rejection of the biological argument.
8. By "dominate," I am not referring to those who engage in BDSM practices after discussing limits, safe words, etc. that ensure the ongoing agreement of the practice. I use the word "domination" because of its historical resonances with lordship, household, and patriarchal control.
9. Young (1990, 38). It is not my argument here, but I think that rape culture is also oppressive in the sense that Young suggests, by inhibiting self-development.
10. Rose 2021, 3–4.
11. Though the question of the meaning of rape is connected to the meaning of sex (and sexual desire), I disentangle them for analytical purposes to help clarify how the myths, discourses, and practices of rape culture reinforce marginalization in the United States. They are necessarily close to ideas about sexuality and desire. Future work might fruitfully re-entangle them to think through their interconnections.
12. Srinivasan 2021, 90.
13. Ibid., 84. Emphasis in original.
14. Ibid., 73.
15. Winton et al. 2014, quoting Rodger's manifesto.
16. Ibid.
17. Ibid. Emphasis in original.
18. Srinivasan 2021, 86.
19. Ging 2019, passim.
20. Jaleel 2021, 14.
21. Richie 2012, 90–91.
22. Wells-Barnett 1895; Douglass 1895; Davis 1978, 1983, 1990; Combahee River Collective (in Moraga and Anzaldúa 2015). Throughout this text, I capitalize the words "Black" and "Indigenous" but not "white." I settled on this imperfect usage to highlight the ways that these two communities of people (often but not always diasporic, often but not always forcibly relocated) came into being *as* Black or Indigenous as a result of the operations of white supremacy, which I want to signify through capitalization, are different from the way that whiteness came into being. Robert Nichols's approach is a guide: when discussing his use of the term "Indigenous" to describe peoples with distinctive histories across vast geographic territories, he notes that being "Indigenous" names "processes and mechanics of . . . dispossession" (2020, 98). I capitalize "Black" and "Indigenous," but not white, to highlight the involuntary subjection to the

processes of white supremacy *and* the creative expression and emergence of distinctive communal identities (such as Blackness) in response to it. This is a sticky point: I am trying to highlight a difference in experience and community formation without denying the agency of the humans who live in (and through) it, nor romanticizing the communal identities that are born from it. While my usage is imperfect, it feels like the best way to reiterate this point throughout the text.

23. Phillips 2017, 15; Google Trends search of "rape culture" on January 28, 2021.
24. See Buchwald et al. 1993, 1; J. Friedman and Valenti 2008, 6; Ridgway 2014; Taub 2014; Harding (citing Buchwald et al.) 2015, 2; Murphy 2016; Gay 2018, xi; Wikipedia 2021 (this date is when I first searched Wikipedia for this term; more recent updates, in mid-2025, as I write this, continue to prioritize gender and sex as primary to understand a rape culture); and Abdulali 2018, 133. These books and articles represent what I call the "mainstream" view. They are written and published for a broad, popular, non-academic audience. Some recent academic texts that emphasize rape culture as primarily about male domination of women include Marcus (in Butler and Scott 1992) and Projansky 2001; more recent academic texts often note that rape culture extends beyond the gender dynamic, though most still emphasize its gendered dimensions. See, for example, Mardorossian 2014; Ferreday 2015; Phillips 2017. More recently, Julia Serano has challenged the mainstream account of rape culture in a way that aligns with my argument, but she does so by arguing that "forms of sexualization that fall shy of sexual assault can nevertheless have very real negative consequences in and of themselves" (2022, 128, 129–30). I agree with Serano and am simply making a different claim about the mainstream account.
25. Taub 2014.
26. Crenshaw explains: "the interpretive work that must be done to make ideas [like intersectionality] work in different contexts is a feature of the discursive environment through which ideas travel rather than a reflection of inherent deficiencies in ideas themselves. It is quite clear that as an idea travels, the ways that it is re-articulated, sized up, written down, adapted, disciplined, and deployed all become part of its discursive history—its travel log as it were" (in Lutz et al. 2011, 223).
27. Wells-Barnett 1895, chap. 1; Davis 1983, 183; Alexander 2012, 28.
28. Douglass 1895, part II.
29. Wells-Barnett 1895, chap. 1.
30. Davis 1978, 27–28.
31. Oklahoma Commission 2001, 57, see also Astor 2020.
32. Oklahoma Commission 2001, 59–62 and passim.
33. A 2025 Department of Justice report on the Tulsa Massacre determined that at least three hundred people were killed and at least another seven hundred were injured (Department of Justice 2025, 51).
34. Wells-Barnett 1895, chap. 6, emphasis added.
35. Curry 2017, 57–58.
36. Ibid., 56–58.
37. In the cases listed here, either the accuser(s) recanted or forensic evidence eventually exonerated the accused. See Patton and Snyder-Yuly 2007.
38. Stansell 2010, 347.
39. Ibid. This myth, invoked in the mid-1970s, is not new. The ancient myth of the rape of Lucretia depends on Lucretia's moral purity and innocence. More recently, those who are considered "innocent victims" are not only white but also middle- or upper-class (their class status doubling as a marker of moral worth). The association of working-class or poor women with immorality often led to the dismissal of their rape allegations during the nineteenth and early twentieth centuries (D'Cruze in J. Brown and Walklate 2012, 32–33, discusses this during the Victorian period in England; Bourke 2007, 109, discusses this in the US context).
40. Stansell 2010, 345.
41. Murphy 2016.
42. Bever 2016. Kate Manne calls this "himpathy" (2018).
43. D. K. King 1988, 47.
44. Harris-Perry 2011, 55–56, 88.
45. Ibid., 59.
46. New York Radical Feminists 1974 (in Connell and Wilson 1974, 60).

47. Ibid., 6.
48. Ibid., 5. This text includes a few essays about popular representations of rape and may be the first time the term "rape culture" is used in print, though the term is only used once and is not defined (103).
49. Ibid., 3.
50. Griffin 1977 (originally published in 1971; in Chappell et al. 1977, 50–51).
51. Ibid., 50.
52. Ibid., 62.
53. Lazarus and Wunderlich (dirs.) 1983. As I hope is clear from my analysis, because I view rape as an assertion of relative entitlement to dominate through sex, I argue that all persons (regardless of gender) can be raped.
54. Combahee River Collective (in Moraga and Anzaldúa 2015, 213).
55. Ibid., 212.
56. Brownmiller 1993, 15.
57. Cohen 2015.
58. Cooke 2018.
59. Remnick 2017.
60. Brownmiller 1993; Davis 1983, 196–99.
61. Brownmiller 1993, 252.
62. Ibid., 247.
63. Ibid.
64. Pérez-Peña 2017.
65. Griffin 1977 (in Chappell et al. 1977, 63).
66. Alexander 2012; Wacquant 2009.
67. Davis 1983, 198. Emphasis in original.
68. Davis 1978, 1983, 177 and 196.
69. Davis 1983, 191.
70. Ibid., 177.
71. Collins 2019, 4, emphasis added.
72. See also Anthony Giddens's "double hermeneutic" (1987, 18).
73. Deborah K. King refers to this kind of thinking as "monist" (1988, 51) and explains that monistic discourses in feminism fail to recognize the multiple "jeopardies" exerted via gender and class subordination, which renders Black women either invisible or marginal in the analysis (57).
74. Inasmuch as I argue that discourses contribute to logics that yield material effects (via practices), this view could be considered loosely Foucauldian.
75. Ortner 2006, 16.
76. Serano 2022, 131–32.
77. Ortner 2006, 16.
78. RAINN 2014, on a page that is no longer published on their website but can be found at the Wayback Machine at https://web.archive.org/web/20210421103451/https://www.rainn.org/news/rainn-urges-white-house-task-force-overhaul-colleges%E2%80%99-treatment-rape.
79. Messina-Dysert 2015.
80. Ortner 2006, 129.
81. Sood 2019, 406, 414.
82. VandenBos 2007.
83. *Oxford English Dictionary* 2025.
84. Marcus (in Butler and Scott 1992, 391).
85. Ibid., 393.
86. I use this language to reflect "intersectionality's working hypothesis of the relational nature of power relations" (Collins 2019, 16).
87. Jaleel 2021, 9. See also Sanyal 2019, 3, 100–01.
88. *Oxford English Dictionary* 2023.
89. While I invoke the precise term "sq*aw," I acknowledge the history and implications of it being "spoken" in my voice as a white settler. I use an asterisk to disrupt my use of the word in order to signify the ways in which it has been appropriated for use by white settlers in a racist and misogynistic way. I have no interest in replicating those patterns.

Chapter Two

1. While this legislation contained regulations unrelated to bathrooms, I refer to them as "bathroom bills" because this aspect gained the most public attention and captures the feature of the bills I am exploring in relation to US rape culture.
2. The 2016 North Carolina bill was partially repealed in 2017 under public pressure, including a National Collegiate Athletic Association (NCAA) boycott of the state (Hanna et al. 2017).
3. Data collected at the Trans Legislation Tracker, updated regularly at https://translegislation.com/learn. Accessed in May 2024. As I write this in 2025, President Trump has just signed an executive order defining "male" and "female" in biological terms, requiring the federal government to enforce sex-based distinctions, and prohibiting the use of federal funds to "promote gender ideology," all in the name of "defend[ing] women's rights and protect[ing] freedom of conscience" (White House 2025).
4. Barnett et al. 2018.
5. Bevacqua 2000, 114–16.
6. Throughout this chapter, I use "mis-association" rather than "false association" to more accurately convey the willful conflation of trans persons and sexual predators.
7. Gorski and Perry 2022. They describe an "'us vs. them' tribalism" that seeks to "redeem and restore a lost world corrupted by 'outsiders,'" often by violent means (p. 7). Although it makes sense to distinguish between Christian nationalism and Christian evangelicalism, as Gorski and Perry do (pp. 9–10), I see these debates as Christian nationalist because they reserve the enactment of violence to preserve a white Christian heteropatriarchal order and white Christian freedom.
8. Ibid., 7.
9. Personal conversation, March 2024.
10. The ADF advocates a wide range of anti-trans legislation, but this chapter focuses on its involvement in the bathroom bills because of their work to advance a discourse about sexual violence (who are its victims, predators, and saviors) and how that discourse reinforces the US rape culture as well as white heteropatriarchy.
11. Michaels 2016.
12. Percelay 2015.
13. The ADF claims it has participated in several such cases, including *Masterpiece Cakeshop* and *Arlene's Flowers* (see ADF Legal n.d.).
14. Barnett et al. 2018, 234–35.
15. Family Research Council 2017.
16. Philipps 2016.
17. Gordon et al. 2017.
18. Lacour 2017.
19. This latter provision of HB2 was repealed the following year after significant pressure from outside organizations, including the NCAA. The repealed version of the bill preserved state authority to regulate public restrooms and changing rooms but did not allow cities to pass additional anti-discrimination measures until December 1, 2020 (Ibid.).
20. The ADF's support for such measures is evinced by its backing of defendants in the recent *Masterpiece Cakeshop, Ltd. v. Colorado Civil Rights Commission* (2018) and *Arlene's Flowers et al. v. Washington et al.* court cases.
21. The ADF advocates "generational wins" in five key areas (right to life; religious freedom; free speech; "God's creative order for marriage, the family, and human sexuality"; and "the fundamental rights of parents to direct the upbringing and education of their children") (ADF Legal n.d.).
22. Stern 2021.
23. Stern 2021; Avery 2021. I focus on the bathroom bills, even though they are only one piece of the anti-trans legislative strategy because they are justified as a way to prevent sexual violence. Thus, they occupy a unique place in US rape culture.
24. The ADF maintains that there has been a shift in the legislative approach to religious liberty: "For many years, religious freedom cases in the United States focused mostly on protecting certain minority religious beliefs. Today, the government has begun legislating in areas that violate core tenets of the Christian, Jewish, and Islamic faiths" (ADF Legal n.d.).
25. Mattise et al. 2021.
26. Sher 2021.

27. Sears and Osten 2003 associate "homosexual behavior" with pedophilia (83); claim that gender non-conforming persons (especially parents) deliberately try to indoctrinate children to "the homosexual agenda" (114), and explicitly connect gender confusion with "sexual dysfunction" (115). See also Dowland 2015, 158.
28. General Assembly of the State of Tennessee HB 1182 debate. 1:51:00. Transcription mine.
29. W. Brown 1992, 16.
30. Currah 2013.
31. Dowland 2015, 18–19.
32. Cavanagh 2010, referencing Butler 1990.
33. Du Mez defines a traditional family in the evangelical Christian tradition as "headed by a white, heterosexual male breadwinner" (2020, 100).
34. For a contextualized discussion of the historic, racialized dimensions of the enactment of legal and extra-legal violence by white persons in the United States, see Beltrán 2020, 23, 52.
35. Spillers 1987, 74. Emphases in the original.
36. Du Mez 2020, 4, 93–4. I draw on Du Mez's definition of Christian nationalism throughout this chapter: "the belief that America is God's chosen nation and must be defended as such." This belief extends to domestic and foreign policy (4).
37. Ibid., 4.
38. Dowland 2015, 11–12.
39. Du Mez 2020, 39.
40. Ibid., 91 and 88; Dowland 2015, 172.
41. Du Mez 2020, 91.
42. Ibid., 67, 83.
43. Ibid., 80; Dowland 2015, 12.
44. Sears and Osten 2003, 96.
45. Du Mez 2020, 67.
46. Ibid., 88.
47. Sears and Osten 2003, 116.
48. Ibid., 115–16.
49. Stolakis 2021 at 15:10, 16:00, and passim; see also Sears and Osten 2003, 3.
50. White House 2025.
51. Lopez 2015.
52. See Dowland 2015, 172.
53. In this discussion, I use the words "predators" and "predatory" cautiously. I am trying to capture the sense of threat that is being invoked. In general, I don't find these terms useful for thinking about sexual violence because they are suggestive of the myth of the "bad man rapist" or the "stranger in the bushes," as if sexual violence is rare rather than commonplace.
54. Barnett et al. 2018.
55. Ibid., 239.
56. Ibid., 235, 236.
57. Family Research Council 2017, emphasis in original.
58. See Rouse and Hamilton 2021; Hird 1996 (reproduced in Stryker and Aizura 2013).
59. See Bettcher 2007.
60. Bettcher 2007.
61. RAINN n.d.
62. Bettcher 2007, 285, quoted in Stryker and Aizura 2013.
63. James et al. 2016, 198.
64. Ibid.
65. Barnett et al. 2018, 234.
66. James et al. 2016, 185.
67. Barnett et al. 2018 report low incidents of sexual violence in public bathrooms and a lack of evidence suggesting that trans persons commit such violence.
68. In the final deliberations of HB 1182, Rudd said his goal is to make Tennessee a "forerunner" of such legislation (General Assembly of the State of Tennessee 1:50:09).
69. ADF Legal n.d.
70. Southern Poverty Law Center, n.d. In response, the ADF put out a disclaimer noting, for example, that it files lawsuits and briefs in defense of jurisdictional claims (e.g., https://www.splcenter.org/sites/default/files/adf-ap-and-others-v-france-echr-brief.pdf).

71. Southern Poverty Law Center 2017. See also Sears and Osten 2003, 83.
72. Glenza 2020.
73. See Dowland 2015, 157. See White House 2025.
74. Spade 2015, 32.
75. See Beauchamp 2019, 89.
76. Enke 2012, 74–75, see also Beauchamp 2019, especially 79–106. Emphasis in original.
77. Beauchamp 2019, 93–94.
78. Wootson 2018.
79. As the time of writing, twenty-six individuals have accused Trump of sexual violence (Hurley 2023).
80. For recent accounts of how settlers use both the force of the law and their claim to be outside the law (i.e., their right to be lawless enactors of violence), see Beltrán 2020; Wolfe 2006. Ida B. Wells identifies this logic in her account of "lynch law," as described in Chapter One.
81. Young 2003, 4.
82. See Du Mez 2020; Dowland 2015.
83. Ibid., 2.
84. Ibid., 4.
85. Du Mez 2020, 51.
86. Young 2003, 13. See also Rose 2021: the determination of who is innocent is mutually constitutive of the determination about who can be violent (2).
87. Richie 2012, 78, emphasis in original.
88. Spade 2015, 73–74.
89. Schmidt 2020.
90. Pauly 2023.
91. Women's Liberation Front n.d.
92. As one example that challenges the view that sexual violence is inevitable, I show in Chapter Three that Indigenous cultures in North America did not demonstrate a tendency to use sexual violence as a strategy of control because they did not have the same heteropatriarchal, white supremacist, or settler values or gender relations. Culture matters.
93. Women's Liberation Front 2024.
94. Beltrán 2020, 49; see also Du Mez 2020, 56.
95. Du Mez 2020, 42, 53.
96. Transcribed by *Time* 2015.
97. Steiger 2015.
98. Transcribed at *New York Times* 2016.
99. Blake 2016.
100. Kogan 2016.
101. Kogan 2016. See also Cavanagh 2010.
102. Crenshaw 1991, 1271; Davis 1983, 176.
103. Crenshaw 1991, 1271.
104. Richie 2012, 94, emphasis added.
105. W. Brown 1992, 9.
106. South Dakota HB1008 2016.
107. Deutsch n.d.
108. M. Mayer 2017.
109. M. Smith 2016, emphasis added.
110. Cavanagh 2010, 64.
111. Centers for Disease Control n.d.
112. Murray et al. 2014, 3.
113. Centers for Disease Control n.d.
114. Seto et al. 2015, 43.
115. Edelman 2004, 11.
116. Ibid.
117. This is one reason why it would be a mistake, in Spade's view (and, I suspect, in the view of other critics of "carceral feminism") to seek "getting protected" as a desired outcome as long as the state has a vested interest in trying to get people to vie for its protection.
118. Du Mez 2020, 42, 53.

Chapter Three

1. The word "Indigenous" is inexact, and I typically use more precise identifications when referring to specific individuals or groups. Robert Nichols cautions against constructing a monolithic Indigenous identity but also notes that "despite—or perhaps because of—the decentralized, heterodox, and fluid nature of the various processes and mechanics of its articulation, dispossession had a relatively stable, predictable, and uniform effect on Indigenous peoples" (2020, 98). Like Nichols, I use the modifier "Indigenous" to indicate this effect.
2. Deer cautions against calling the high incidence of sexual violence an "epidemic" because it suggests a recent, biological problem and "deflects responsibility because it fails to acknowledge the agency of perpetrators and those who allow the problem to continue" (2015, x).
3. Deer 2015.
4. See Deer 2015, chap. 1, for an accounting of the data on violence against Native Americans. See also Lucchesi and Echo-Hawk 2018.
5. Black 2018, 215.
6. Esterhuyse et al. 2022; Holzman 2011; Meng 2017; US Geological Survey 2022.
7. These effects are compounded when concentrated in small, rural areas (Ruddell and Britto 2020, 207).
8. Lim 2018; Archbold et al. 2014; Pippert and Zimmer Schneider 2018; Parson and Ray 2020.
9. Wolfe 2006, 388.
10. Voyles 2015, 9–10.
11. Tallbear 2018 in Clarke and Haraway 2018, 146–47; see also S. Hunt 2015, 28.
12. L. B. Simpson 2017, 45, emphasis in original.
13. Nichols (2020) writes: "one cannot help but be struck by the relatively *uniform effect* of all these different micro-practices" (90) that, like all racist practices, sustain "long-standing patterns of group-differentiated vulnerability" (88).
14. Deer 2015; A. Simpson 2016; L. B. Simpson 2017; A. Smith 2015; Estes et al. 2021.
15. A. Simpson 2016, emphasis added.
16. As I noted in Chapter one, while I invoke the term "sq∗aw," I acknowledge the history and implications of it being "spoken" in my voice as a white settler. I use an asterisk to disrupt my use of the word to signify how it has been appropriated for use by white settlers in a racist and misogynistic way. When the word is used by another author, I have bracketed the asterisk to signify that this is my usage, not the author's.
17. L. B. Simpson 2017, 29.
18. Bruyneel 2021, xiii.
19. S. Hunt 2015, 27.
20. A. Simpson 2016. Sarah Deer also notes "precolonial gender balance" that is disrupted by settler heteropatriarchy (2015, 25). See also Barman 1997/1998, 243 and 258 and L. B. Simpson 2017, 52.
21. Tallbear in Clarke and Haraway 2018, 159; S. Hunt 2015, 27, 33; Barman 1997/1998, 242; A. Smith 2003, 76–78; Arvin et al. 2013, 22–23.
22. L. B. Simpson 2017, 96–97.
23. Agtuca, quoted in Amnesty International 2007, 15.
24. A. Smith 2003, 78, 82. I refer to the settler "state" or "project" enacted by individuals who assert their power and needs over others, not all of whom are white men. The settler "project" that does not want its heteropatriarchal notions of womanhood and maternity to be challenged is at least partly upheld by the white women who benefit (or think they benefit) from these notions (L. B. Simpson 2017, 96–97).
25. A. Simpson 2016, Section "Bodies".
26. A. Smith 2003, 76. Indigenous scholars like Audra Simpson have recently referenced Smith's valuable historical work on this topic. In response to questions about Smith's claim to membership in the Cherokee community, I follow Simpson's practice of identifying Smith as a feminist scholar, without identifying her as a member of an Indigenous community. I am in no position to participate in discussions of Indigenous community membership and wish to do no harm to those involved in this discussion. I draw on Smith's work here because I believe she has done important archival research which needs to be included in this analysis.
27. Deer 2015, 25. See also Barman 1997/1998, 243, 258; L. B. Simpson 2017, 52.
28. Rosay 2016, 2.

29. Ibid., 11. See also Deer 2015, 6, citing a study by Greenfield and Smith.
30. This statistic describes how many respondents reported having been assaulted by an interracial perpetrator, *not* the percentage of all reported rapes by an interracial perpetrator.
31. Shippen 2021.
32. Urban Indian Health Institute 2020.
33. Ibid.
34. Ibid.
35. Deer 2015, 4.
36. Women's Earth Alliance and Native Youth Sexual Health Network 2016, 33. Lim 2018 reports some complicating evidence that connects the temporary population increase in the Bakken region to the increased rates of sexual violence. This report nevertheless does not contradict the fact that Indigenous women and girls face disproportionate rates of sexual violence and that it is typically perpetrated by a non-Indigenous person. Further, Lim's study draws on FBI uniform crime reports statistics (those reported to law enforcement, including tribal police) but does not challenge the claim, suggested by the DOJ report cited above that non-Indigenous persons are targeting Indigenous persons.
37. See Maracle 1996, 55; Women's Earth Alliance and Native Youth Sexual Health Network 2016, 32; S. Hunt 2015, 33; and the documentary short film *Nuuca* (Latimer 2018).
38. S. Hunt 2016, 20:00-21:00. See also Maracle 1996, 55; Deer 2015, 5.
39. Ruddell and Britto 2020, 206. This study surveys all long-term residents and does not disaggregate by race.
40. Rosay 2016. See also Women's Earth Alliance and Native Youth Sexual Health Network 2016; Amnesty International 2007.
41. Deer 2015, xi.
42. L. B. Simpson 2017, 80; Urban Indian Health Institute 2020, 14; Women's Earth Alliance and Native Youth Sexual Health Network 2016, 3.
43. Hunt 2016, 20:08.
44. C. R. King 2003, 12.
45. C. R. King 2003, 6. The same language is not used to describe people in the colonized Pacific Islands, suggesting that Pacific Islanders are racialized and sexualized *differently* from Indigenous persons in North America, as exotic objects of fascination. See Trask 1999, 143.
46. Goddard 1997. See also Deloria 1998, 33.
47. C. R. King 2003, 3–4. See also Deloria 1998, 33.
48. C. R. King 2003, 3–4.
49. A. Simpson 2016, Section "Grief".
50. In Barman 1997/1998, 239.
51. See Beltrán 2020.
52. A. Smith 2003, 77.
53. Rowlandson 1682.
54. Barman 1997/1998, 240.
55. Ibid.
56. Barman 1997/1998, 245.
57. A. Smith 2003, 78.
58. Green 1975.
59. Ibid., 711.
60. Ibid., 713.
61. Parezo and Jones 2009, 379; Merskin 2010, 353.
62. Nichols 2020, 58.
63. A. Smith 2003, 73.
64. Ibid. 78.
65. Arvin et al. 2013, 23.
66. Simpson 2016.
67. Driskill et al. 2011, 25; see also Finley in Driskill et al. 2011, 40.
68. Parezo and Jones 2009, 378.
69. Rosay 2016.
70. Finley in et al. 2011, 35.
71. S. Hunt 2016, 11:15.
72. Croisy 2017, 6.

73. Matera 2018.
74. A. Smith 2003, 80.
75. WeRNative.org n.d.
76. Maracle 1996. See also Deer 2015, 7–8.
77. Maracle 1996, 54.
78. S. Hunt 2015, 33.
79. Ibid.
80. Farley et al. 2011.
81. A. Simpson 2016, Section "Grief". Emphasis in original.
82. I quote this line because it is important to highlight this specific racialization in the film. As with the word "sq*aw," I am mindful of who this word references and who is speaking it (and where I fit into these categories). I have also "disrupted" this word with an asterisk in my text because I believe that some white people (including some scholars) have a subconscious desire to "say" the N word without saying it, by putting it into someone else's mouth. My practice here is imperfect, but it is my way of trying to show how anti-Blackness is functioning in this racialization. The word is harmful when "spoken" in the voice of a character (as intended in the film), but I am trying not to replicate that harm as a white scholar.
83. Sheridan 2017a, 98.
84. Lucchesi and Echo-Hawk 2018, 6.
85. Lucchesi 2019, 12–13. This joint study of the Sovereign Bodies Institute and the Brave Heart Society was part of the preparatory reading materials distributed to members for the first meeting of the DOJ's MMIW Task Force in 2020.
86. Shippen 2021.
87. Native Hope 2019.
88. Yellow Bird 2009; see also Dura 2021.
89. MHA Nation 2018.
90. Ibid.
91. Ibid. I note that Sakakawea is a figure who is most often valorized in alignment with the myth of "Indian princess" who assisted white settlers nobly.
92. Murdoch 2020, 116.
93. Ibid., 43.
94. Climate in Berthold, North Dakota n.d.
95. Murdoch 2020, 354. See also Grann 2017, passim.
96. According to Arvin et al. 2013, 21, "land is knowing and knowledge."
97. L. B. Simpson 2017, 43.
98. Coulthard 2014, 60. Emphasis in original.
99. Ibid., 61.
100. Coulthard and Simpson 2016, 251–52; L. B. Simpson 2017, 75.
101. Coulthard 2014, 38–41.
102. Ibid., 8–11. See also Nichols 2020, 57.
103. Coulthard 2014, 9–11. See also Nichols 2020, 83–84.
104. Nichols 2020, 8.
105. Locke 2003, §42. See also §38, §49.
106. Ibid., §32.
107. Ibid., §34. For additional examples of this logic in the US colonies, see A. Smith 2005, 56–57.
108. Klein 2014, 169–70.
109. Lisa Brunner, White Earth Ojibwe, quoted in Pember 2018, describing the relationship between extractive industries and sexual violence.
110. I refer to this land as the Bakken when describing it as a site of industrial activity rather than as one of tradition, homeland, relation, and care.
111. INCITE! Women of Color against Violence 2016, 84–85.
112. Merchant 1989, 173.
113. Ibid., 168–70.
114. Ibid., 177–80.
115. Saidero 2017.
116. McHenry 2021, 199. See also Black 2018, 215.
117. The popular remake of the TV series *Battlestar Galactica* used the word "frak" to signify "fuck." Although this usage apparently preceded the widespread use of the term "fracking" to describe

hydraulic fracturing, according to the Sierra Club it has helped turn "fracking" into a dirty word. Today, the association is widespread (Rauber 2014).

118. McHenry 2021, 200.
119. Ibid.; Parson and Ray 2020; Pippert and Zimmer Schneider 2018.
120. Sigurdson 2014, 249–50, 263–64.
121. Ibid., 250.
122. Ibid., 265.
123. Phillips 2013, 47.
124. Ibid., 55–56.
125. Arvin et al. 2013, 12.
126. Native Governance Center 2022.
127. Gilmore 2007, 28.
128. A. Smith 2005, 16; Wolfe 2006, 388.
129. See Carpio 2004.
130. Arias et al. 2023, 3.
131. See L. B. Simpson 2017, 25; Coulthard 2014, 60.
132. Moran and Gies 2015.
133. Murdoch 2020, 190.
134. Ibid., 159.
135. Marathon Oil 2012.
136. Klein 2014, 311.
137. Sheridan 2017a, 94.
138. Connell and Messerschmidt 2005, 832.
139. Ibid., 846.
140. Connell 1993, 611–12, citing Phillips 1980. Recent scholarly work has located frontier masculinity in workplace practices within the oil industry (Miller 2004), discourse and practices of gun use and ownership (Stroud 2012), and wildlife management (Anahita and Mix 2006). Ruddell and Britto 2020, 213–14, describe a "frontier masculinity" that is connected to resource extraction.
141. Arvin et al. 2013, 18. I detail many aspects of the heteropatriarchal family and the binary gender roles it enforces in Chapter Two.
142. L. B. Simpson 2017, 128–29.
143. Brooks 2018, 265.
144. For a discussion of settler violence and the law, see Beltrán 2020, 51–60.
145. Ibid., 53. Emphasis in original.
146. Bird 1990, 66; Arvin et al. 2013, 14; A. Smith 2003, 76–78. Also, see my discussion of the sq*aw above, citing Jean Barman.
147. This line is in the screenplay (Sheridan 2017a, 6) but not the film.
148. When he has caught Pete, Cory convinces him to confess by saying, "Hey, look, I'm not the law here" (Sheridan 2017b, 1:26:20).
149. Ibid., 1:23:20
150. Ibid., 1:35:00.
151. McHenry 2021, 199.
152. Murdoch 2020, 53.
153. Filteau 2015, 447.
154. Ruddell and Britto 2020, 213.
155. Murdoch 2020, 197.
156. Ferree and Smith 2013.
157. Garofalo 2022.
158. Caraher et al. 2017, 274, 276.
159. Pippert and Zimmer Schneider 2018, 236; Archbold et al. 2014, 399.
160. Caraher et al. 2017, passim.
161. Ibid.
162. Filteau 2014. 409.
163. Ibid., 409. See also McHenry 2021, 200.
164. Lim 2018; Lucchesi 2019, 5 and 13; Ruddell et al. 2014.
165. Pippert and Zimmer Schneider 2018, 241.

166. Jayasundara et al. 2018, 65. This challenges the conclusion of Lim 2018, whose analysis is based on FBI universal crime reports.
167. See also Deer 2015.
168. Murdoch 2020, 151–52.
169. Ibid., 159.
170. Ibid., 245.
171. Pippert and Zimmer Schneider 2018. 245.
172. Ibid., 246.
173. Ruddell and Britto 2020, 210.
174. Running Horse Buckley 2015.
175. Jayasundara et al. 2018, 67.
176. Ibid., 70.
177. Pippert and Zimmer Schneider 2018, 239–40, 245.
178. Beltrán 2020, 52–53.
179. Pippert and Zimmer Schneider 2018, 241.
180. L. B. Simpson 2017, 52. Emphasis in original.
181. Maracle 1996, 20.

Chapter Four

1. Parts of this chapter are reproduced from Kessel 2020. Copyright © 2019, Springer Nature Limited.
2. Jones 2013.
3. See Freedman 2013; Bourke 2007.
4. My use of the word "magic" is inspired by a line by Bonnie Honig in *Democracy and the Foreigner* (2001, 17: "By what magic are dependent, not yet fully formed followers supposed to become the responsible, active citizens that democracy requires?"), which, for me, also brings to mind Joan Didion's idea of "magical thinking." I think of discursive magic as a kind of political magical thinking, in which the magic wand of consent is waved over the issue of widespread sexual violence, and society no longer has a rape problem.
5. I have learned a great deal about the nuances and complexities of legally permissible but morally questionable sex from Zoe Moss's 2024 dissertation, "Bad Sex." See also Garcia 2023 (especially chap. 1).
6. Ribiero et al. 2021.
7. Ging 2019.
8. Mamié et al. 2021.
9. Ribeiro et al. 2021.
10. Mamié et al. 2021.
11. Frost 2013. Without evidence, another *Return of Kings* contributor, Jon Anthony, suggests that "dozens of men are falsely accused every day" (2016).
12. Zuboff 2019, 9.
13. As Manon Garcia recently noted, contracts create obligations in *civil* law, but "sexual consent belongs to criminal law" (2023, 29).
14. De Zutter et al. 2017. A meta-analysis by Ferguson and Malouff 2016 reveals a similar rate.
15. Harsey and Freyd 2022.
16. Frost 2013.
17. Keating describes compensatory domination as a mode of rule in which the most powerful actors (including, but in my view not limited to, state actors) "use ideological conditioning (and sometimes force) to pressure or entice dominant members of a structurally subordinate group to exercise command as part of the process of manufacturing consent, or at least of establishing acquiescence" (2011, 6).
18. Frost 2013.
19. Ibid.
20. Srinivasan 2021, 5.
21. Ibid., 14.
22. See Laiou 1993. Since I am limiting my focus to US rape culture, I begin with this history but am not suggesting that other mythic traditions did not have stories about rape and consent or

that the European mythic tradition emerged wholly untouched by travel, migrations, explorations, and colonizations from non-European places, which may have informed and changed these myths over time.
23. Brundage 1987, 64–65.
24. Dunn 2012, 53.
25. J. Brown and Walklate 2012, 32–33.
26. Dunn 2012, 24.
27. Brundage 1987, 22.
28. Laiou 1993, 50. See also Dunn 2012, 61.
29. Laiou 1993, 25–26.
30. Ibid., 28. See also Dunn 2012, who describes the lack of legal protections afforded to "lower-status women" relative to higher-status men (62) and their likely difficulties in successfully prosecuting a rape charge.
31. Brundage 1987, 48.
32. Laiou 1993, 25–26.
33. Brundage 1987, 56.
34. Dunn 2012; Hawkes 1995.
35. Dunn 2012, 42.
36. Brundage 1987, 209.
37. Hawkes 2007, 117.
38. Ibid., 130.
39. Brundage 1987, 532.
40. Ibid., 470.
41. Ibid., 107, 470. See also Laiou 1993, 24.
42. Laiou 1993, 32–33.
43. Ehrlich 2001, 65; Estrich 1986, 1122.
44. McGregor 2005, 29.
45. Ibid., 29, 33.
46. Davis 1978, 25.
47. Estrich 1986, 1090.
48. Freedman 2013, 47. See also Crenshaw 1991, 1269–71.
49. Kendall 2021. According to this *Washington Post* story, "A former Minnesota prosecutor reviewed Kansas law for the Smiths and concluded that the attack qualified for a rape charge. 'I would contend that it is clear that if while strangling someone, they are pulling on your hands and gasping for breath, and they are crying, none of that sounds consensual to me,' said Julie Germann, who specialized in sexual assault cases. 'I would not have a hard time taking that case to a jury at all.'"
50. Davis 1983 177.
51. Combahee River Collective (in Moraga and Anzaldúa 2015, 210).
52. Historian Sharon Block argues that enslaved Black and servant white women in the United States might, in some important ways, be subject to the same kinds of sexual coercion and the same presumptions about their right to refuse consent to unwanted sexual advances (in Hodes 1999, 143). This equation of experiences is a mistake: enslavement is a radically different political position than servanthood, even if the latter is also subject to some related forms of domination.
53. Srinivasan 2021, 17–18.
54. Wolf 1997.
55. Chang 2021; Trask 1999.
56. Harris-Perry 2011.
57. Settles et al. 2008, 459–60.
58. Buchanan et al. 2008, 355.
59. Ibid., 349.
60. Haag 1999, xv.
61. For examples of critical contract arguments, see Pateman 1988; Mills 1999; Simplican 2015. By exploring the social contract and its implicit assumptions about personhood, each reveals different grounds for inequality within the contract tradition.
62. W. Brown 1995, 162–63.
63. Mills 1999, 56.

64. Mills 1999, 56.
65. For more on the hyper-sexualization of Black women as one mode of misrecognition (Black woman as Jezebel) which justified the intensive and unabashed "brutality of Southern white men," see Harris-Perry 2011, 55.
66. Blinder 2018.
67. Crenshaw in Morrison 1992, 416.
68. Ibid., 410–11, 414.
69. Ibid., 420–22. See also Richie 2012, 46.
70. Mills 2017, 29, 31. See also Christine Keating 2011, 7, on "compensatory domination."
71. See, for example, Harris-Perry 2011; Richie 2012.
72. Fischel and O'Connell 2015, 430.
73. Ibid.
74. Haag 1999, 25.
75. Ibid., citing Lawrence Friedman.
76. Ibid., chap. 2, passim.
77. Ibid., 45.
78. Ibid., 26.
79. See, for example, Brownmiller 1993, 163; D'Cruze in Laiou 1993, 25–26; Brundage 1987, 209.
80. Donovan and Brown 2014.
81. Brundage 1987, 396.
82. Laiou 1993, 27; M. D. Smith 2001, 29.
83. Haag 1999, 14.
84. Bourke 2007, 41.
85. Dunn 2012, 68.
86. Ibid., 64.
87. Levy 2013.
88. Radin 2013, 56.
89. Radin 2013, chap. 4, provides a good overview.
90. *Restatement (Second) of Contracts* 1.1. (Perillo 2014) This account, which emphasizes that contracts represent an obligation that parties make to each other about the future, is not universally accepted. See Fried 1981 for a defense of the view and Macneil 1980 for a critique. Radin 2013 argues that the philosophical debates about the meaning of contracts seem divorced from the contemporary realities of their enforcement (57).
91. Perillo 2014, 19, 57.
92. Perillo., 58. See Fried 1981, 31, for a discussion of "mutuality."
93. Perillo 2014, 4.
94. Ibid., 1.4.
95. Fried 1981, 42.
96. See Perillo 1.4.e, referencing the Chicago school.
97. Ibid.
98. Brundage 1987, 209.
99. Rudolph 2000, 161, 167, 171.
100. Ibid., 177.
101. Ibid.
102. Jones 2013.
103. While Jones does not specifically mention race, she references two instances of what she calls false rape accusations in sports (Kobe Bryant and the Duke Lacrosse case). These cases are very different, both in how race, gender, and class function and in the extent (and manner) to which the accusations were adjudicated to be false. If read intersectionally, these instances raise complicating questions about consent, the false rape accusation, and the myth of the false accuser that Jones does not address. Her column is written as general advice for parents but not intended as a commentary on gender, sex, and consent.
104. Jones 2013.
105. Ibid.
106. Anthony 2016.
107. Ibid.
108. Jones 2016.
109. Abramson 2014, 10.

110. Ibid.
111. LegalFling. January 12, 2018. Accessed through the Way Back Machine. https://web.archive.org/web/20180112005815/https://legalfling.io/.
112. The extent to which violation of the LegalFling agreement represents a breach of contract depends on jurisdiction. The "smart contract" produced as code on a blockchain is not yet legally binding in all places. Recent analysis of the viability of "smart contracts" suggests that their coded nature makes them reasonable for simple contracts (such as an exchange of currency for goods) but less so for more complex agreements: "In more complex, long-term, relational, and ambiguous contract types coding is highly problematic" (DiMatteo et al. 2020, 8–9). DiMatteo et al. note that, at this point, the legality of a smart contract likely depends on the precise contract itself, though innovations in coding may eventually produce legally binding, complex smart contracts. LegalFling's smart contract seems to be a fairly simple contract that belies the relationality and complexity of sexual consent: LegalFling's website claims that the blockchain ledger documents a transaction hash and a timestamp (https://legalfling.io/, accessed November 23, 2021; as of August 2024, the website for LegalFling and its parent company, LegalThings (https://legalthings.com/), no longer seemed to contain functioning links).
113. LegalFling. January 12, 2018. Emphasis added. Accessed through the Way Back Machine. https://web.archive.org/web/20180112005815/https://legalfling.io/
114. LegalFling. March 3, 2018. Boldface emphasis was in the original; italicized emphasis added. Accessed through the Way Back Machine. https://web.archive.org/web/20180303184132/https://legalfling.io/
115. DiMatteo et al. 2020, 7.
116. Srinivasan 2021, 29.
117. Manne 2020, 66.
118. Horneich 2016a.
119. Horneich 2016d.
120. Horneich 2016e.
121. Ibid., emphasis in original.
122. Horneich, 2016a.
123. Horneich 2016d.
124. Bourke 2007, 24.
125. Ibid.

Chapter Five

1. Hamilton et al. 2023, 1.
2. Marcus 2022.
3. Bruner 2021.
4. Marcus 2022.
5. Groce 2021. See also Laurin 2019, 74.
6. Groce 2021.
7. Kibbe 2020.
8. Marcus 2022.
9. Wilkinson 2017, 983.
10. Hamilton et al. 2023, sect. 4.3.
11. Berg 2021, 4.
12. Wilkinson 2017, 986.
13. Glick 2000, 28.
14. I use "both/and" here, rather than "either/or," to dwell on the contradiction as it is always present, rather than to suggest that sometimes it can be resolved in one direction and other times in the other.
15. Wynne 2021.
16. Reuters 2023.
17. Kibbe 2020.
18. Mae 2021. See also #payforyourporn: https://www.payforyourporn.org/.
19. Head 2021.
20. Wynne 2021.
21. Decaro et al. 2024, 1226.

22. Wilkinson 2017, 994n8.
23. Decaro et al. 2024, 1226, 1229.
24. Morris 2020.
25. Hamilton et al. 2023, 1.
26. Spangler 2022.
27. Marcus 2022. A report in *Time* in 2021 notes that: "Twitch, for instance, takes a 50% cut of any subscriptions. Only-Fans says the 20% it takes helps offset the costs of the security and privacy features that adult content in particular requires. Patreon takes 5% to 12%; Substack takes 10%, minus processing fees" (Bruner 2021).
28. Bruner 2021.
29. Shane 2021.
30. I thank Cristina Beltrán for helping me think through this point in a panel at the 2023 annual conference of the Association for Political Theory. She pointed out that the flip side of this logic is the tendency for entitled men to want to punish women who have what they do not or who represent what they lack. I discuss this dynamic with respect to Elliot Rodger in Chapter One. These apparent contradictions make sense in a rape culture in which some entitled men may want to embrace a certain fantasy (as if the subscriber were somehow responsible for the conspicuous consumption of "their" fantasy), while desiring to punish economic or other forms of independence in reality.
31. Berg 2021, 97.
32. Shane 2021.
33. Hamilton et al. 2023, sect. 4.3; Laurin 2019, 73; Cardoso et al. in Krijnen et al. 2023, 181–82.
34. W. Brown 2017, 65.
35. Ibid., 80, emphasis added.
36. Berg 2021, 110, cf. 118.
37. W. Brown 2017, 34.
38. Litam et al. 2022, 3098.
39. Ibid., 11. See also Wilkinson 2017, 983.
40. Berg 2021, 142.
41. Berg 2021, 117.
42. Ibid.
43. Ibid., 12–13.
44. Marcus 2022.
45. Ibid. "Simp" is a slang term for a man who does too much for a woman he likes, that is, a submissive and pathetic fool who gets played by a woman who strings him along (https://www.urbandictionary.com/define.php?term=Simp).
46. Marcus 2022.
47. Hamilton et al. 2023, sect. 4.2.
48. Avery Center 2021, 13.
49. Shane 2021.
50. Hamilton et al. 2023, sect. 4.2.
51. Berg 2021, 137.
52. A "camming" site is a site where individuals perform acts (often sexual) on camera for compensation.
53. Marcus 2022.
54. ThinkExpansion 2024; Marcus 2022; see also Brand Partner Agency 2021.
55. Marcus 2022.
56. Ibid.
57. Ibid.
58. Montemurro and Siefken 2012, 368.
59. Ibid., 367–68.
60. M. Friedman 2014, 52.
61. Ibid.
62. Ibid., 50.
63. Berg 2021, 116.
64. Drenten et al. 2020, 42 (citing Duffy 2017).
65. Pezzutto 2019, 35, cf. 37 and 40.
66. Jones 2021, 244.

67. Ibid.
68. Ibid., 249–50.
69. Hamilton et al. 2023, sect. 4.2.
70. Berg 2021, 116, 142.
71. Ibid., 142–43.
72. Drenten et al. 2020, 60.
73. Pezzutto 2019, 40.
74. Ibid., 35.
75. Ibid., 40.
76. Ibid., 40–41.
77. In a different context, philosopher C. Thi Nguyen refers to this as "value capture" (2020, 189).
78. M. G. Hunt et al. 2018.
79. Lee et al. 2022.
80. Berg 2021, 13–14.
81. Marcus 2022.
82. Litam et al. 2022, 3094.
83. See, for example, Federici 2014.
84. Hamilton et al. 2023, sect. 4.2.
85. W. Brown 2017, 33.
86. Swords et al. 2023, 278; Laurin 2019, 63; Bonifacio et al. 2023, 2687.
87. Bonofacio et al. 2023 (citing Craig and Cunningham 2019), 2685-6.
88. Drenten et al. 2020; Laurin 2019; Berg 2021.
89. Laurin 2019, 64–65.
90. Bernstein 2007, 103–05.
91. Groce 2021.
92. Bernstein 2007. See also Laurin 2019, 71–72.
93. Bernstein 2007, 6–7.
94. Berg 2021; Pezzuto 2019.
95. I thank Sara Rushing for this observation, which she shared as a comment in a panel at the 2023 Western Political Science Association annual conference.
96. Berg 2021, 2.
97. Manne 2020, 11. Emphasis in original.
98. Entitlement is not the same thing as *privilege* (as in "white privilege"), which refers to the unearned advantages of growing up white in a white supremacist society.
99. Manne 2018.
100. Bailey 2021, 1.
101. Serano 2009, 14–15.
102. I focus on men here because, as I noted above, they are the majority of OnlyFans customers. And, as I noted, claims to entitlement are not limited to claims to male entitlement. While I build on Manne's account, entitlement can be imposed on the basis of class, race, sexuality, and more. My analysis should thus be understood to apply to any customers on OnlyFans, not just men.
103. Tolentino 2023.
104. Manne 2020, 36–38.
105. Ibid., 45–48.
106. Ibid., 66.
107. Avery Center 2021, 13, emphasis added.
108. Bernstein 2007, 129–30.
109. Laurin 2019, 70.
110. Hernandez and Morton 2021.
111. Bindel 2020.
112. Tolentino 2023.
113. Ibid.
114. Lorenz 2023.
115. Tolentino 2023.
116. Ibid.
117. Lorenz 2023.
118. Carolus et al. 2021.

119. Costa and Ribas 2019.
120. Lorenz 2023.
121. Nelken-Zitser 2023.
122. Lorenz 2023.
123. Cole 2023.
124. Comella 2017, 10.

Chapter Six

1. Rose 2021, 3–4.
2. Mary James of Reed College shared this insight in a training at my university many years ago. It has stuck with me ever since.
3. Bailey 2021.
4. Bell 2022, episode 4, 40:40.
5. Ibid., episode 4, 41:51.
6. Collins 2000, 34. See also Collins and Bilge 2016, 32.
7. Hancock 2016, 27, 38, 185. Here, Hancock references G. Chezia Carraway's 1991 article, "Violence against Women of Color," in the *Stanford Law Review*'s remarkable issue *Women of Color at the Center: Selections from the Third National Conference of Women of Color and the Law.*
8. Combahee River Collective in Moraga and Anzaldúa 2015, 210.
9. Many texts speak to this point, including Sojourner Truth, "Ain't I a Woman?" (n.d.); Francis Beal, "Double Jeopardy" (2008); the Combahee River Collective's "Black Feminist Statement" reprinted in Taylor 2017; Kimberlé Crenshaw, "Mapping the Margins" (1991); Patricia Hill Collins, *Black Feminist Thought* (2000); Audre Lorde, *Sister Outsider* (2020); and Angela Y. Davis, *Women, Race, and Class* (1983). Rather than suggest a fractured self, these feminists understand the multiplicity of subject-positions (subjecting them to racism as well as heterosexism, for example) as simultaneous and mutually reinforcing.
10. I read Spillers's "misnaming," Harris-Perry's "misrecognition," and Collins's "controlling images" in similar light.
11. Spillers 1987, 65.
12. Ibid., 72.
13. Ibid., 80. Emphasis in original.
14. See Hartman 2016, 166.
15. Harris-Perry 2011, 33 and passim.
16. In Morrison 1992, 335. See discussions of the Moynihan Report in Lubiano in Morrison 1992; Spillers 1987; Hartman 2016.
17. Hine 1989, 915.
18. Spillers 1987, 67
19. Ibid., 70.
20. Painter in Morrison 1992, 204.
21. Davis 1971-2, 100 and passim.
22. Ibid. See also Collins 2000, 84–85.
23. Collins 2000, 89.
24. Crenshaw in Morrison 1992, 403.
25. Crenshaw in Morrison 1992, 416.
26. Crenshaw in Morrison 1992, 417.
27. Thomas 1991.
28. Collins 2000.
29. See Lubiano in Morrison 1992, 349; Painter in Morrison 1992, 209.
30. I thank my colleague Regina Duthely for sharing this insight with me.
31. Lubiano in Morrison 1992, 331.
32. Ibid., 342.
33. Famuyiwa 2016, 1:16. Although in some ways fictionalized, the film gives a new generation of people access to the Thomas confirmation hearing and reintroduces core moments into the current popular cultural imagination. In that sense, the film serves as its own cultural text for consideration.
34. Wallace-Wells 2018.
35. Graham 2018.

36. See remarks of Orrin Hatch (R-UT). "Senate Judiciary Committee Hearing on the Nomination of Brett M. Kavanaugh" 2018.
37. Collins 2000, 91.
38. Collins 2000, 89; Lubiano in Morrison 1992, 335.
39. Lubiano in Morrison 1992, 334. As of this writing, Thomas serves as an honorary board member of the Horatio Alger Association (https://horatioalger.org/leadership/, accessed June 18, 2024). And Thomas was not, in fact, self-made: his achievements were only possible because of the erasure of another Black woman: his sister, who stayed home and cared for ailing family members while Thomas was sent to private school and then on to college, unburdened by family care obligations (Morrison 1992, 202).
40. Ibid., 342.
41. Lubiano in Morrison 1992, 343. See also Collins 2000, 89.
42. Hill 1997, 85–87.
43. Crenshaw in Morrison 1992, 410.
44. Hill 1991 at 11:06.
45. Crenshaw in Morrison 1992, 420. Emphasis added.
46. Hill 1997, 191.
47. Lubiano in Morrison 1992, 345–47.
48. Crenshaw in Morrison 1992, 409–10; J. Mayer 2015.
49. Ransby 2018.
50. Hill 1997, 1.
51. Ibid., 195.
52. Epstein et al. 2017.
53. Noble 2018, 4–5, 10–11.
54. McGuire 2010, 40.
55. McGuire 2010 details each of these cases.
56. Davis 1983, 174.
57. Crenshaw in Morrison 1992, 413.
58. Schwab 2015.
59. In my research, I came across a Facebook group dedicated to Holtzclaw's innocence, which posted the photos (usually booking photos) of all of his accusers and cast the character of each into doubt.
60. Testa 2015.
61. Holtzclaw v. State 2019; Kaplan 2015; Schwab 2015. The courts have protected the identities of Holtzclaw's accusers, but a Facebook group called "In Defense of Daniel Holtzclaw" posted images of him in uniform and what appear to be his accusers' booking photos. This common strategy is meant to emphasize Holtzclaw's lawfulness against his accusers' lawlessness.
62. Kaplan 2015.
63. Fenwick and Schwarz 2015.
64. See, for example, https://www.holtzclawtrial.com/untold-story and https://www.uncufftheinnocent.org/daniel-holtzclaw (accessed August 24, 2024).
65. Kaplan 2015.
66. "Holtzclaw Verdict" 2015.
67. Oklahoma Senate 2019.
68. I thank my colleague Regina Duthely for sharing this insight with me.
69. Tillman et al. 2010, 63–65.
70. Hine 1989.
71. The words "rapeable" and "unrapeable" (like "flammable" and "inflammable") appear to be opposites but mean the same thing. To call a person "rapeable" is to say that they can be raped with impunity. To call a person "unrapeable" is to say that their assault will not rise to the level of rape. In either case, the implication is that a rape can happen without consequence for the rapist.
72. McElya 2007, 162.
73. Harris-Perry 2011, 56, 71.
74. Collins 2000, 92.
75. Ibid., 90–91.
76. Ibid., 91–92.
77. Crenshaw in Morrison 1992, 420.

78. Rodriguez 2020.
79. Nugent 2020; Aniftos 2023.
80. National PREA Resource Center 2017.
81. Bailey 2021, 12.
82. Hill 2021, 20.
83. Collins 2000, 92.
84. See Tillman et al. 2010 for a review of the literature on non-disclosure of sexual assault by women of color.
85. Carraway 1991, 1303.
86. Ibid., 1302.
87. Burke 2019.
88. Davis et al. 2022, 14–16, 145.
89. Survivors' Agenda 2020.
90. Burke 2019.
91. I see this idea implicit in the Survivors' Agenda Initiative, but because it is not explicit, I note that the rejection of violence does not necessarily preclude certain forms of violent resistance that are not undertaken to facilitate domination or political control.
92. Hine 1989, 916. See also Tillman et al. 2010, 60, who suggest "the need for prevention strategies that address not only individuals but systems that indirectly or directly support the violation of African American women."
93. Urban Indian Health Institute 2020, 8.
94. Minnesota Indian Women's Sexual Assault Coalition, n.d.
95. Urban Indian Health Institute 2020, 9.
96. Ibid., 14.
97. This symbol has other histories related to violence. Until the mid-2000s, the California Polytechnic San Luis Obispo (Cal Poly SLO) campus had a "red handprint campaign," which seems to have emerged after a Cal Poly SLO student named Kristin Smart disappeared from in front of her dorm in 1996. The campaign involved painting red handprints on locations where students had reported being sexually assaulted (CalPoly n.d.). Undergraduate students at Cal Poly SLO have recently reconvened this practice (Meyerhoff 2019). This is a local practice, one that (as far as I can tell) has not extended to other campuses or groups. The image was also used in Ohio in 2020 to call attention to police violence, where it reflected the activist chant "hands up, don't shoot" (NBC4 Staff 2020). In this case, as at Cal Poly SLO, the image was always stamped onto a building, rather than pressed over one's mouth.
98. Abdeldaiem 2019.
99. African American Policy Forum, n.d.
100. Trimmer 2019.
101. Roberts 2020. The image of weight is a powerful one that seems always to have resonated with another activist, Emma Sulkowicz, in 2014–15 who carried a mattress in protest to the resolution of a student conduct hearing at Columbia University. Sulkowicz named her performance art piece "Carry That Weight" (Nathanson 2014).
102. Roberts 2020.
103. Ibid.
104. See Johnson 2020.
105. Saunooke 2020, 23.
106. Alicia Garza tells a similar cautionary tale about the dangers of well-intended but non-Black marginalized groups adopting the Black Lives Matter slogan and hashtag for their purposes without permission; this replicates the very problem the slogan identifies and challenges (in K-Y Taylor 2017).
107. See Burke and Brown 2021.
108. Harvard Kennedy School 2020, 9.
109. Burke and Brown 2018.
110. Ruíz 2024, 32.
111. Tuerkheimer 2022.
112. Collins 2000, 135.
113. Ibid., 136–37.
114. Hartman 2019, 227–28.
115. Spillers 1987.

116. Hartman 2019, 83.
117. Ibid., 65.
118. Ibid., 153, 129, 186.
119. Davis et al. 2022, 172.
120. Davis 1971-2, 89.
121. Spillers 1987, 73.
122. Hill 1997, 69–70.
123. Hill 1997, 6.
124. Jensen 2018.
125. Survivors' Agenda 2020. See also Davis et al. 2022, 117; Combahee River Collective in Moraga and Anzaldúa 2015, 217–18.

Bibliography

Abdeldaiem, Aala. "Q&A: Jordan Daniel on Raising Native American Awareness through Running, Boston Marathon 2019." *Sports Illustrated*, April 29, 2019. https://www.si.com/edge/2019/04/29/jordan-daniel-native-american-rights-awareness-running-boston-marathon-2019.

Abdulali, Sohaila. *What We Talk about When We Talk about Rape*. New York: New Press, 2018.

Abramson, Kate. "Turning up the Lights on Gaslighting." *Philosophical Perspectives* 28 (December 2014): 1–30.

African American Policy Forum. "#Sayhername." n.d. Accessed October 8, 2022. https://www.aapf.org/sayhername.

Alcoff, Linda Martín. *Rape and Resistance: Understanding the Complexities of Sexual Violation*. Cambridge: Polity Press, 2018.

Alexander, Michelle. *The New Jim Crow: Mass Incarceration in the Age of Colorblindness*. New York: New Press, 2012.

Alliance Defending Freedom. "About ADF—I Am ADF." n.d. Accessed July 6, 2021. https://iamadf.org/about/.

Alliance Defending Freedom. "Devastating News: U.S. Supreme Court Declines to Hear Barronelle Stutzman's Case." 2021. Accessed July 6, 2021. https://adflegal.org/blog/devastating-news-us-supreme-court-declines-hear-barronelle-stutzmans-case.

Alliance Defending Freedom Legal. "About Us." n.d. Accessed July 6, 2021. https://adflegal.org/about-us.

Alter, Charlotte. "Mike Huckabee Joked about Pretending to Be Transgender to Shower with Girls after Gym Class." *Time*. June 2, 2015.

Amnesty International. *Maze of Injustice: The Failure to Protect Indigenous Women from Sexual Violence in the USA*. London: Amnesty International, 2007. Accessed August 31, 2024. https://www.amnesty.org/fr/wp-content/uploads/2021/05/AMR510352007ENGLISH.pdf.

Anahita, Sine, and Tamara L. Mix. "Retrofitting Frontier Masculinity for Alaska's War against Wolves." *Gender and Society* 20, no. 3 (2006): 332–53. Accessed April 26, 2022. https://www.jstor.org/stable/27640894.

Angel, Katherine. *Tomorrow Sex Will Be Good Again*. London: Verso, 2021.

Aniftos, Rania. "Cardi B Recalls 'WAP' Backlash, Getting 'Almost Sued' by FCC." *Billboard*, June 28, 2023. Accessed August 27, 2024. https://www.billboard.com/music/music-news/cardi-b-recalls-wap-backlash-1235363724/.

Anthony, Jon. "5 Tips to Avoid a False Rape Accusation on Campus." 2016. *Return of Kings* (July 8). Accessed April 25, 2025. https://theredarchive.com/blog/Return-of-Kings/5-tips-to-avoid-a-false-rape-accusation-on-campus.19528#google_vignette

Archbold, Carol A., Thorvald Dahle, and Rachel Jordan. "Policing 'The Patch': Police Response to Rapid Population Growth in Oil Boomtowns in Western North Dakota." *Police Quarterly* 17, no. 4 (December 2014): 386–413. Accessed September 2, 2022. https://doi.org/10.1177/1098611114549629.

Arias, Elizabeth, Kenneth D. Kochanek, Jiaquan Xu, and Betzaida Tejada-Vera. *Provisional Life Expectancy Estimates for 2022.* Vital Statistics Rapid Release no. 31. Hyattsville, MD: National Center for Health Statistics, 2023.

Arvin, Maile, Eve Tuck, and Angie Morrill. "Decolonizing Feminism: Challenging Connections between Settler Colonialism and Heteropatriarchy." *Feminist Formations* 25, no. 1 (Spring 2013): 8–34.

Associated Press. "Missouri Couple Who Waved Guns at Protesters Plead Guilty." CBC, June 17, 2021. Accessed July 16, 2021. https://www.cbc.ca/news/world/mccloskey-st-louis-couple-guns-guilty-1.6070260.

Astor, Maggie. "What to Know about the Tulsa Greenwood Massacre." *New York Times*, June 20, 2020. Accessed September 2, 2022. https://www.nytimes.com/2020/06/20/us/tulsa-greenwood-massacre.html.

Avery Center. *OnlyFans: A Case Study of Exploitation in the Digital Age.* Avery Center, December 2021.

Avery, Dan. "State Anti-transgender Bills Represent Coordinated Attack, Advocates Say." *NBC News*, February 17, 2021. Accessed Jun 30, 2021. https://www.nbcnews.com/feature/nbc-out/state-anti-transgender-bills-represent-coordinated-attack-advocates-say-n1258124.

Baig, Edward C. "Does 'Yes' Mean 'Yes?' Can You Give Consent to Have Sex to an App?" *USA Today*, September 26, 2018. Accessed September 21, 2021. https://www.usatoday.com/story/tech/columnist/baig/2018/09/26/proof-yes-means-yes-sexual-consent-apps-let-users-agree-have-sex/1420208002/.

Bailey, Moya. 2021. *Misogynoir Transformed: Black Women's Digital Resistance.* New York: New York University Press.

Barman, Jean. "Taming Aboriginal Sexuality: Gender, Power, and Race in British Columbia, 1850–1900." *BC Studies* no. 115/116 (1997/1998): 237–66.

Barnett, Brian S., Ariana E. Nesbit, and Renée M. Sorrentino. "The Transgender Bathroom Debate at the Intersection of Politics, Law, Ethics, and Science." *Journal of the American Academy of Psychiatry and the Law* 46, no. 2 (2018): 232–41.

Barrett, Paul. "White Thumbs, Black Bodies: Race, Violence, and Neoliberal Fantasies in *Grand Theft Auto: San Andreas*." *Review of Education, Pedagogy, and Cultural Studies* 28, no. 1 (2006): 95–119. Accessed Sep 2, 2022. https://doi.org/10.1080/10714410600552902.

Barthélemy, Hélène. "How Men's Rights Groups Helped Rewrite Regulations on Campus Rape." *The Nation*, August 14, 2020. Accessed September 17, 2021. https://www.thenation.com/article/politics/betsy-devos-title-ix-mens-rights/.

Basu, Tanya. "The 'Manosphere' Is Getting More Toxic as Angry Men Join the Incels." *Technology Review*, February 7, 2020. Accessed September 17, 2021. https://www.technologyreview.com/2020/02/07/349052/the-manosphere-is-getting-more-toxic-as-angry-men-join-the-incels/.

Beal, Frances M. "Double Jeopardy: To Be Black and Female." *Meridians* 8, no. 2 (2008): 166–76.

Beauchamp, Toby. *Going Stealth: Transgender Politics and U.S. Surveillance Practices.* Durham, NC: Duke University Press, 2019.

Beitsch, Rebecca. "#MeToo Movement Has Lawmakers Talking about Consent." Stateline, January 23, 2018. https://stateline.org/2018/01/23/metoo-movement-has-lawmakers-talking-about-consent/. Accessed April 25, 2025.

Bell, W. Kamau, dir. *We Need to Talk about Cosby.* Showtime, 2022.

Beltrán, Cristina. *Cruelty as Citizenship: How Migrant Suffering Sustains White Democracy.* Minneapolis: University of Minnesota Press, 2020.

Berg, Heather. *Porn Work: Sex, Labor, and Late Capitalism.* Chapel Hill: University of North Carolina Press, 2021.

Berlant, Lauren Gail. *Cruel Optimism.* Durham, NC: Duke University Press, 2011.

Bernstein, Elizabeth. *Temporarily Yours: Intimacy, Authenticity, and the Commerce of Sex.* Chicago: University of Chicago Press, 2007. Accessed August 27, 2024. https://alliance-pugetsound.primo.exlibrisgroup.com/discovery/fulldisplay?docid=alma99121010770001451&context=L&vid=01ALLIANCE_UPUGS:UPUGS&lang=en&search_scope=Collins_Summit&adaptor=Local%20Search%20Engine&tab=Collins_Summit&query=any,contains,bernstein,%20elizabeth&offset=0.

Bettcher, Talia Mae. "Evil Deceivers and Make-Believers: On Transphobic Violence and the Politics of Illusion." *Hypatia* 22, no. 3 (2007): 43–65.

Bevacqua, Maria. *Rape on the Public Agenda: Feminism and the Politics of Sexual Assault.* Evanston, IL: Northeastern University Press, 2000.

Bever, Lindsey. "'You Took away My Worth': A Sexual Assault Victim's Powerful Message to Her Stanford Attacker." *Washington Post*, June 4, 2016. Accessed July 3, 2024. https://www.washingtonpost.com/news/early-lead/wp/2016/06/04/you-took-away-my-worth-a-rape-victim-delivers-powerful-message-to-a-former-stanford-swimmer/.

Bindel, Julie. "There's Nothing 'Empowering' about the Sex Work on OnlyFans." *The Spectator*, April 15, 2020. Accessed August 27, 2024. https://www.spectator.co.uk/article/there-s-nothing-empowering-about-the-sex-work-on-onlyfans/.

Bird, S. Elizabeth. "Gendered Construction of the American Indian in Popular Media." *Journal of Communication* 49, no. 3 (1999): 61–83.

Black, Megan. *The Global Interior: Mineral Frontiers and American Power.* Cambridge, MA: Harvard University Press, 2018.

Blake, Aaron. "Three Dozen Republicans Have Now Called for Donald Trump to Drop Out." *Washington Post*, October 9, 2016. Accessed September 2, 2022. https://www.washingtonpost.com/news/the-fix/wp/2016/10/07/the-gops-brutal-responses-to-the-new-trump-video-broken-down/.

Blinder, A. "U.S. Reopens Emmett Till Investigation, Almost 63 Years after His Murder." *New York Times*, July 12, 2018.

Bonifacio, Ross, Lee Hair, and Donghee Yvette Wohn. "Beyond Fans: The Relational Labor and Communication Practices of Creators on Patreon." *New Media & Society* 25, no. 10 (2023): 2684–2703.

Bourke, Joanna. *Rape: Sex, Violence, History.* Emeryville, CA: Shoemaker & Hoard, 2007.

Bracho-Sanchez, Edith. "Transgender Teens in Schools with Bathroom Restrictions Are at Higher Risk of Sexual Assault, Study Says." CNN, May 6, 2019. Accessed June 28, 2021. https://www.cnn.com/2019/05/06/health/trans-teens-bathroom-policies-sexual-assault-study/index.html.

Bradley, Laura. "Critics of Sansa's Rape Scene on *Game of Thrones* Are Missing the Point." Slate, May 19, 2015. https://slate.com/culture/2015/05/the-rape-scene-on-sundays-game-of-thrones-was-necessary-and-sansa-deserves-more-credit.html.

Brand Partner Agency. "How to Get More OnlyFans Subscribers and Increase Your OnlyFans Income." *Village Voice*, August 21, 2021.

Brodsky, A. "Rape-Adjacent: Imagining Legal Responses to Nonconsensual Condom Removal." *Columbia Journal of Gender and Law* 32, no. 2 (2017): 183–210.

Brooks, Lisa. *Our Beloved Kin: A New History of King Philip's War*. New Haven, CT: Yale University Press, 2018.

Brown, April. "South Dakota Considers Legislating Transgender Access to Restrooms." *PBS News Hour*, February 29, 2016. Accessed July 13, 2021. https://www.pbs.org/newshour/show/south-dakota-considers-legislating-transgender-access-to-rest rooms.

Brown, Jennifer, and Sandra Walklate, eds. *Handbook on Sexual Violence*. Abingdon, UK: Routledge, 2012.

Brown, Wendy. "Finding the Man in the State." *Feminist Studies* 18, no. 1 (1992): 7–34.

Brown, Wendy. *States of Injury: Power and Freedom in Late Modernity*. Princeton, NJ: Princeton University Press, 1995.

Brown, Wendy. *Undoing the Demos: Neoliberalism's Stealth Revolution*. Princeton, NJ: Princeton University Press, 2017.

Brownmiller, Susan. *Against Our Will: Men, Women, and Rape*. First Ballentine Books edition. New York: Fawcett Books, 1993.

Brundage, James A. *Law, Sex, and Christian Society in Medieval Europe*. Chicago: University of Chicago Press, 1987.

Bruner, Raisa. "How 'Subscribe to Me' Became the Future of Work." *Time*, December 1, 2021. Accessed August 27, 2024. https://time.com/6124508/creator-economy-onlyfans-twitch-future/.

Bruyneel, Kevin. *Settler Memory: The Disavowal of Indigeneity and the Politics of Race in the United States*. Chapel Hill: University of North Carolina Press, 2021.

Buchanan, NiCole T., Isis H. Settles, and Krystle C. Woods. "Comparing Sexual Harassment Subtypes among Black and White Women by Military Rank: Double Jeopardy, the Jezebel, and the Cult of True Womanhood." *Psychology of Women Quarterly* 32 (2008): 347–61.

Buchwald, Emilie, Pamela R. Fletcher, and Martha Roth, eds. *Transforming a Rape Culture*. Minneapolis, MN: Milkweed Editions, 1993.

Buist, Erica. "Can 'Sexual Consent' App Good2Go Really Reduce Assaults on Campus?" *The Guardian*, September 30, 2014. Accessed September 21, 2021. http://www.theguardian.com/technology/shortcuts/2014/sep/30/consent-app-good2go-bad.

Burke, Tarana. "The 'Me Too' Movement's Success Took a Decade of Work, not Just a Hashtag. And There's More to Do." *NBC News.* December 31, 2019. https://www.nbcnews.com/think/opinion/me-too-movement-s-success-took-decade-work-not-just-ncna1108206.

Burke, Tarana. "Year 19: For Toyin and All the Black Girls Whose Lives Have Been Stolen." *Essence*, July 16, 2020. Accessed August 31, 2024. https://www.essence.com/feature/toyin-salau-tarana-burke/.

Burke, Tarana, and Brené Brown, eds. *You Are Your Best Thing: Vulnerability, Shame Resilience, and the Black Experience—An Anthology.* New York: Random House, 2021.

Burke, Tarana, and S. Tia Brown. "Me Too Founder Tarana Burke: 'Survivors Need to Know They're Worthy of Life, Dignity and Protection.'" ESPN, October 17, 2018. Accessed October 8, 2022. https://www.espn.com/espnw/voices/story/_/id/25008114/survivors-need-know-worthy-life-dignity-protection.

Butler, Judith. *Gender Trouble: Feminism and the Subversion of Identity.* New York: Routledge, 1990.

Butler, Judith, and Joan Wallach Scott, eds. *Feminists Theorize the Political.* New York: Routledge, 1992.

CalPoly. "What Is SAFER?" n.d. Accessed August 27, 2024. https://safer.calpoly.edu/what-is-safer.

Caraher, William R., Bret Weber, Kostis Kourells, and Richard Rothaus. "The North Dakota Man Camp Project: The Archaeology of Home in the Bakken Oil Fields." *Historical Archaeology* 51 (2017): 267–87.

Carolus, Astrid, Carolin Wienrich, Anna Törke, Tobias Friedel, Christian Schwietering, and Mareike Sperzel. "'Alexa, I Feel for You!' Observers' Empathetic Reactions towards a Conversational Agent." *Frontiers in Computer Science* 3 (2021): 682982. Accessed August 27, 2024. https://www.frontiersin.org/journals/computer-science/articles/10.3389/fcomp.2021.682982/full.

Carpio, Myla Vicenti. "The Lost Generation: American Indian Women and Sterilization Abuse." *Social Justice* 31, no. 4 (2004): 40–53.

Carraway, G. Chezia. "Violence against Women of Color." *Stanford Law Review* 43, no. 6 (1991): 1301–09.

Cavanagh, Sheila L. *Queering Bathrooms: Gender, Sexuality, and the Hygienic Imagination.* Toronto: University of Toronto Press, 2010.

Centers for Disease Control. "Preventing Child Sexual Abuse." n.d. Accessed July 14, 2021. https://www.cdc.gov/violenceprevention/childsexualabuse/fastfact.html.

Chang, Ailsa. "A Sociologist's View on the Hyper-sexualization of Asian Women in American Society." *All Things Considered*, March 19, 2021. Accessed October 21, 2021. https://www.npr.org/2021/03/19/979340013/a-sociologists-view-on-the-hyper-sexualization-of-asian-women-in-american-societ.

Chappell, Duncan, Robley Geis, and Gilbert Geis, eds. *Forcible Rape: The Crime, the Victim, and the Offender.* New York: Columbia University Press, 1977.

Clarke, Adele E., and Donna Haraway, eds. *Making Kin not Population.* Chicago: Prickly Paradigm Press, 2018.

Climate in Berthold, North Dakota. Bestplaces, n.d. Accessed October 8, 2022. https://www.bestplaces.net/climate/city/north_dakota/berthold.

Closson, Troy. "Amy Cooper Falsely Accused Black Bird-Watcher in 2nd 911 Conversation." *New York Times*, October 14, 2020. https://www.nytimes.com/2020/10/14/nyregion/amy-cooper-false-report-charge.html.

Cohen, Sascha. "The Book That Changed the Way We Talk about Rape." *Time*, October 7, 2015. Accessed July 3, 2024. https://time.com/4062637/against-our-will-40/.

Cole, Samantha. "Replika CEO Says AI Companions Were not Meant to Be Horny. Users Aren't Buying It." *Vice*, February 17, 2023. Accessed August 27, 2024. https://www.vice.com/en/article/replika-ceo-ai-erotic-roleplay-chatgpt3-rep/.

Collins, Patricia Hill. *Black Feminist Thought: Knowledge, Consciousness, and the Politics of Empowerment*. Rev. tenth anniv. ed.; 2nd ed. New York: Routledge, 2000.

Collins, Patricia Hill. *Intersectionality as Critical Social Theory*. Durham, NC: Duke University Press, 2019.

Collins, Patricia Hill, and Sirma Bilge. *Intersectionality*. Chichester, UK: Wiley, 2016.

Comella, Lynn. *Vibrator Nation: How Feminist Sex-Toy Stores Changed the Business of Pleasure*. Durham, NC: Duke University Press, 2017.

Connell, Noreen, and Cassandra Wilson, eds. *Rape: The First Sourcebook for Women*. New York: New American Library, 1974.

Connell, R. W. "The Big Picture: Masculinities in Recent World History." *Theory and Society* 22, no. 5 (1993): 597–623.

Connell, R. W., and James W. Messerschmidt. "Hegemonic Masculinity: Rethinking the Concept." *Gender and Society* 19, no. 6 (2005): 829–59.

Cooke, Rachel. "U.S. Feminist Susan Brownmiller on Why Her Groundbreaking Book on Rape Is Still Relevant." *The Guardian*, February 18, 2018. Accessed September 2, 2022. https://www.theguardian.com/world/2018/feb/18/susan-brownmiller-against-our-will-interview-metoo.

Costa, Pedro, and Luísa Ribas. "AI Becomes Her: Discussing Gender and Artificial Intelligence." *Technoetic Arts* 17, no. 1–2 (2019): 171–93. Accessed August 27, 2024. https://intellectdiscover.com/content/journals/10.1386/tear_00014_1.

Coulthard, Glen Sean. *Red Skin, White Masks: Rejecting the Colonial Politics of Recognition*. Minneapolis: University of Minnesota Press, 2014.

Coulthard, Glen, and Leann Betasamosake Simpson. "Grounded Normativity/Place-Based Solidarity." *American Quarterly* 68, no. 2 (2016): 249–55. https://muse.jhu.edu/article/622080/pdf.

Crenshaw, Kimberle. "Mapping the Margins: Intersectionality, Identity Politics, and Violence against Women of Color." *Stanford Law Review* 43, no. 6 (1991): 1241–99.

Croisy, Sophie. "Fighting Colonial Violence in 'Indian Country': Deconstructing Racist Sexual Stereotypes of Native American Women in American Popular Culture and History." *Angles: New Perspectives on the Anglophone World* 5 (2017): 1–16.

Currah, Paisley. "Homonationalism, State Rationalities, and Sex Contradictions." *Theory and Event* 16, no. 1 (2013). https://muse.jhu.edu/pub/1/article/501864. Accessed April 26, 2025.

Currah, Paisley. *Sex Is as Sex Does.* New York: NYU Press, 2022. Accessed January 27, 2024. https://nyupress.org/9780814717103/sex-is-as-sex-does.

Curry, Tommy J. *The Man-Not: Race, Class, Genre, and the Dilemmas of Black Manhood.* Philadelphia: Temple University Press, 2017.

Davis, Angela Y. "Rape, Racism, and the Capitalist Setting." *Black Scholar* 9, no. 7 (1978): 24–30.

Davis, Angela Y. "Reflections on the Black Woman's Role in the Community of Slaves." *Massachusetts Review* 13, no. 1/2 (1971-1972): 81–100.

Davis, Angela Y. *Women, culture, & politics.* New York: Vintage Books, 1990.

Davis, Angela Y. *Women, race & class.* New York: Vintage Books, 1983.

Davis, Angela Y., Gina Dent, Erica R. Meiners, and Beth E. Richie. *Abolition. Feminism. Now.* Chicago: Haymarket Books, 2022.

DeBonis, Mike. "The Push for LGBTQ Civil Rights Stalls in the Senate as Advocates Search for Republican Support." *Washington Post,* June 20, 2021. Accessed July 6, 2021. https://www.washingtonpost.com/politics/senate-lgbtq-equality-act/2021/06/19/887a4134-d038-11eb-a7f1-52b8870bef7c_story.html.

Decaro, Sofia Pavanello, Daniel Michael Portolani, Greta Toffoli, Antonio Prunas, and Annalisa Anzani. "'There Is No One Way to Be Transgender and to Live Sex': Transgender and Non- binary Individuals' Experiences with Pornography." *Journal of Sex Research* 61, no. 8 (2024): 1222–32.

Deer, Sarah. *The Beginning and End of Rape: Confronting Sexual Violence in Native America.* Minneapolis: University of Minnesota Press, 2015.

Deloria, Philip Joseph. *Playing Indian.* New Haven, CT: Yale University Press, 1998.

Department of Justice. "Review and Evaluation: Tulsa Race Massacre." January 17, 2025. https://www.justice.gov/crt/media/1383756/dl.

Deutsch, Fred. "Defending Traditional Values." n.d. Accessed August 25, 2021. https://www.freddeutsch.com/defending-family-values.

De Zutter, Andre, Robert Horselenberg, and Peter J. van Koppen. "The Prevalence of False Allegations of Rape in the United States from 2006–2010." *Journal of Forensic Psychology* 2, no. 2 (2017): 1000119.

DiMatteo, Larry A., Michel Cannarsa, and Cristina Poncibò, eds. *The Cambridge Handbook of Smart Contracts, Blockchain Technology and Digital Platforms.* Cambridge: Cambridge University Press, 2020.

Donovan, K., and J. Brown. "CBC Fires Jian Ghomeshi over Sex Allegations." *Toronto Star,* October 26, 2014.

Douglass, Frederick. *Why Is the Negro Lynched?* 1895. Project Gutenberg, March 24, 2019. Accessed February 7, 2021. https://www.gutenberg.org/files/59116/59116-h/59116-h.htm.

Dowland, Seth. *Family Values and the Rise of the Christian Right.* Philadelphia: University of Pennsylvania Press, 2015.

Drenten, Jenna M., Lauren Gurrieri, and Meagan Tyler. "Sexualized Labour in Digital Culture: Instagram Influencers, Porn Chic and the Monetization of Attention." *Gender, Work & Organization* 27, no. 1 (2020): 41–66.

Driskill, Qwo-Li, Chris Finley, Brian Joseph Gilley, and Scott Lauria Morgensen, eds. *Queer Indigenous Studies: Critical Interventions in Theory, Politics, and Literature.* Tucson, AZ: University of Arizona Press, 2011.

Du Mez, Kristin Kobes. *Jesus and John Wayne: How White Evangelicals Corrupted a Faith and Fractured a Nation.* New York: Liveright Publishing, 2020.

Dunn, Caroline. *Stolen Women in Medieval England: Rape, Abduction, and Adultery c. 1100–1500.* Cambridge: Cambridge University Press, 2012.

Dura, Jack. "Bighorn Sheep Herds Show Promise on North Dakota Reservation." *US News & World Report*, February 1, 2021. Accessed October 8, 2022. www.usnews.com/news/best-states/north-dakota/articles/2021-02-01/bighorn-sheep-herds-show-promise-on-north-dakota-reservation.

Dworkin, Andrea. *Intercourse.* New York: Free Press, 1988.

Edelman, Lee. *No Future: Queer Theory and the Death Drive.* Durham, NC: Duke University Press, 2004.

Ehrlich, Susan. *Representing Rape: Language and Sexual Consent.* London: Routledge, 2001.

Enke, Anne, ed. *Transfeminist Perspectives in and beyond Transgender and Gender Studies.* Philadelphia: Temple University Press, 2012.

Epstein, Rebecca, Jamilia J. Blake, and Thalia González. *Girlhood Interrupted: The Erasure of Black Girls' Childhood.* Washington DC: Georgetown Law Center on Poverty and Inequality, 2017. Accessed August 27, 2024. https://www.law.georgetown.edu/poverty-inequality-center/wp-content/uploads/sites/14/2017/08/girlhood-interrupted.pdf.

Esterhuyse, S., D. Vermeulen, and J. Glazewski. "Developing and Enforcing Fracking Regulations to Protect Groundwater Resources." *NPJ Clean Water* 5, no. 1 (2022): 3. Accessed August 26, 2024. https://www.nature.com/articles/s41545-021-00145-y.

Estes, Nick, Melanie K. Yazzie, Jennifer Denetdale, and David Correia. *Red Nation Rising: From Bordertown Violence to Native Liberation.* Oakland, CA: PM Press, 2021.

Estrich, Susan. "Rape." *Yale Law Journal* 95, no. 6 (1986): 1087–1184.

Evans, Sophie J., and Victoria Woollaston. "No so Good2Go: Consensual Sex App Closes after Apple Pulls It." *Daily Mail*, October 9, 2014. Accessed September 21, 2021. https://www.dailymail.co.uk/sciencetech/article-2786605/No-Good2Go-Consensual-sex-app-shuts-Apple-pulls-store.html.

Family Research Council. "Issue Brief: Bathroom Incidents." April 2017. Accessed August 31, 2024. https://downloads.frc.org/EF/EF16F27.pdf.

Famuyiwa, Rick, dir. *Confirmation.* HBO Films, 2016.

Farley, Melissa, Nicole Matthews, Sarah Deer, Guadalupe Lopez, Christine Stark, and Eileen Hudon. *Garden of Truth: The Prostitution and Trafficking of Native Women in Minnesota.* Lame Deer, MT: National Indigenous Women's Resource Center, 2011. Accessed August 31, 2024. https://www.niwrc.org/resources/report/garden-truth-prostitution-and-trafficking-native-women-minnesota.

Federici, Silvia. *Caliban and the Witch.* Brooklyn, NY: Autonomedia, 2014.

Fenwick, Ben, and Alan Schwarz. "In Rape Case of Oklahoma Officer, Victims Hope Conviction Will Aid Cause." *New York Times*, December 11, 2015. Accessed August

31, 2024. https://www.nytimes.com/2015/12/12/us/daniel-holtzclaw-oklahoma-police-rape-case.html#:~:text=In%20Rape%20Case%20of%20Oklahoma%20Officer%2C%20Victims%20Hope%20Conviction%20Will%20Aid%20Cause,-Share%20full%20article&text=OKLAHOMA%20CITY%20%E2%80%94%20Jannie%20Ligons%20stood,car%20during%20a%20traffic%20stop.

Ferguson, Claire E., and John M. Malouff. "Assessing Police Classifications of Sexual Assault Reports: A Meta-analysis of False Reporting Rates." *Archives of Sexual Behavior* 45 (2016): 1185–93.

Ferreday, Debra. "*Game of Thrones*, Rape Culture and Feminist Fandom." *Australian Feminist Studies* 30, no. 83 (2015): 21–36.

Ferree, Paul, and Peter W. Smith. "Employment and Wage Changes in Oil-Producing Counties in the Bakken Formation, 2007–2011." *Employment & Unemployment* 2, no. 11 (2013). Accessed June 16, 2022. https://www.bls.gov/opub/btn/volume-2/employment-wages-bakken-shale-region.htm.

Filteau, Matthew R. "A Localized Masculine Crisis: Local Men's Subordination within the Marcellus Shale Region's Masculine Structure." *Rural Sociology* 80, no. 4 (2015): 431–55.

Filteau, Matthew R. "Who Are Those Guys? Constructing the Oilfied's New Dominant Masculinity." *Men and Masculinities* 17, no. 5 (2014), 396-416.

Fischel, Joseph J., and Hilary R. O'Connell. "Disabling Consent, or Reconstructing Sexual Autonomy." *Columbia Journal of Gender and Law* 30, no. 2 (2015): 428–528. https://journals.library.columbia.edu/index.php/cjgl/article/view/2735.

Fitzgerald, Tami. "Statement: NC Values Coalition Statement on NCAA's Threat to Pull More Championship Games." n.d. Accessed July 13, 2021. https://www.ncvalues.org/nc_values_statement_on_ncaa.

Fountain, Aaron G., Jr. "It's not Just White Incels. We Need to Talk about the Black Manosphere, Too." The Black Youth Project. 2018. Accessed September 20, 2021. http://blackyouthproject.com/its-not-just-white-incels-we-need-to-talk-about-the-black-manosphere-too/.

Freedman, Estelle B. *Redefining Rape: Sexual Violence in the Era of Suffrage and Segregation.* Cambridge, MA: Harvard University Press, 2013.

Fried, Charles. *Contract as Promise: A Theory of Contractual Obligation*. Cambridge, MA: Harvard University Press, 1981.

Friedman, Jaclyn, and Jessica Valenti, eds. *Yes Means Yes! Visions of Female Sexual Power & a World without Rape.* Berkeley, CA: Seal Press, 2008.

Friedman, May. "Beyond MILF: Exploring Sexuality and Feminism in Public Motherhood." *Atlantis* 36, no. 2 (2014): 49–60.

Frost. "The Truth about False Rape Accusations That All Men Should Know." *Return of Kings* (blog), December 10, 2013. https://www.returnofkings.com/22079/the-truth-about-false-rape-accusations-that-all-men-should-know. Accessed September 17, 2021.

Garcia, Manon. *The Joy of Consent: A Philosophy of Good Sex.* Cambridge, MA: Belknap Press of Harvard University Press, 2023.

Garofalo, Eve. "Trigger Warning: Work Camps Are Linked to Increased Sexual Violence." *My Sea to Sky*, June 23, 2022. Accessed October 8, 2022. https://myseatosky.org/news/trigger-warning-work-camps-are-linked-to-increased-sexual-violence/.

Gash, Alison. "Anti-transgender Bills Are Latest Version of Conservatives' Long-time Strategy to Rally Their Base." The Conversation, May 6, 2021. Accessed June 28, 2021. http://theconversation.com/anti-transgender-bills-are-latest-version-of-conservatives-longtime-strategy-to-rally-their-base-158296.

Gay, Roxane. *Not That Bad: Dispatches from Rape Culture*. New York: Harper, 2018.

General Assembly of North Carolina. Public Facilities Privacy & Security Act. Second Extra Session 2016 (March 23, 2016).

General Assembly of the State of Tennessee. House Bill 1182. 112th General Assembly Session 2021 (March 29, 2021).

Giddens, Anthony. *Social Theory and Modern Sociology*. Stanford, CA: Stanford University Press, 1987.

Gilmore, Ruth Wilson. *Golden Gulag: Prisons, Surplus, Crisis, and Opposition in Globalizing California*. Berkeley: University of California Press, 2007.

Ging, Debbie. "Alphas, Betas, and Incels: Theorizing the Masculinities of the Manosphere." *Men and Masculinities* 22, no. 4 (2019): 638–57.

Glenza, Jessica. "The Multimillion-Dollar Christian Group Attacking LGBTQ+ Rights." *The Guardian*, February 21, 2020. Accessed July 6, 2021. https://www.theguardian.com/world/2020/feb/20/alliance-defending-freedom-multimillion-dollar-conservative-christian-group-attacking-lgbtq-rights.

Glick, Elisa. "Sex Positive: Feminism, Queer Theory, and the Politics of Transgression." *Feminist Review* no. 64 (2000): 19–45.

Goddard, I. "The True History of the Word Squaw." *News from Indian Country*, April 1997.

Gordon, Michael, Mark S. Price, and Katie Peralta. "Understanding HB2: North Carolina's Newest Law Solidifies State's Role in Defining Discrimination." *Charlotte Observer*, March 26, 2017 (updated March 30, 2017). Accessed July 20, 2021. https://www.charlotteobserver.com/news/politics-government/article68401147.html.

Gorski, Philip S., and Samuel L. Perry. *The Flag and the Cross: White Christian Nationalism and the Threat to American Democracy*. New York: Oxford University Press, 2022.

Graham, Lindsay. "Transcript of Graham's Remarks on Kavanaugh Nomination." September 27, 2018. https://www.lgraham.senate.gov/public/index.cfm/2018/9/transcript-of-graham-s-remarks-on-kavanaugh-nomination.

Grandoni, Dino. "The Disturbing New Trend in 'Grand Theft Auto' Is Virtual Rape." HuffPost, August 12, 2014. Accessed September 2, 2022. https://www.huffpost.com/entry/grand-theft-auto-rape_n_5671400.

Grann, David. *Killers of the Flower Moon: The Osage Murders and the Birth of the FBI*. New York: Doubleday, 2017.

Green, Rayna. "The Pocahontas Perplex: The Image of Indian Women in American Culture." *Massachusetts Review* 16, no. 4 (1975): 698–714.

Groce, Alex. "Pay for Your Porn!" Medium, January 15, 2021. Accessed August 27, 2024. https://medium.com/15-01-20/pornhub-1df497c9112.

Haag, Pamela. *Consent: Sexual Rights and the Transformation of American Liberalism.* Ithaca, NY: Cornell University Press, 1999.

Halberstam, Jack. *Female Masculinity.* Twentieth anniv. ed. Durham, NC: Duke University Press, 2018.

Hamilton, Vaughn, Ananta Soneji, Allison McDonald, and Ellisa M. Redmiles. "'Nudes? Shouldn't I Charge for These?': Motivations of New Sexual Content Creators on OnlyFans." In *CHI '23: Proceedings of the 2023 CHI Conference on Human Factors in Computing Systems, Hamburg, Germany, April 2023.* Accessed August 31, 2024. https://dl.acm.org/doi/fullHtml/10.1145/3544548.3580730.

Hancock, Ange-Marie. *Intersectionality: An Intellectual History.* New York: Oxford University Press, 2016.

Hanna, Jason, Madison Park, and Eliott C. McLaughlin. "North Carolina Repeals 'Bathroom Bill.'" CNN, March 30, 2017. Accessed July 21, 2021. https://www.cnn.com/2017/03/30/politics/north-carolina-hb2-agreement/index.html.

Harding, Kate. *Asking for It: The Alarming Rise of Rape Culture—And What We Can Do about It.* Boston: Da Capo Lifelong, 2015.

Harris-Perry, Melissa. *Sister Citizen.* New Haven, CT: Yale University Press, 2011.

Harsey, Sarah, and Jennifer J. Freyd. "Deny, Attack, Blame: The Prosecution of Women Reporting Rape." *Ms*, November 28, 2022. Accessed August 27, 2024. https://msmagazine.com/2022/11/28/darvo-deny-attack-blame-prosecution-women-report-rape/.

Hartman, Saidiya. "The Belly of the World: A Note on Black Women's Labors." *Souls* 18, no. 1 (2016): 166–73.

Hartman, Saidiya. *Wayward Lives, Beautiful Experiments: Intimate Histories of Social Upheaval.* New York: W.W. Norton & Company, 2019.

Harvard Kennedy School. "Leading with Empathy: Tarana Burke and the Making of the Me Too Movement." HKS Case 2197.0. November 16, 2020. https://case.hks.harvard.edu/leading-with-empathy-tarana-burke-and-the-making-of-the-me-too-movement/. Accessed April 26, 2025.

Hasenbush, Amira, Andrew R. Flores, and Jody L. Herman. "Gender Identity Nondiscrimination Laws in Public Accommodations: A Review of Evidence Regarding Safety and Privacy in Public Restrooms, Locker Rooms, and Changing Rooms." *Sexuality Research & Social Policy* 16, no. 1 (2019): 70–83.

Hauter, Wenonah. *Frackopol: The Battle for the Future of Energy and the Environment.* New York: New Press, 2016.

Hawkes, Emma. "Preliminary Notes on Consent in the 1382 Rape and Ravishment Laws of Richard II." *Legal History* 11 (2007): 117–32.

Hawkes, Emma. "'She Was Ravished against Her Will, What so Ever She Say': Female Consent in Rape and Ravishment in Late-Medieval England." *Limina* 1 (1995): 47–53.

Head, Ally. "Ever Heard of Ethical Porn? Here's Where, Exactly, to Find It, Plus Why You'll Want to Get behind It." *Marie Claire*, May 28, 2021. Accessed August 27, 2024. https://www.marieclaire.co.uk/life/sex-and-relationships/ethical-porn-474913.

Hernandez, Natalie M. and Morton, Ivannia A. "Growing Pains on OnlyFans: A Coming of Age Story" (2021). *CUNY Academic Works.* https://academicworks.cuny.edu/gj_etds/552. Accessed Arpil 26, 2025.

Hill, Anita. *Believing: Our Thirty-Year Journey to End Gender Violence.* New York: Penguin Publishing Group, 2021.

Hill, Anita. *Speaking Truth to Power.* New York: Doubleday, 1997.

Hill, Anita. "Thomas Second Hearing Day 1, Part 2." October 11, 1991. Accessed August 26, 2024. https://www.c-span.org/video/?22097-1/clarence-thomas-confirmation-hearing.

Hine, Darlene Clark. "Rape and the Inner Lives of Black Women in the Middle West." *Signs* 14, no. 4 (1989): 912–20.

Hodes, Martha, ed. *Sex, Love, Race: Crossing Boundaries in North American History.* New York: NYU Press, 1999.

Hoffman, Bruce, Jacob Ware, and Ezra Shapiro. "Assessing the Threat of Incel Violence." *Studies in Conflict and Terrorism* 43, no. 7 (2020): 565–87.

Holtzclaw v. State, 448 P.3d 1134 Okla. Crim. App. (2019). https://casetext.com/case/holtzclaw-v-state-3.

"Holtzclaw Verdict." Posted December 10, 2015, by Law and Crime Network. YouTube, 6 min., 15 sec. https://www.youtube.com/watch?v=MtY0fVneWuU.

Holzman, David C. "Methane Found in Well Water Near Fracking Sites." *Environmental Health Perspectives* 119, no. 7 (2011): A289. Accessed August 26, 2024. https://pubmed.ncbi.nlm.nih.gov/21719376/.

Honig, Bonnie. *Democracy and the Foreigner.* Princeton, NJ: Princeton University Press, 2001.

Horneich, Sam. "Affirmative Consent App SaSie Provides Alternative Recourse for College Students." PRWeb, September 1, 2016a. Accessed November 22, 2021. https://www.prweb.com/releases/2016/09/prweb13648984.htm.

Horneich, Sam. "Affirmative Consent for Parents: What You Need to Know." Medium, August 14, 2016b. Accessed November 22, 2021. https://medium.com/only-yes/affirmative-consent-for-parents-what-you-need-to-know-18f1c120971d.

Horneich, Sam. "Affirmative Consent for Parents: What You Need to Know Part 2." Medium, August 24, 2016c. Accessed November 22, 2021. https://medium.com/only-yes/affirmative-consent-for-parents-what-you-need-to-know-part-2-8b52e02ec4eb.

Horneich, Sam. "The (not so) Crazy Reasons Students Need an App for Sexual Relationships." Medium, August 25, 2016d. Accessed November 22, 2021. https://medium.com/only-yes/the-not-so-crazy-reasons-students-need-an-app-for-sex-b8924f653d51.

Horneich, Sam. "We Believe Consent Shouldn't Be Fun or Sexy at College- (Even though the Sex Is)." Medium, September 16, 2016e. Accessed November 22, 2021. https://medium.com/only-yes/we-believe-consent-shouldnt-be-fun-or-sexy-at-college-even-though-the-sex-is-d612b23ac4f3.

Hunt, Melissa G., Rachel Marx, Courtney Lipson, and Jordyn Young. "No More FOMO: Limiting Social Media Decreases Loneliness and Depression." *Journal of Social and Clinical Psychology* 37, no. 10 (2018): 751–68.

Hunt, Sarah. "Decolonizing the Roots of Rape Culture: Reflections on Consent, Sexual Violence and University Campuses." Emma Talks Podcast, 2016. https://soundcloud.com/user-210912628/sarah-hunt-decolonizing-the-roots-of-rape-culture, Accessed April 26, 2025.

Hunt, Sarah. "Representing Colonial Violence: Trafficking, Sex Work, and the Violence of Law." *Atlantis: Critical Studies in Gender, Culture & Social Justice* 37, no. 2 (2015): 25–39. Accessed September 2, 2022. https://www.academia.edu/9127880/Representing_Colonial_Violence_Trafficking_Sex_Work_and_the_Violence_of_Law.

Hurley, Bevan. "A Sexual Abuse Ruling. 26 Accusations. Yet Donald Trump Is Still Frontrunner to Be the Next US President." *The Independent*, May 10, 2023. Accessed August 26, 2024. https://www.independent.co.uk/news/world/americas/donald-trump-loses-lawsuit-sexual-abuse-b2336239.html.

INCITE! Women of Color against Violence. *Color of Violence: The INCITE! Anthology*. Durham, NC: Duke University Press, 2016.

Jaleel, Rana M. *The Work of Rape*. Durham, NC: Duke University Press, 2021.

James, S. E., J. L. Herman, S. Rankin, M. Keisling, L. Mottet, and M. Anafi. *The Report of the 2015 U.S. Transgender Survey*. Washington DC: National Center for Transgender Equality, 2016.

Jayasundara, Dheeshana, Elizabeth Legerski, and Fran S. Danis. "The Impact of Oil Development on Sexual Assault in the Bakken." *Family and Intimate Partner Violence Quarterly* 10, no. 4 (2018): 63–72.

Jensen, Phyllis Graber. "Look What We Found: Leslie Hill's Prized Document of Protest by African American Women." Bates, January 24, 2018. Accessed August 27, 2024. https://www.bates.edu/news/2018/01/24/look-what-we-found-leslie-hills-prized-proclamation-of-protest/.

Johnson, Rhiannon. "Widespread Use of Red Handprints to Represent MMIWG Sparks Debate among Advocates." *CBC News*, March 9, 2020. Accessed October 8, 2022. https://www.cbc.ca/news/indigenous/red-handprints-mmiwg-1.5483955#:~:text=A%20red%20handprint%20across%20the,the%20United%20States%20and%20beyond.

Jones, Angela. "Cumming to a Screen Near You: Transmasculine and Non-binary People in the Camming Industry." *Porn Studies* 8, no. 2 (2021): 239–54.

Jones, Roxanne. "Young men, get a 'yes' text before sex." CNN. November 26, 2013. Accessed April 21, 2025. https://www.cnn.com/2013/11/26/opinion/jones-sex-consent-texting/index.html.

Kaplan, Sarah. "A Serial Rapist Cop's 'Mistake': Assaulting the Grandmother Who Finally Reported Him." *Washington Post*, December 11, 2015. https://www.washingtonpost.com/news/morning-mix/wp/2015/12/11/daniel-holtzclaws-mistake-assaulting-the-grandmother-who-finally-reported-him/.

Keating, Christine. *Decolonizing Democracy: Transforming the Social Contract in India*. University Park: Pennsylvania State University Press, 2011.

Kendall, Peter. "A Prosecutor Says No to a Rape Charge, so a College Student Calls Her Own Grand Jury." *Washington Post*, May 19, 2021. Accessed September 23, 2021.

https://www.washingtonpost.com/national/a-prosecutor-says-no-to-a-rape-charge-so-a-college-student-calls-her-own-grand-jury/2021/05/18/2ea9a130-b766-11eb-a5fe-bb49dc89a248_story.html.

Kessel, Alisa. "The Cruel Optimism of Sexual Consent." *Contemporary Political Theory* 19 (2020): 359–80.

Kessel, Alisa. "Rethinking Rape Culture: Revelations of Intersectional Analysis." *American Political Science Review* 116, no. 1 (2022): 131–43.

Kibbe, Kahla. "Mia Khalifa, OnlyFans and the Politics of Ethical Porn." InsideHook, July 24, 2020. Accessed August 27, 2024. https://www.insidehook.com/sex-and-dating/mia-khalifa-onlyfans-and-the-debate-around-ethical-porn.

King, C. Richard. "De/scribing Squ*w: Indigenous Women and Imperial Idioms in the United States." *American Indian Culture and Research Journal* 27, no. 2 (2003): 1–16.

King, Deborah K. "Multiple Jeopardy, Multiple Consciousness: The Context of a Black Feminist Ideology." *Signs: Journal of Women in Culture and Society* 14, no. 1 (1988): 42–72.

Klein, Naomi. *This Changes Everything: Capitalism vs. the Climate.* New York: Simon & Schuster, 2014.

Kogan, Terry S. "How Did Public Bathrooms Get to Be Separated by Sex in the First Place?" The Conversation, May 26, 2016. Accessed July 9, 2021. http://theconversation.com/how-did-public-bathrooms-get-to-be-separated-by-sex-in-the-first-place-59575.

Krijnen, Tonny, Paul G. Nixon, Michelle D. Ravenscroft, and Cosimo Marco Scarcelli, eds. *Identities and Intimacies on Social Media.* London: Taylor & Francis, 2023. Accessed August 27, 2024. https://alliance-pugetsound.primo.exlibrisgroup.com/discovery/fulldisplay?docid=alma99900572365101854&context=L&vid=01ALLIANCE_UPUGS:UPUGS&lang=en&search_scope=Collins_Summit&adaptor=Local%20Search%20Engine&tab=Collins_Summit&query=any,contains,identities%20and%20intimacies%20on%20social%20media&offset=0.

Lacour, Greg. "HB2: How North Carolina Got Here (Updated)." *Charlotte Magazine*, March 3, 2017. Accessed July 20, 2021. https://www.charlottemagazine.com/hb2-how-north-carolina-got-here-updated/.

Laiou, Angeliki E., ed. *Consent and Coercion to Sex and Marriage in Ancient and Medieval Societies.* Washington, DC: Dumbarton Oaks Research Library and Collection, 1993.

Latimer, Michelle, dir. *Nuuca.* 12 min. Streel Films, 2018. https://www.streelfilms.com/nuuca. Accessed April 25, 2025.

Laurin, Daniel. "Subscription Intimacy: Amateurism, Authenticity and Emotional Labour in Direct-to-Consumer Gay Pornography." *AG: About Gender* 8, no. 16 (2019): 61–79.

Lazarus, Margaret and Renner Wunderlich, dirs. *Rape Culture.* Cambridge Documentary Films, 1983.

LegalFling. https://legalfling.io. Accessed April 22, 2025 through the Way Back Machine. https://web.archive.org/web/20180501000000*/legalfling.io.

Lee, Youngrong, Ye Jin Jeon, Sunghyuk Kang, Jae Il Shin, Young-Chul Jung, and Sun Jae Jung. "Social Media Use and Mental Health during the COVID-19 Pandemic in

Young Adults: A Meta-analysis of 14 Cross-sectional Studies." *BMC Public Health* 22, no. 1 (2022): 995.

Levy, Ariel. "Trial by Twitter." *The New Yorker*, July 29, 2013. Accessed September 29, 2021. http://www.newyorker.com/magazine/2013/08/05/trial-by-twitter.

Lewis, Helen. "To Learn about the Far Right, Start with the 'Manosphere.'" *The Atlantic*, August 7, 2019. Accessed September 17, 2021. https://www.theatlantic.com/international/archive/2019/08/anti-feminism-gateway-far-right/595642/.

Lim, Siew Hoon. "Does Shale Energy Development Mean More Crime? The Case of the Bakken Oil Boom." *Growth and Change* 49, no. 3 (2018): 413–41.

Litam, Stacey Diane Aranez, Megan Speciale, and Richard S. Balkin. "Sexual Attitudes and Characteristics of OnlyFans Users." *Archives of Sexual Behavior* 51 (2022): 3093–3103.

Locke, John. *Two Treatises of Government and a Letter Concerning Toleration*. Edited by Ian Shapiro. New Haven, CT: Yale University Press, 2003.

Lopez, German. "Mike Huckabee: I Wish I Could've Said I'm Transgender in High School to Shower with Girls." *Vox*, June 2, 2015. Accessed August 26, 2024. https://www.vox.com/2015/6/2/8711051/mike-huckabee-transgender-showers.

Lorde, Audre. *Sister Outsider*. New York: Penguin Books, 2020.

Lorenz, Taylor. "An Influencer's AI Clone Will Be Your Girlfriend for $1 a Minute." *Washington Post*, May 13, 2023. Accessed August 27, 2024. https://www.washingtonpost.com/technology/2023/05/13/caryn-ai-technology-gpt-4/.

Lucchesi, Annita. *Zuya Winyan Wicayuonihan: Honoring Warrior Women*. Eureka, CA: Sovereign Bodies Institute, 2019.

Lucchesi, Annita, and Abigail Echo-Hawk. *Missing and Murdered Indigenous Women and Girls: A Snapshot of Data from 71 Urban Cities in the United States*. Seattle, WA: Urban Indian Health Institute, 2018.

Lutz, Helma, Maria Teresa Herrera Vivar, and Linda Supik. *Framing Intersectionality: Debates on a Multi-faceted Concept in Gender Studies*. Farnham, UK: Ashgate, 2011.

MacKinnon, Catharine. *Feminism Unmodified: Discourses on Life and Law*. Cambridge, MA: Harvard University Press, 1987.

MacKinnon, Catharine. "Rape Redefined." *Harvard Law and Policy Review* 10 (2016): 431–77.

MacKinnon, Catharine. *Women's Lives, Men's Laws*. Cambridge, MA: Belknap Press of Harvard University Press, 2005.

Macneil, Ian R. *The New Social Contract: An Inquiry into Modern Contractual Relations*. New Haven, CT: Yale University Press, 1980.

Mae, Kristen. "Yes, Feminist Porn Exists—Here's Where to Find It." *Scary Mommy* (blog), March 24, 2021. Accessed August 27, 2024. https://www.scarymommy.com/feminist-ethical-porn-where-to-find.

Majumdar, Mayukh. "Now, Consent Apps Let You Sign a Digital Contract before Having Sex." Man's World, April 17, 2018. Accessed October 28, 2021. https://www.mansworldindia.com/more/sexuality-relationships/legal-fling-digital-consent-apps/.

Mamié, Robin, Manoel Horta Ribeiro, and Robert West. "Feminist Communities Gateways to the Far Right? Evidence from Reddit and YouTube." arXiv:2012.12837, February 25, 2021. Accessed August 31, 2024. https://arxiv.org/abs/2102.12837.

Manne, Kate. *Down Girl: The Logic of Misogyny*. New York: Oxford University Press, 2018.

Manne, Kate. *Entitled: How Male Privilege Hurts Women*. New York: Crown, 2020.

Maracle, Lee. *I Am Woman: A Native Perspective on Sociology and Feminism*. Vancouver, Canada: Press Gang Publishers, 1996.

Marathon Oil. *Animation of Hydraulic Fracturing (Fracking)*. Houston: Marathon Oil, 2012.

Marcotte, A. "For Once, *Game of Thrones* Treats Rape with the Gravity It Deserves." *Slate*, May 18, 2015. https://slate.com/human-interest/2015/05/another-major-character-is-raped-on-game-of-thrones-this-time-it-works-for-the-story.html.

Marcus, Ezra. "The 'E-Pimps' of OnlyFans." *The New York Times Magazine*, May 16, 2022. Accessed August 27, 2024. https://www.nytimes.com/2022/05/16/magazine/e-pimps-onlyfans.html.

Mardorossian, Carine M. *Framing the Rape Victim: Gender and Agency Reconsidered*. New Brunswick, NJ: Rutgers University Press, 2014.

Martin, D. "Breaking Down Jaime and Cersi's Controversial Scene with Last Night's *Game of Thrones* Director." *Vulture*. April 21, 2014. https://www.vulture.com/2014/04/game-of-thrones-director-on-the-rape-sex-scene.html.

Matera, Avery. "5 Times Victoria's Secret Was Accused of Cultural Appropriation." *Teen Vogue*. November 7, 2018.

Mattise, Jonathan, Kimberlee Kruesi, and Lindsay Whitehurst. "Tennessee Moves to the Forefront with Anti-transgender Laws." *AP News*, May 23, 2021. Accessed April 26, 2025. https://apnews.com/article/tennessee-transgender-laws-b8d81d56287d6ed9d56c5da2203596b0.

Mayer, Jane. "What Joe Biden Hasn't Owned Up to about Anita Hill." *New Yorker*, April 27, 2015.

Mayer, Marissa. "The Unintended Victims of Bathroom Bills and Open Locker Room Policies." Alliance Defending Freedom, October 17, 2017. Accessed April 26, 2025. https://web.archive.org/web/20220201033450/https://adflegal.org/blog/unintended-victims-bathroom-bills-and-open-locker-room-policies.

McElya, Micki. *Clinging to Mammy: The Faithful Slave in Twentieth-Century America*. Cambridge, MA: Harvard University Press, 2007.

McGregor, Joan. *Is It Rape? On Acquaintance Rape and Taking Women's Consent Seriously*. Burlington, VT: Ashgate, 2005.

McGuire, Danielle L. *At the Dark End of the Street: Black Women, Rape, and Resistance—A New History of the Civil Rights Movement from Rosa Parks to the Rise of Black Power*. New York: Vintage Books, 2010.

McHenry, Kristen Abatsis. "Getting Fracked: Gender Politics in Fracking Discourse." *Signs: Journal of Women in Culture and Society* 47, no. 1 (2021): 191–207.

McRae, Elizabeth Gillespie. *Mothers of Massive Resistance: White Women and the Politics of White Supremacy*. New York: Oxford University Press, 2018.

Meng, Qingmin. "The Impacts of Fracking on the Environment: A Total Environmental Study Paradigm." *Science of the Total Environment* 580 (2017): 953–57.

Merchant, Carolyn. *The Death of Nature: Women, Ecology, and the Scientific Revolution.* New York: Harper & Row, 1989.

Merskin, Debra. "The S-Word: Discourse, Stereotypes, and the American Indian Woman." *Howard Journal of Communications* 21 (2010): 345–66.

Messina-Dysert, Gina. *Rape Culture and Spiritual Violence: Religion, Testimony, and Visions of Healing.* Hoboken, NJ: Taylor and Francis, 2015.

Meyerhoff, Amelia. *The Clapback.* 2019. Accessed August 27, 2024. https://the-clapback.com/.

MHA Nation. "History." 2018. Accessed October 8, 2022. https://www.mhanation.com/history.

Michaels, Samantha. "We Tracked down the Lawyers behind the Recent Wave of Anti-trans Bathroom Bills." *Mother Jones*, April 25, 2016. Accessed June 30, 2021. https://www.motherjones.com/politics/2016/04/alliance-defending-freedom-lobbies-anti-lgbt-bathroom-bills/.

Miller, Gloria E. "Frontier Masculinity in the Oil Industry: The Experience of Women Engineers." *Gender, Work and Organization* 11, no. 1 (2004): 47–73.

Mills, Charles W. *Black Rights/White Wrongs: The Critique of Racial Liberalism.* New York: Oxford University Press, 2017.

Mills, Charles W. *The Racial Contract.* Ithaca, NY: Cornell University Press, 1999.

Minnesota Indian Women's Sexual Assault Coalition. "Barrette Project." n.d. Accessed October 8, 2022. https://www.miwsac.org/barrette-project-living-memorial/.

Montemurro, Beth, and Jenna Marie Siefken. "MILFs and Matrons: Images and Realities of Mothers' Sexuality." *Sexuality and Culture* 16 (2012): 366–88.

Moraga, Cherríe, and Gloria Anzaldúa, eds. *This Bridge Called My Back: Writings by Radical Women of Color.* Albany, NY: SUNY Press, 2015.

Moran, Sandra, and Heather Gies. "Interview: Resource Extraction Destroys Guatemala Social Fabric." December 13, 2015. https://www.telesurenglish.net/opinion/Interview-Resource-Extraction-Destroys-Guatemala-Social-Fabric-20151213-0018.html.

Moreau, Jordan. "Grand Theft Auto 6 Trailer: Franchise's First Female Protagonist, Vice City Return and 2025 Release Date." *Variety*, December 4, 2023. https://variety.com/2023/digital/news/grand-theft-auto-6-trailer-video-game-1235821088/.

Morris, Seren. "What Is OnlyFans, Who Uses It and How Does It Work?" *Newsweek*, July 23, 2020.

Morrison, Toni, ed. *Race-ing Justice, En-gendering Power: Essays on Anita Hill, Clarence Thomas, and the Construction of Social Reality.* New York: Pantheon Books, 1992.

Moss, Zoe. "Bad Sex." PhD diss., University of Colorado Boulder, 2024.

Murdoch, Sierra Crane. "On Indian Land, Criminals Can Get Away with Almost Anything." *The Atlantic*, February 22, 2013.

Murdoch, Sierra Crane. *Yellow Bird: Oil, Murder, and a Woman's Search for Justice in Indian Country.* New York: Random House, 2020.

Murphy, Meghan. "Rape Culture Is Brock Turner's Father Describing Sexual Assault as '2 Minutes of Action.'" Feminist Current, June 6, 2016. Accessed March 14, 2017. http://www.feministcurrent.com/2016/06/06/rape-culture-is-brock-turner-father-20-minutes-action/.

Murray, Laura K., Amanda Nguyen, and Judith A. Cohen. "Child Sexual Abuse." *Child and Adolescent Psychiatric Clinics of North America* 23, no. 2 (2014): 321–37.

Nathanson, Rebecca. "How 'Carry That Weight' Is Changing the Conversation on Campus Sexual Assault." *Rolling Stone*, December 1, 2014.

National Archives. "American Indian Urban Relocation." 2016. Accessed April 6, 2022. https://www.archives.gov/education/lessons/indian-relocation.html.

National PREA Resource Center. "86 Percent of Women in Jail Are Sexual-Violence Survivors." November 11, 2017. Accessed August 26, 2024. https://www.prearesourcecenter.org/resource/86-percent-women-jail-are-sexual-violence-survivors.

Native Governance Center. "Blood Quantum and Sovereignty: A Guide." 2022. Accessed August 26, 2024. https://nativegov.org/resources/blood-quantum-and-sovereignty-a-guide/.

Native Hope. "Missing and Murdered Indigenous Women." 2019. Accessed October 8, 2022. https://www.nativehope.org/missing-and-murdered-indigenous-women-mmiw.

NBC4 Staff. "Red Handprints Stamped on Steps and Walls of Ohio Statehouse." *2 News WDTN.COM*, June 19, 2020. Accessed October 8, 2022. https://www.wdtn.com/news/ohio/red-handprints-stamped-on-steps-and-walls-of-ohio-statehouse/.

Nelken-Zitser, Joshua. "Influencer Who Created AI Version of Herself Says It's Gone Rogue and She's Working 'around the Clock' to Stop It Saying Sexually Explicit Things." *Business Insider*, May 11, 2023. Accessed August 27, 2024. https://www.businessinsider.com/carynai-ai-virtual-girlfriend-chat-gpt-rogue-filthy-things-influencer-2023-5.

New York Times. "Transcript: Donald Trump's Taped Comments about Women." October 8, 2016. Accessed August 26, 2024. https://www.nytimes.com/2016/10/08/us/donald-trump-tape-transcript.html.

Nguyen, C. Thi. *Games: Agency as Art*. New York: Oxford University Press, 2020.

Nichols, Robert. *Theft Is Property! Dispossession and Critical Theory*. Durham, NC: Duke University Press, 2020.

Noble, Safiya Umoja. *Algorithms of Oppression: How Search Engines Reinforce Racism*. New York: New York University Press, 2018.

Nugent, Annabel. "Megan Thee Stallion Responds to Right-Wing Criticism of 'WAP': 'Tune out, 'Cause I Didn't Ask You to Tune in.'" *The Independent*, September 25, 2020. Accessed August 27, 2024. https://www.independent.co.uk/arts-entertainment/music/news/megan-thee-stallion-wap-cardi-b-right-wing-backlash-candace-owens-b594131.html.

Oklahoma Commission to Study the Tulsa Race Riot of 1921. *Tulsa Race Riot: A Report by the Oklahoma Commission to Study the Tulsa Race Riot of 1921*. Tulsa: Oklahoma

Commission to Study the Tulsa Race Riot of 1921, 2001. Accessed August 31, 2024. https://www.okhistory.org/research/forms/freport.pdf.

Oklahoma Senate. *Oklahoma Statutes Title 21. Crimes and Punishments.* N.d. Accessed April 26, 2025. https://oksenate.gov/sites/default/files/2019-12/os21.pdf.

Ortner, Sherry B. *Anthropology and Social Theory: Culture, Power, and the Acting Subject.* Durham, NC: Duke University Press, 2006.

Osberg, Molly. "How Men's Rights Activists Swallowed the World." *Jezebel*, October 13, 2020. Accessed September 17, 2021. https://jezebel.com/how-mens-rights-activists-swallowed-the-world-1845348223.

Oxford English Dictionary, "practice (*n.*), sense 2.a," March 2025, https://doi.org/10.1093/OED/1201903376.

Oxford English Dictionary, "fantastic (*adj.*), sense 1," July 2023, https://doi.org/10.1093/OED/4553644455.

Panagia, Davide. "On the Possibilities of a Political Theory of Algorithms." *Political Theory* 49, no. 1 (2021): 109–33.

Paquette, Danielle. "What Happens to Boys Who Kill Women in Video Games." *Washington Post*, April 15, 2016. Accessed September 2, 2022. https://www.washingtonpost.com/news/wonk/wp/2016/04/15/what-happens-to-boys-who-kill-women-in-video-games/.

Parezo, Nancy J., and Angelina R. Jones. "What's in a Name? The 1940s–1950s 'Squaw Dress.'" *American Indian Quarterly* 33, no. 3 (2009): 373–404.

Parson, Sean, and Emily Ray. "Drill Baby Drill: Labor, Accumulation, and the Sexualization of Resource Extraction." *Theory & Event* 23, no. 1 (2020): 248–70.

Patel, Nina J. "Reality or Fiction?" Medium, December 21, 2021. Accessed September 2, 2022. https://medium.com/kabuni/fiction-vs-non-fiction-98aa0098f3b0.

Pateman, Carole. "Women and Consent." *Political Theory* 8, no. 2 (1980): 149–68.

Pateman, Carole. *The Sexual Contract.* Cambridge: Polity, 1988.

Patton, Tracey Owens, and Julie Snyder-Yuly. "Any Four Black Men Will Do: Rape, Race, and the Ultimate Scapegoat." *Journal of Black Studies* 37, no. 6 (2007): 859–95.

Pauly, Madison. "Inside the Secret Working Group That Helped Push Anti-trans Laws across the Country." *Mother Jones*, March 8, 2023. Accessed August 26, 2024. https://www.motherjones.com/politics/2023/03/anti-trans-transgender-health-care-ban-legislation-bill-minors-children-lgbtq/.

Pearson, Catherine, Emma Gray, and Alanna Vagianos. "A Running List of the Women Who've Accused Donald Trump of Sexual Misconduct." *Huffington Post*, December 12, 2017. Accessed July 14, 2021. https://www.huffpost.com/entry/a-running-list-of-the-women-whove-accused-donald-trump-of-sexual-misconduct_n_57ffae1fe4b0162c043a7212.

Pember, Mary Annette. "Brave Heart Women Fight to Ban Man-Camps, Which Bring Rape and Abuse." *Indian Country News*, September 12, 2018. Accessed June 16, 2022. https://indiancountrytoday.com/archive/brave-heart-women-fight-to-ban-man-camps-which-bring-rape-and-abuse.

Percelay, Rachel. "A 'Religious Freedom' Legal Powerhouse Is Leading the National Fight against Transgender Student Rights." Media Matters, November 5, 2015. Accessed

June 30, 2021. https://www.mediamatters.org/alliance-defending-freedom/religious-freedom-legal-powerhouse-leading-national-fight-against.

Pérez-Peña, Richard. "Woman Linked to 1955 Emmett Till Murder Tells Historian Her Claims Were False." *New York Times*, January 27, 2017. Accessed September 2, 2022. https://www.nytimes.com/2017/01/27/us/emmett-till-lynching-carolyn-bryant-donham.html.

Perillo, Joseph M. *Contracts*. 7th ed. St. Paul, MN: West Academic Publishing, 2014.

Petrilla, M. "Can an App Help Reduce Sexual Assault on College Campuses?" *Fortune*, September 1, 2015.

Pezzutto, Sophie. "From Porn Performer to Porntropreneur: Online Entrepreneurship, Social Media Branding, and Selfhood in Contemporary Trans Pornography." *AG: About Gender* 8, no. 16 (2019): 30–60.

Philipps, Dave. "North Carolina Bans Local Anti-discrimination Policies." *New York Times*, March 23, 2016. Accessed July 20, 2021. https://www.nytimes.com/2016/03/24/us/north-carolina-to-limit-bathroom-use-by-birth-gender.html.

Phillips, Anne. *Our Bodies, Whose Property?* Princeton, NJ: Princeton University Press, 2013.

Phillips, Nickie D. *Beyond Blurred Lines: Rape Culture in Popular Media*. Lanham, MD: Rowman and Littlefield, 2017.

Pippert, Timothy, and Rachel Zimmer Schneider. "'Have You Been to Walmart?' Gender and Perceptions of Safety in North Dakota Boomtowns." *The Sociological Quarterly* 59. no. 2 (2018): 234–49.

Pitkin, Hanna. "Obligation and Consent—I." *American Political Science Review* 59, no. 4 (1965): 990–99.

Planty, Michael, Lynn Langton, Christopher Krebs, Marcus Berzofsky, and Hope Smiley-Mcdonald. *Female Victims of Sexual Violence, 1994–2010*. Washington, DC: Bureau of Justice Statistics, 2013.

Projansky, Sarah. *Watching Rape: Film and Television in Postfeminist Culture*. New York: New York University Press, 2001.

Radin, Margaret Jane. *Boilerplate the Fine Print, Vanishing Rights, and the Rule of Law*. Princeton, NJ: Princeton University Press, 2013.

RAINN. "Perpetrators of Sexual Violence: Statistics." n.d. Accessed August 26, 2024. https://rainn.org/statistics/perpetrators-sexual-violence.

RAINN. "RAINN Urges White House Task Force to Overhaul Colleges' Treatment of Rape." March 6, 2014. Accessed April 26, 2025. https://web.archive.org/web/20210410130821/https://www.rainn.org/news/rainn-urges-white-house-task-force-overhaul-colleges%E2%80%99-treatment-rape.

Ransby, Barbara. "What the Defamation of Anita Hill Can Teach Us about the Kavanaugh Hearings." *Democracy Now!*, September 24, 2018. https://www.democracynow.org/2018/9/24/dr_barbara_ransby_what_the_defamation.

Rauber, Paul. "How *Battlestar Galactica* Fought Fracking." *Sierra: The Magazine of the Sierra Club*, December 5, 2014.

Remnick, David. "The Weinstein Moment and the Trump Presidency." *New Yorker*, November 12, 2017.

Reuters. "Pornhub Owner MindGeek Sold to Canada's Ethical Capital." March 16, 2023. Accessed August 27, 2024. https://www.reuters.com/markets/deals/pornhub-owner-mindgeek-sold-canadas-ethical-capital-2023-03-16/.

Ribeiro, Manoel Horta, Jeremy Blackburn, Barry Bradlyn, et al. "The Evolution of the Manosphere across the Web." *Proceedings of the Fifteenth International AAAI Conference on Web and Social Media* 15 (2021): 196–207.

Richie, Beth. *Arrested Justice: Black Women, Violence, and America's Prison Nation.* New York: New York University Press, 2012.

Ridgway, Shannon. "25 Everyday Examples of Rape Culture." Everyday Feminism, March 10, 2014. Accessed September 2, 2022. https://everydayfeminism.com/2014/03/examples-of-rape-culture/.

Rifkin, Mark. *Beyond Settler Time: Temporal Sovereignty and Indigenous Self-determination.* Durham, NC: Duke University Press, 2017.

Riofrancos, Thea. "Extractivismo Unearthed: A Genealogy of a Radical Discourse." *Cultural Studies* 31, no. 2–3 (2017): 277–306.

Roberts, Averi. "Lending a Hand(print): Athletes Raise Awareness for Missing, Murdered Indigenous Women." *Cronkite News*/Arizona PBS, December 31, 2020. https://cronkitenews.azpbs.org/2020/12/31/lending-a-handprint-athletes-raise-awareness-for-missing-murder-indigenous-women/.

Rockstar Games. "Grand Theft Auto V." n.d. Accessed September 2, 2022. https://www.rockstargames.com/gta-v.

Rodriguez, Karla. "Snoop Dogg Criticizes Cardi B and Megan Thee Stallion's Hit Song 'WAP.'" Revolt, December 12, 2020. Accessed August 27, 2024. https://www.revolt.tv/article/2020-12-12/63965/snoop-dogg-criticizes-cardi-b-and-megan-thee-stallions-hit-song-wap.

Rosay, Andre B. *Violence against American Indian and Alaska Native Women and Men: 2010 Findings from the National Intimate Partner and Sexual Violence Survey.* Washington DC: US Department of Justice, 2016.

Rose, Jacqueline. *On Violence and on Violence against Women.* New York: Farrar, Straus and Giroux, 2021.

Rouse, Melvin, Jr., and Evan Hamilton. "Rethinking Sex and the Brain: How to Create an Inclusive Discourse in Neuroscience." *Mind, Brain, and Education* 15, no. 2 (2021): 163–67.

Rowlandson, Mary. *Narrative of the Captivity and Restoration of Mrs. Mary Rowlandson.* 1682. Project Gutenberg, November 3, 2009. https://www.gutenberg.org/files/851/851-h/851-h.htm.

Ruddell, Rick, and Sarah Britto. "A Perfect Storm: Violence toward Women in the Bakken Oil Patch." *International Journal of Rural Criminology* 5, no. 2 (2020): 204–27.

Ruddell, Rick, Dheeshana S. Jayasundara, Roni Mayzer, and Thomasine Heitkamp. "Drilling Down: An Examination of the Boom–Crime Relationship in Resource-Based Boom Counties." *Western Criminology Review* 15, no. 1 (2014): 3–17.

Rudolph, Julia. "Rape and Resistance: Women and Consent in Seventeenth-Century English Legal and Political Thought." *Journal of British Studies* 39, no. 2 (2000): 157–84.

Ruíz, Elena Flores. *Structural Violence: The Makings of Settler Colonial Impunity*. New York: Oxford University Press, 2024.

Running Horse Buckley, Damon. "A Personal Story: Grace Her Many Norses, Newtown, North Dakota." *Preserve the Beartooth Front* (blog), March 24, 2015. Accessed October 8, 2022. https://preservethebeartoothfront.com/2015/03/24/a-personal-story-grace-her-many-horses-newtown-north-dakota/.

Saar, Malika Saada, Rebecca Epstein, Lindsay Rosenthal, and Yasmin Vafa. *The Sexual Abuse to Prison Pipeline: The Girls' Story*. Washington DC: Georgetown Law Center on Poverty and Inequality, 2015. Accessed August 31, 2024. https://genderjusticeandopportunity.georgetown.edu/wp-content/uploads/2020/06/The-Sexual-Abuse-To-Prison-Pipeline-The-Girls%E2%80%99-Story.pdf.

Saidero, Deborah. "'Violence against the Earth Is Violence against Women': The Rape Theme in Women's Eco-narratives." *Le Simplegadi* 15, no. 17 (2017): 263–73.

Sanyal, Mithu M. *Rape: From Lucretia to #Metoo*. London: Verso, 2019.

Saunooke, Robert O. "Running for Missing and Murdered Native Women: Expansion of Tribal Court Criminal Jurisdiction." *The Judges' Journal* 59, no. 2 (2020): 22–25.

Schmidt, Samantha. "Conservatives Find Unlikely Ally in Fighting Transgender Rights: Radical Feminists." *Washington Post*, February 7, 2020. Accessed August 26, 2024. https://www.washingtonpost.com/dc-md-va/2020/02/07/radical-feminists-conservatives-transgender-rights/.

Schwab, Kyle. "Holtzclaw Accusers Speak out after Verdicts in Oklahoma City." *The Oklahoman*, December 11, 2015. Accessed August 31, 2024. https://www.oklahoman.com/story/news/crime/2015/12/11/holtzclaw-accusers-speak-out-after-verdicts-in-oklahoma-city/60704400007/.

Sears, Alan, and Craig Osten. *The Homosexual Agenda: Exposing the Principal Threat to Religious Freedom Today*. Nashville: Broadman & Holman Publishers, 2003.

Secwepemcul'ecw Assembly. "Historic Secwepemc Declaration against Kinder Morgan." Vancouver Ecosocialists, June 28, 2017. Accessed August 26, 2024. https://ecosocialistsvancouver.org/article/historic-secwepemc-declaration-against-kinder-morgan.

"Senate Judiciary Committee Hearing on the Nomination of Brett M. Kavanaugh to be an Associate Justice of the Supreme Court, Day 5, Focusing on Allegations of Sexual Assault." *Washington Post*, September 27, 2018. Accessed August 31, 2024. https://www.washingtonpost.com/news/national/wp/2018/09/27/kavanaugh-hearing-transcript/.

Serano, Julia. *Excluded: Making Feminist and Queer Movements More Inclusive*. Berkeley, CA: Seal Press, 2013.

Serano, Julia. *Sexed up: How Society Sexualizes Us, and How We Can Fight Back*. New York: Seal Press, 2022.

Serano, Julia. *Whipping Girl: A Transsexual Woman on Sexism and the Scapegoating of Femininity*. Seal Press, 2009.*ProQuest Ebook Central*, https://ebookcentral.proquest.com/lib/ups/detail.action?docID=679998.

Seto, Michael X., Kelly M. Babchishin, Lesleigh E. Pullman, and Ian V. McPhail. "The Puzzle of Intrafamilial Child Sexual Abuse: A Meta-analysis Comparing Intrafamilial and Extrafamilial Offenders with Child Victims." *Clinical Psychology Review* 39 (2015): 42–57.

Settles, Isis H., Jennifer S. Pratt-Hyatt, and NiCole T. Buchanan. "Through the Lens of Race: Black and White Women's Perceptions of Womanhood." *Psychology of Women Quarterly* 32 (2008): 454–68.

Shane, Charlotte. "OnlyFans Isn't Just Porn." *New York Times Magazine*, May 18, 2021.

Shanks, Torrey. "Affect, Critique, and the Social Contract." *Theory and Event* 18, no. 1 (2015). https://muse.jhu.edu/article/566087. Accessed April 25, 2025.

Sharpe, Christina Elizabeth. *In the Wake: On Blackness and Being*. Durham, NC: Duke University Press, 2016.

Sheldon, Rebekah. *The Child to Come: Life after the Human Catastrophe*. Minneapolis: University of Minnesota Press, 2016.

Shen, Michelle. "Sexual Harassment in the Metaverse? Woman Alleges Rape in Virtual World." *USA Today*, January 31, 2022. Accessed September 2, 2022. https://www.usatoday.com/story/tech/2022/01/31/woman-allegedly-groped-metaverse/9278578002/.

Sher, Andy. "Tennessee Transgender 'Business Bathroom Bill' Threatens Criminal Penalties if Violations not Fixed in 30 Days." *Chattanooga Times Free Press*, May 24, 2021. Accessed August 12, 2021. https://www.timesfreepress.com/news/local/story/2021/may/24/tennessee-transgender-business-bathroom-bill/547464/.

Sheridan, Taylor. *Wind River*, Script. 2017a. https://www.scriptslug.com/assets/scripts/wind-river-2017.pdf.

Sheridan, Taylor, dir. *Wind River*, Film. 2017b.

Shippen, Nichole. "If Indigenous Women Counted: Critical Thoughts on Murdered and Missing Indigenous Women Legislation." Paper presented at the November 11–13, 2021 annual meeting of the Association for Political Theory, Amherst, MA.

Sigurdson, Erika Ruth. "Violence and Historical Authenticity: Rape (and Pillage) in Popular Viking Fiction." *Scandinavian Studies* 86, no. 3 (2014): 249–67.

Silman, A. "'Game of Thrones' Stars Defend Disturbing Sex Scene: 'It Wasn't Rape.'" Salon, April 8, 2015. https://www.salon.com/2015/04/07/game_of_thrones_stars_defend_cersei_and_jaimes_disturbing_sex_scene_it_wasnt_rape/.

Simplican, Stacy Clifford. *The Capacity Contract: Intellectual Disability and the Question of Citizenship*. Minneapolis: University of Minnesota Press, 2015.

Simpson, Audra. "The State Is a Man: Theresa Spence, Loretta Saunders and the Gender of Settler Sovereignty." *Theory and Event* 19, no. 4 (2016). https://muse.jhu.edu/article/633280. Accessed April 25, 2025.

Simpson, Leanne Betasamosake. *As We Have Always Done: Indigenous Freedom through Radical Resistance*. Minneapolis: University of Minnesota Press, 2017.

Smith, Andrea. *Conquest: Sexual Violence and American Indian Genocide*. Durham, NC: Duke University Press, 2005.

Smith, Andrea. "Not an Indian Tradition: The Sexual Colonization of Native Peoples." *Hypatia* 18, no. 2 (2003): 70–85.

Smith, Andrea, and Luana Ross. "Introduction: Native Women and State Violence." *Social Justice* 31, no. 4 (2004): 1–7.

Smith, Merril D. *Sex without Consent: Rape and Sexual Coercion in America.* New York: New York University Press, 2001.

Smith, Mitch. "South Dakota Bill on Transgender Students' Bathroom Access Draws Ire." *New York Times*, February 25, 2016. Accessed September 2, 2022. https://www.nytimes.com/2016/02/26/us/south-dakota-bill-on-transgender-students-bathroom-access-draws-ire.html.

Sood, Raema. "Biases behind Sexual Assault: A Thirteenth Amendment Solution to Under-enforcement of the Rape of Black Women." *University of Maryland Law Journal of Race, Religion, Gender, and Class* 18, no. 2 (2019): 405–28.

South Dakota HB1008, 2016 Regular Session. LegiScan, 2016. Accessed July 9, 2021. https://legiscan.com/SD/text/HB1008/id/1340969.

Southern Poverty Law Center. Alliance Defending Freedom. n.d. Accessed June 30, 2021. https://www.splcenter.org/fighting-hate/extremist-files/group/alliance-defending-freedom.

Southern Poverty Law Center. Alliance Defending Freedom through the Years. July 24, 2017. Accessed July 6, 2021. https://www.splcenter.org/hatewatch/2017/07/24/alliance-defending-freedom-through-years.

Spade, Dean. *Normal Life: Administrative Violence, Critical Trans Politics, and the Limits of Law.* Rev. exp. ed. Durham, NC: Duke University Press, 2015.

Spangler, Todd. "OnlyFans Creators Earned $3.9 Billion in 2021, Swelling 115% Year over Year." *Variety*, September 1, 2022. Accessed August 31, 2024. https://money.yahoo.com/onlyfans-creators-earned-3-9-184050221.html#:~:text=OnlyFans%20creators%20earned%20%243.86%20billion,the%20year%20ended%20November%202021.

Spillers, Hortense J. "Mama's Baby, Papa's Maybe: An American Grammar Book." *Diacritics* 17, no. 2 (1987): 64–81.

Srinivasan, Amia. *The Right to Sex: Feminism in the Twenty-First Century.* New York: Farrar, Straus and Giroux, 2021.

Stansell, Christine. *The Feminist Promise: 1792 to the Present.* New York: Modern Library, 2010.

Steiger, Kay. "Church Shooting Suspect Identified: Dylann Storm Roof." Think Progress, June 18, 2015. Accessed September 2, 2022. https://archive.thinkprogress.org/church-shooting-suspect-identified-dylann-storm-roof-362d497191f8/.

Stern, Mark J. "It Wasn't about Bathrooms, and It's not about Women's Sports." Slate, April 7, 2021. Accessed June 29, 2021. https://slate.com/news-and-politics/2021/04/transgender-rights-bathrooms-sports-alliance-defending-freedom.html.

Stewart, E. "Sen. Martha McSally Coming forward about Her Rape Could Be a Watershed Moment for Republican Women." *Vox*, March 7, 2019.

Stolakis, Kristine, dir. *Pray Away.* Netflix, 2021.

Stroud, Angela. "Good Guys with Guns: Hegemonic Masculinity and Concealed Handguns." *Gender and Society* 26, no. 2 (2012): 216–38.

Stryker, Susan, and Aren Z. Aizura, eds. *The Transgender Studies Reader 2.* New York: Routledge, 2013.

Survivors' Agenda. "Culture & Narrative Shift." 2020. Accessed October 8, 2022. https://survivorsagenda.org/agenda/full-agenda/#culture-narrative-shift.

Swords, Jon, Mary Laing, and Ian R. Cook. "Platforms, Sex Work and Their Interconnectedness." *Sexualities* 26, no. 3 (2023): 277–97.

Taub, Amanda. "Rape Culture Isn't a Myth. It's Real, and It's Dangerous." *Vox*, December 15, 2014. Accessed September 2, 2022. https://www.vox.com/2014/12/15/7371737/rape-culture-definition.

Taylor, Goldie. "White Cop Convicted of Serial Rape of Black Women." *The Daily Beast*, June 26, 2017.

Taylor, Keeanga-Yamahtta. "How Black Feminists Defined Abortion Rights." *The New Yorker*, February 22, 2022. Accessed July 14, 2022. https://www.newyorker.com/news/essay/how-black-feminists-defined-abortion-rights.

Taylor, Keeanga-Yamahtta. *How We Get Free: Black Feminism and the Combahee River Collective.* Chicago: Haymarket Books, 2017.

Testa, Jessica. "The 13 Women Who Accused a Cop of Sexual Assault, in Their Own Words." Buzz Feed News, December 10, 2015. https://www.buzzfeednews.com/article/jtes/daniel-holtzclaw-women-in-their-ow.

Think Expansion. "About Us." June 27, 2024. Accessed August 27, 2024. https://thinkexpansion.com/about-us/.

Thomas, Clarence. "Statement before the Senate Judiciary Committee." *American Rhetoric*, October 11, 1991. Accessed August 27, 2024. https://www.americanrhetoric.com/speeches/clarencethomashightechlynching.htm.

Tillman, Shaquita, Thema Bryant-Davis, Kimberly Smith, and Alison Marks. "Shattering Silence: Exploring Barriers to Disclosure for African American Sexual Assault Survivors." *Trauma, Violence, and Abuse* 11, no. 2 (2010): 59–70.

Time. "Here's Donald Trump's Presidential Announcement Speech." June 16, 2015. Accessed August 26, 2024. https:/time.com/3923128/donald-trump-announcement-speech/.

Tolentino, Daysia. "Snapchat Influencer Launches an AI-Powered 'Virtual Girlfriend' to Help 'Cure Loneliness.'" *NBC News*, May 12, 2023. Accessed August 27, 2024. https://www.nbcnews.com/tech/ai-powered-virtual-girlfriend-caryn-marjorie-snapchat-influencer-rcna84180.

Trans Legislation Tracker. "Anti-trans Bills: Trans Legislation Tracker." n.d. Accessed August 26, 2024. https://translegislation.com.

Trask, Haunani-Kay. *From a Native Daughter: Colonialism and Sovereignty in Hawai'i.* Revised ed. Honolulu: University of Hawaii Press, 1999.

Trimmer, Dave. "'When I Run about It, People Will Notice': Rosalie Fish Runs for Missing and Murdered Indigenous Women." *Seattle Times*, June 7, 2019. Accessed October 8, 2022. https://www.seattletimes.com/sports/high-school/but-when-i-run-about-it-people-will-notice-muckleshoot-tribals-rosalie-fish-runs-for-missing-and-murdered-indigenous-women/.

Trotta, Daniel. "Massive, landmark survey finds 60% of transgender Americans have avoided public bathrooms for fear of being harassed. *Business Insider*, December 8, 2016. Accessed June 28, 2021. https://www.businessinsider.com/r-us-transgender-people-harassed-in-public-restrooms-landmark-survey-2016-12.

Trudy. "Explanation of Misogynoir." 2014. Accessed September 22, 2021. https://www.gradientlair.com/post/84107309247/define-misogynoir-anti-black-misogyny-moya-bailey-coined.

Tuerkheimer, Deborah. "Op-ed: No Matter How the Heard/Depp Trial Ends, Defamation Lawsuits against Accusers Are Here to Stay." *LA Times*. May 23, 2022. Accessed August 27, 2024. https://www.latimes.com/opinion/story/2022-05-23/amber-heard-johnny-depp-trial-accusers-defamation.

Urban Indian Health Institute. "Protecting the Sacred: Addressing Sexual Violence and Gender-Based Violence against Natives during the COVID-19 Pandemic." 2020. Accessed March 25, 2022. https://www.uihi.org/projects/protecting-the-sacred/.

US Geological Survey. "Induced Earthquakes Overview." March 9, 2022. Accessed April 4, 2022. https://www.usgs.gov/programs/earthquake-hazards/science/induced-earthquakes-overview.

US Sentencing Commission. "Quick Facts: Sexual Abuse Offenders." 2018. https://www.ussc.gov/sites/default/files/pdf/research-and-publications/quick-facts/Sexual_Abuse_FY18.pdf.

VandenBos, Gary R. *APA Dictionary of Psychology*. Washington, DC: American Psychological Association, 2007.

Voyles, Traci Brynne. *Wastelanding: Legacies of Uranium Mining in Navajo Country*. Minneapolis: University of Minnesota Press, 2015.

Wacquant, Loïc J. D. *Punishing the Poor: The Neoliberal Government of Social Insecurity*. Durham, NC: Duke University Press, 2009.

Wallace-Wells, Benjamin. "The Mute Republicans at the Kavanaugh–Ford Hearing." *New Yorker*. September 17, 2018.

Wells-Barnett, Ida B. *The Red Record*. 1895. Project Gutenberg, February 8, 2005. https://www.gutenberg.org/files/14977/14977-h/14977-h.htm.

WeRNative.org. "Lateral Violence." n.d. Accessed August 26, 2024. https://www.wernative.org/articles/lateral-violence.

White House. "Defending Women from Gender Ideology and Extremism and Restoring Biological Truth to the Federal Government." January 20, 2025. https://www.whitehouse.gov/presidential-actions/2025/01/defending-women-from-gender-ideology-extremism-and-restoring-biological-truth-to-the-federal-government/.

Wikipedia. "Rape Culture." January 26, 2021. Accessed April 26, 2025. https://web.archive.org/web/20210126213410/https://en.wikipedia.org/wiki/Rape_culture.

Wilkinson, Eleanor. "The Diverse Economies of Online Pornography: From Paranoid Readings to Post-capitalist Futures." *Sexualities* 20, no. 8 (2017): 981–98.

Winton, Richard, Rosanna Xia, and Rong-Gong Lin II. "Isla Vista Shooting: Read Elliot Rodger's Graphic, Elaborate Attack Plan." *Los Angeles Times*, May 25, 2014. Accessed September 2, 2022. https://www.latimes.com/local/lanow/la-me-ln-isla-vista-document-20140524-story.html.

Wolf, Naomi. *Promiscuities: The Secret Struggle for Womanhood.* New York: Random House, 1997.

Wolfe, Patrick. "Settler Colonialism and the Elimination of the Native." *Journal of Genocide Research* 8, no. 4 (2006): 387–409.

Women's Earth Alliance and Native Youth Sexual Health Network. *Violence on the Land, Violence on our Bodies: Building an Indigenous Response to Environmental Violence.* Berkeley, CA: Women's Earth Alliance and Native Youth Sexual Health Network, 2016.

Women's Liberation Front. "A Mother's Concern for Her Daughters." February 26, 2024. Accessed August 26, 2024. https://womensliberationfront.org/letters-from-the-front-submissions/a-mothers-concern-for-her-daughters.

Women's Liberation Front. "Women's Bill of Rights." n.d. Accessed August 26, 2024. https://womensliberationfront.org/womens-bill-of-rights-full-text.

Wootson, Cleve R., Jr. "Trump and Biden Are Both Openly Fantasizing about Who Would Win in a Fistfight." *Washington Post,* March 22, 2018. Accessed September 2, 2022. https://www.washingtonpost.com/news/powerpost/wp/2018/03/21/joe-biden-cant-stop-talking-about-beating-up-donald-trump/.

Wright, Aaron, and Primavera De Filippi. *Blockchain and the Law: The Rule of Code.* Cambridge, MA: Harvard University Press, 2018.

Wynne, Griffin. "Here's Why Experts Are Torn about the Ethics of OnlyFans." *Bustle,* April 8, 2021. Accessed August 27, 2024. https://www.bustle.com/wellness/onlyfans-ethical-porn-experts.

Yellow Bird. "A Tale from the Fort Berthold Reservation." 2009. Accessed October 8, 2022. https://www.indianz.com/News/2009/06/03/yellow_bird_a_tale_from_the_fo.asp.

Young, Iris Marion. *Justice and the Politics of Difference.* Princeton, NJ: Princeton University Press, 1990.

Young, Iris Marion. "The Logic of Masculinist Protection: Reflections on the Current Security State." *Signs* 29, no. 1 (2003): 1–25.

Yurcaba, Jo. "Judge Blocks Tennessee's Transgender Bathroom Sign Law." NBC News, July 9, 2021. Accessed August 12, 2021. https://www.nbcnews.com/nbc-out/out-news/judge-blocks-tennessees-transgender-bathroom-sign-law-rcna1384.

Zarya, V. "Is Blockchain the Answer to Consensual Sex?" *Fortune,* January 16, 2018. Accessed August 31, 2024. https://finance.yahoo.com/news/blockchain-answer-sexual-consent-230544393.html.

Zuboff, Shoshana. *The Age of Surveillance Capitalism: The Fight for a Human Future at the New Frontier of Power.* New York: Public Affairs Hachette Book Group, 2019.

Index

For the benefit of digital users, indexed terms that span two pages (e.g., 52–53) may, on occasion, appear on only one of those pages.